Beautiful Security

Beautiful Security

Edited by Andy Oram and John Viega

O'REILLY®

Beijing · Cambridge · Farnham · Köln · Sebastopol · Tokyo

Beautiful Security

Edited by Andy Oram and John Viega

Copyright © 2009 O'Reilly Media, Inc. All rights reserved.
Printed in the United States of America.

Published by O'Reilly Media, Inc., 1005 Gravenstein Highway North, Sebastopol, CA 95472.

O'Reilly books may be purchased for educational, business, or sales promotional use. Online editions are also available for most titles (*http://my.safaribooksonline.com/*). For more information, contact our corporate/institutional sales department: 800-998-9938 or *corporate@oreilly.com*.

Production Editor:	Sarah Schneider	**Indexer:**	Lucie Haskins
Copyeditor:	Genevieve d'Entremont	**Cover Designer:**	Mark Paglietti
Proofreader:	Sada Preisch	**Interior Designer:**	David Futato
		Illustrator:	Robert Romano

Printing History:

April 2009:   First Edition.

ISBN: 978-0-596-52748-8

[LSI]   [2011-02-04]

1296499055

All royalties from this book will be donated to the Internet Engineering Task Force (IETF).

CONTENTS

PREFACE   XI

1   PSYCHOLOGICAL SECURITY TRAPS   1
        by Peiter "Mudge" Zatko

        Learned Helplessness and Naïveté   2
        Confirmation Traps   10
        Functional Fixation   14
        Summary   20

2   WIRELESS NETWORKING: FERTILE GROUND FOR SOCIAL ENGINEERING   21
        by Jim Stickley

        Easy Money   22
        Wireless Gone Wild   28
        Still, Wireless Is the Future   31

3   BEAUTIFUL SECURITY METRICS   33
        by Elizabeth A. Nichols

        Security Metrics by Analogy: Health   34
        Security Metrics by Example   38
        Summary   60

4   THE UNDERGROUND ECONOMY OF SECURITY BREACHES   63
        by Chenxi Wang

        The Makeup and Infrastructure of the Cyber Underground   64
        The Payoff   66
        How Can We Combat This Growing Underground Economy?   71
        Summary   72

5   BEAUTIFUL TRADE: RETHINKING E-COMMERCE SECURITY   73
        by Ed Bellis

        Deconstructing Commerce   74
        Weak Amelioration Attempts   76
        E-Commerce Redone: A New Security Model   83
        The New Model   86

6   SECURING ONLINE ADVERTISING: RUSTLERS AND SHERIFFS IN THE NEW WILD WEST 89
        by Benjamin Edelman

        Attacks on Users   89
        Advertisers As Victims   98

Creating Accountability in Online Advertising 105

7 THE EVOLUTION OF PGP'S WEB OF TRUST 107
by Phil Zimmermann and Jon Callas

PGP and OpenPGP 108
Trust, Validity, and Authority 108
PGP and Crypto History 116
Enhancements to the Original Web of Trust Model 120
Interesting Areas for Further Research 128
References 129

8 OPEN SOURCE HONEYCLIENT: PROACTIVE DETECTION OF CLIENT-SIDE EXPLOITS 131
by Kathy Wang

Enter Honeyclients 133
Introducing the World's First Open Source Honeyclient 133
Second-Generation Honeyclients 135
Honeyclient Operational Results 139
Analysis of Exploits 141
Limitations of the Current Honeyclient Implementation 143
Related Work 144
The Future of Honeyclients 146

9 TOMORROW'S SECURITY COGS AND LEVERS 147
by Mark Curphey

Cloud Computing and Web Services: The Single Machine Is Here 150
Connecting People, Process, and Technology: The Potential for Business Process Management 154
Social Networking: When People Start Communicating, Big Things Change 158
Information Security Economics: Supercrunching and the New Rules of the Grid 162
Platforms of the Long-Tail Variety: Why the Future Will Be Different for Us All 165
Conclusion 168
Acknowledgments 169

10 SECURITY BY DESIGN 171
by John McManus

Metrics with No Meaning 172
Time to Market or Time to Quality? 174
How a Disciplined System Development Lifecycle Can Help 178
Conclusion: Beautiful Security Is an Attribute of Beautiful Systems 181

11 FORCING FIRMS TO FOCUS: IS SECURE SOFTWARE IN YOUR FUTURE? 183
by Jim Routh

Implicit Requirements Can Still Be Powerful 184
How One Firm Came to Demand Secure Software 185
Enforcing Security in Off-the-Shelf Software 190
Analysis: How to Make the World's Software More Secure 193

12 OH NO, HERE COME THE INFOSECURITY LAWYERS! 199
by Randy V. Sabett

Culture   200

Balance   202

Communication   207

Doing the Right Thing   211

13   BEAUTIFUL LOG HANDLING   213
   by Anton Chuvakin

Logs in Security Laws and Standards   213

Focus on Logs   214

When Logs Are Invaluable   215

Challenges with Logs   216

Case Study: Behind a Trashed Server   218

Future Logging   221

Conclusions   223

14   INCIDENT DETECTION: FINDING THE OTHER 68%   225
   by Grant Geyer and Brian Dunphy

A Common Starting Point   226

Improving Detection with Context   228

Improving Perspective with Host Logging   232

Summary   237

15   DOING REAL WORK WITHOUT REAL DATA   239
   by Peter Wayner

How Data Translucency Works   240

A Real-Life Example   243

Personal Data Stored As a Convenience   244

Trade-offs   244

Going Deeper   245

References   246

16   CASTING SPELLS: PC SECURITY THEATER   247
   by Michael Wood and Fernando Francisco

Growing Attacks, Defenses in Retreat   248

The Illusion Revealed   252

Better Practices for Desktop Security   257

Conclusion   258

CONTRIBUTORS   259

INDEX   269

Preface

IF ONE BELIEVES THAT NEWS HEADLINES REVEAL TRENDS, THESE ARE INTERESTING times for computer security buffs. As *Beautiful Security* went to press, I read that a piece of software capable of turning on microphones and cameras and stealing data has been discovered on more than 1,200 computers in 103 countries, particularly in embassies and other sensitive government sites. On another front, a court upheld the right of U.S. investigators to look at phone and Internet records without a warrant (so long as one end of the conversation is outside the U.S.). And this week's routine vulnerabilities include a buffer overflow in Adobe Acrobat and Adobe Reader—with known current exploits—that lets attackers execute arbitrary code on your system using your privileges after you open their PDF.

Headlines are actually not good indicators of trends, because in the long run history is driven by subtle evolutionary changes noticed only by a few—such as the leading security experts who contributed to this book. The current directions taken by security threats as well as responses can be discovered in these pages.

All the alarming news items I mentioned in the first paragraph are just business as usual in the security field. Yes, they are part of trends that should worry all of us, but we also need to look at newer and less dramatic vulnerabilities. The contributors to this book have, for decades, been on the forefront of discovering weaknesses in our working habits and suggesting unconventional ways to deal with them.

Why Security Is Beautiful

I asked security expert John Viega to help find the authors for this book out of frustration concerning the way ordinary computer users view security. Apart from the lurid descriptions of break-ins and thefts they read about in the press, average folks think of security as boring.

Security, to many, is represented by nagging reminders from system administrators to create backup folders, and by seemingly endless dialog boxes demanding passwords before a web page is displayed. Office workers roll their eyes and curse as they read the password off the notepad next to their desk (lying on top of the budget printout that an office administrator told them should be in a locked drawer). If this is security, who would want to make a career of it? Or buy a book from O'Reilly about it? Or think about it for more than 30 seconds at a time?

To people tasked with creating secure systems, the effort seems hopeless. Nobody at their site cooperates with their procedures, and the business managers refuse to allocate more than a pittance to security. Jaded from the endless instances of zero-day exploits and unpatched vulnerabilities in the tools and languages they have to work with, programmers and system administrators become lax.

This is why books on security sell poorly (although in the last year or two, sales have picked up a bit). Books on hacking into systems sell much better than books about how to protect systems, a trend that really scares me.

Well, this book should change that. It will show that security is about the most exciting career you can have. It is not tedious, not bureaucratic, and not constraining. In fact, it exercises the imagination like nothing else in technology.

Most of the programming books I've edited over the years offer a chapter on security. These chapters are certainly useful, because they allow the author to teach some general principles along with good habits, but I've been bothered by the convention because it draws a line around the topic of security. It feeds the all-too-common view of security as an add-on and an afterthought. *Beautiful Security* demolishes that conceit.

John chose for this book a range of authors who have demonstrated insight over and over in the field and who had something new to say. Some have designed systems that thousands rely on; some have taken high-level jobs in major corporations; some have testified on and worked for government bodies. All of them are looking for the problems and solutions that the rest of us know nothing about—but will be talking about a lot a few years from now.

The authors show that effective security keeps you on your toes all the time. It breaks across boundaries in technology, in cognition, and in organizational structures. The black hats in security succeed by exquisitely exercising creativity; therefore, those defending against them must do the same.

With the world's infosecurity resting on their shoulders, the authors could be chastised for taking time off to write these chapters. And indeed, many of them experienced stress trying to balance their demanding careers with the work on this book. But the time spent was worth it, because this book can advance their larger goals. If more people become intrigued with the field of security, resolve to investigate it further, and give their attention and their support to people trying to carry out organizational change in the interest of better protection, the book will have been well worth the effort.

On March 19, 2009, the Senate Committee on Commerce, Science, and Transportation held a hearing on the dearth of experts in information technology and how that hurts the country's cybersecurity. There's an urgent need to interest students and professionals in security issues; this book represents a step toward that goal.

Audience for This Book

This book is meant for people interested in computer technology who want to experience a bit of life at the cutting edge. The audience includes students exploring career possibilities, people with a bit of programming background, and those who have a modest to advanced understanding of computing.

The authors explain technology at a level where a relatively novice reader can get a sense of the workings of attacks and defenses. The expert reader can enjoy the discussions even more, as they will lend depth to his or her knowledge of security tenets and provide guidance for further research.

Donation

The authors are donating the royalties from this book to the Internet Engineering Task Force (IETF), an organization critical to the development of the Internet and a fascinating model of enlightened, self-organized governance. The Internet would not be imaginable without the scientific debates, supple standard-making, and wise compromises made by dedicated members of the IETF, described on their web page as a "large open international community of network designers, operators, vendors, and researchers." O'Reilly will send royalties to the Internet Society (ISOC), the longtime source of funding and organizational support for the IETF.

Organization of the Material

The chapters in this book are not ordered along any particular scheme, but have been arranged to provide an engaging reading experience that unfolds new perspectives in hopefully surprising ways. Chapters that deal with similar themes, however, are grouped together.

Chapter 1, *Psychological Security Traps*, by Peiter "Mudge" Zatko

Chapter 2, *Wireless Networking: Fertile Ground for Social Engineering*, by Jim Stickley

Chapter 3, *Beautiful Security Metrics*, by Elizabeth A. Nichols

Chapter 4, *The Underground Economy of Security Breaches*, by Chenxi Wang

Chapter 5, *Beautiful Trade: Rethinking E-Commerce Security*, by Ed Bellis

Chapter 6, *Securing Online Advertising: Rustlers and Sheriffs in the New Wild West*, by Benjamin Edelman

Chapter 7, *The Evolution of PGP's Web of Trust*, by Phil Zimmermann and Jon Callas

Chapter 8, *Open Source Honeyclient: Proactive Detection of Client-Side Exploits*, by Kathy Wang

Chapter 9, *Tomorrow's Security Cogs and Levers*, by Mark Curphey

Chapter 10, *Security by Design*, by John McManus

Chapter 11, *Forcing Firms to Focus: Is Secure Software in Your Future?*, by James Routh

Chapter 12, *Oh No, Here Come the Infosecurity Lawyers!*, by Randy V. Sabett

Chapter 13, *Beautiful Log Handling*, by Anton Chuvakin

Chapter 14, *Incident Detection: Finding the Other 68%*, by Grant Geyer and Brian Dunphy

Chapter 15, *Doing Real Work Without Real Data*, by Peter Wayner

Chapter 16, *Casting Spells: PC Security Theater*, by Michael Wood and Fernando Francisco

Conventions Used in This Book

The following typographical conventions are used in this book:

Italic
> Indicates new terms, URLs, filenames, and Unix utilities.

`Constant width`
> Indicates the contents of computer files and generally anything found in programs.

Using Code Examples

This book is here to help you get your job done. In general, you may use the code in this book in your programs and documentation. You do not need to contact us for permission unless you're reproducing a significant portion of the code. For example, writing a program that uses several chunks of code from this book does not require permission. Selling or distributing a CD-ROM of examples from O'Reilly books does require permission. Answering a question by citing this book and quoting example code does not require permission. Incorporating a significant amount of example code from this book into your product's documentation does require permission.

We appreciate, but do not require, attribution. An attribution usually includes the title, author, publisher, and ISBN. For example: "*Beautiful Security*, edited by Andy Oram and John Viega. Copyright 2009 O'Reilly Media, Inc., 978-0-596-52748-8."

If you feel your use of code examples falls outside fair use or the permission given here, feel free to contact us at *permissions@oreilly.com*.

Safari® Books Online

When you see a Safari® Books Online icon on the cover of your favorite technology book, that means the book is available online through the O'Reilly Network Safari Bookshelf.

Safari offers a solution that's better than e-books. It's a virtual library that lets you easily search thousands of top tech books, cut and paste code samples, download chapters, and find quick answers when you need the most accurate, current information. Try it for free at *http://my.safaribooksonline.com/*.

How to Contact Us

Please address comments and questions concerning this book to the publisher:

O'Reilly Media, Inc.
1005 Gravenstein Highway North
Sebastopol, CA 95472
800-998-9938 (in the United States or Canada)
707-829-0515 (international or local)
707-829-0104 (fax)

We have a web page for this book, where we list errata, examples, and any additional information. You can access this page at:

http://www.oreilly.com/catalog/9780596527488

To comment or ask technical questions about this book, send email to:

bookquestions@oreilly.com

For more information about our books, conferences, Resource Centers, and the O'Reilly Network, see our website at:

http://www.oreilly.com

CHAPTER ONE

Psychological Security Traps

Peiter "Mudge" Zatko

DURING MY CAREER OF ATTACKING SOFTWARE AND THE FACILITIES THEY POWER, many colleagues have remarked that I have a somewhat nonstandard approach. I tended to be surprised to hear this, as the approach seemed logical and straightforward to me. In contrast, I felt that academic approaches were too abstract to realize wide success in real-world applications. These more conventional disciplines were taking an almost completely random tack with no focus or, on the opposite end of the spectrum, spending hundreds of hours reverse-engineering and tracing applications to (hopefully) discover their vulnerabilities before they were exploited out in the field.

Now, please do not take this the wrong way. I'm not condemning the aforementioned techniques. In fact I agree they are critical tools in the art of vulnerability discovery and exploitation. However, I believe in applying some shortcuts and alternative views to envelope, enhance, and—sometimes—bypass these approaches.

In this chapter I'll talk about some of these alternative views and how they can help us get inside the mind of the developer whose code or system we engage as security professionals.

Why might you want to get inside the mind of the developer? There are many reasons, but for this chapter we will focus on various constraints that are imposed on the creation of code and the people who write it. These issues often result in suboptimal systems from the security viewpoint, and by understanding some of the environmental, psychological, and philosophical frameworks in which the coding is done, we can shine a spotlight on which areas of a system are more likely to contain vulnerabilities that attackers can exploit. Where appropriate, I'll share anecdotes to provide examples of the mindset issue at hand.

My focus for the past several years has been on large-scale environments such as major corporations, government agencies and their various enclaves, and even nation states. While many of the elements are applicable to smaller environments, and even to individuals, I like to show the issues in larger terms to offer a broader social picture. Of course, painting with such a broad brush requires generalizations, and you may be able to find instances that contradict the examples. I won't cite counterexamples, given the short space allotted to the chapter.

The goal here is not to highlight particular technologies, but rather to talk about some environmental and psychological situations that caused weak security to come into being. It is important to consider the external influences and restrictions placed on the implementers of a technology, in order to best understand where weaknesses will logically be introduced. While this is an enjoyable mental game to play on the offensive side of the coin, it takes on new dimensions when the defenders also play the game and a) prevent errors that would otherwise lead to attacks or b) use these same techniques to game the attackers and how they operate. At this point, the security game becomes what I consider *beautiful*.

The mindsets I'll cover fall into the categories of learned helplessness and naïveté, confirmation traps, and functional fixation. This is not an exhaustive list of influencing factors in security design and implementation, but a starting point to encourage further awareness of the potential security dangers in systems that you create or depend on.

Learned Helplessness and Naïveté

Sociologists and psychologists have discovered a phenomenon in both humans and other animals that they call *learned helplessness*. It springs from repeated frustration when trying to achieve one's goals or rescue oneself from a bad situation. Ultimately, the animal subjected to this extremely destructive treatment stops trying. Even when chances to do well or escape come along, the animal remains passive and fails to take advantage of them.

To illustrate that even sophisticated and rational software engineers are subject to this debilitating flaw, I'll use an example where poor security can be traced back to the roots of backward compatibility.

Backward compatibility is a perennial problem for existing technology deployments. New technologies are discovered and need to be deployed that are incompatible with, or at the very least substantially different from, existing solutions.

At each point in a system's evolution, vendors need to determine whether they will forcibly end-of-life the existing solutions, provide a migration path, or devise a way to allow both the legacy and modern solutions to interact in perpetuity. All of these decisions have numerous ramifications from both business and technology perspectives. But the decision is usually driven by business desires and comes down as a decree to the developers and engineers.* When this happens, the people responsible for creating the actual implementation will have the impression that the decision has already been made and that they just have to live with it. No further reevaluation or double guessing need take place.

Imagine that the decision was made to maintain compatibility with the legacy technology in its replacement. Management further decrees that no further development or support work will take place on the legacy solution, in order to encourage existing customers to migrate to the replacement.

Although such decisions place burdens on the development in many ways—with security implications—they are particularly interesting when one solution, usually the new technology, is more secure than the other. In fact, new technologies are often developed *explicitly* to meet the need for greater security—and yet the old technology must still be supported. What security problems arise in such situations?

There are different ways to achieve backward compatibility, some more secure than others. But once the developers understand that the older, less secure technology is allowed to live on, solutions that would ease the risk are often not considered at all. The focus is placed on the new technology, and the legacy technology is glued into it (or vice versa) with minimal attention to the legacy's effects. After all, the team that is implementing the new technology usually didn't develop the legacy code and the goal is to ultimately supplant the legacy solution anyway—right?

The most direct solution is to compromise the robustness and security strength of the new technology to match that of the legacy solution, in essence allowing both the modern and legacy technology to be active simultaneously. Learned helplessness enters when developers can't imagine that anything could be done—or worse, even should be done—to mitigate the vulnerabilities of the legacy code. The legacy code was forced on them, it is not perceived to be their bailiwick (even if it impacts the security of the new technology by reducing it to the level of the old), and they feel they are powerless to do anything about it anyway due to corporate decree.

A Real-Life Example: How Microsoft Enabled L0phtCrack

Years ago, to help system administrators uncover vulnerabilities, I wrote a password-cracking tool that recovered Microsoft user passwords. It was called L0phtCrack at the time, later to be renamed LC5, and then discontinued by Symantec (who had acquired the rights to it) due to concerns that it could be considered a munition under the International Tariff on Arms Regulations (ITAR).† Many articles on the Net and passages in technical books have been written about how L0phtCrack worked, but none have focused on *why* it worked in the first

---

* Or at least it often appears to the developers and engineers that this is the case.

† This might not be the end of L0phtCrack....

place. What were some of the potential influences that contributed to the vulnerabilities that L0phtCrack took advantage of in Microsoft Windows?

In fact, the tool directly exploited numerous problems in the implementation and use of cryptographic routines in Windows. All these problems originated in the legacy LAN Manager (or LANMAN) hash function that continued to be used in versions of Windows up to Vista. Its hash representation, although based on the already aging Data Encryption Standard (DES), contained no salt. In addition, passwords in LANMAN were case-insensitive. The function broke the 14-character or shorter password into two 7-byte values that were each encrypted against the same key and then concatenated. As I described in a post to BugTraq in the late 1990s, the basic encryption sequence, illustrated in Figure 1-1, is:

1. If the password is less than 14 characters, pad it with nulls to fill out the allocated 14-character space set aside for the password. If the password is greater than 14 characters, in contrast, it is truncated.

2. Convert the 14-character password to all uppercase and split it into two 7-character halves. It should be noted that if the original password was 7 or fewer characters, the second half will always be 7 nulls.

3. Convert each 7-byte half to an 8-byte parity DES key.

4. DES encrypt a known constant ("KGS!@#$%") using each of the previously mentioned keys.

5. Concatenate the two outputs to form the LM_HASH representation.

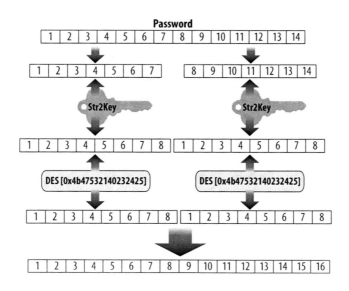

FIGURE 1-1. Summary of old LANMAN hash algorithm

This combination of choices was problematic for many technical reasons.

The developers of Windows NT were conscious of the weaknesses in the LANMAN hash and used a stronger algorithm for its storage of password credentials, referred to as the NT hash. It maintained the case of the characters, allowed passwords longer than 14 characters, and used the more modern MD4 message digest to produce its 16-byte hash.

Unfortunately, Windows systems continued to store the weaker version of each password next to the stronger one—and to send both versions over the network each time a user logged in. Across the network, both the weaker 16-byte LANMAN hash and the stronger 16-byte NT hash underwent the following process, which is represented in Figure 1-2:

1. Pad the hash with nulls to 21 bytes.

2. Break the 21-byte result into three 7-byte subcomponents.

3. Convert each 7-byte subcomponent to 8-byte parity DES keys.

4. Encrypt an 8-byte challenge, which was visibly sent across the network, using the previously mentioned DES keys.

5. Concatenate the three 8-byte outputs from step 4 to make a 24-byte representation that would be sent over the network.

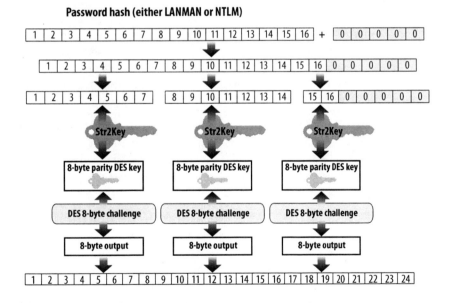

FIGURE 1-2. Handling both LANMAN and NT hashes over the network

Microsoft preferred for all their customers to upgrade to newer versions of Windows, of course, but did not dare to cut off customers using older versions or even retrofit them with the new hash function. Because the password was a key part of networking, they had to assume that, for the foreseeable future, old systems with no understanding of the new hash function would continue to connect to systems fitted out with the more secure hash.

If systems on both sides of the login were new systems with new hash functions, they could perform the actual authentication using the stronger NT hash. But a representation of the older and more vulnerable LANMAN hash was sent right alongside its stronger sibling.

By taking the path of least resistance to backward compatibility and ignoring the ramifications, Microsoft completely undermined the technical advances of its newer security technology.

L0phtCrack took advantage of the weak LANMAN password encoding and leveraged the results against the stronger NTLM representation that was stored next to it. Even if a user chose a password longer than 14 characters, the cracking of the LANMAN hash would still provide the first 14, leaving only a short remnant to guess through inference or brute force. Unlike LANMAN, the NT hash was case-sensitive. But once the weak version was broken, the case specifics of the password in the NT hash could be derived in a maximum of 2^x attempts (where x is the length of the password string) because there were at most two choices (uppercase or lowercase) for each character. Keep in mind that x was less than or equal to 14 and thus trivial to test exhaustively.

Although NTLM network authentication introduced a challenge that was supposed to act as a salt mechanism, the output still contained too much information that an attacker could see and take advantage of. Only two bytes from the original 16-byte hash made it into the third 7-byte component; the rest was known to be nulls. Similarly, only one byte—the eighth— made it from the first half of the hash into the second 7-byte component.

Think of what would happen if the original password were seven characters or less (a very likely choice for casual users). In the LANMAN hash, the second group of 7 input bytes would be all nulls, so the output hash bytes 9 through 16 would always be the same value. And this is further propagated through the NTLM algorithm. At the very least, it takes little effort to determine whether the last 8 bytes of a 24-byte NTLM authentication response were from a password that was less than eight characters.

In short, the problems of the new modern security solution sprang from the weaker LANMAN password of the legacy system and thus reduced the entire security profile to its lowest common denominator. It wasn't until much later, and after much negative security publicity, that Microsoft introduced the capability of sending only one hash or the other, and not both by default—and even later that they stopped storing both LANMAN and NT hashes in proximity to each other on local systems.

Password and Authentication Security Could Have Been Better from the Start

My L0phtCrack story was meant to highlight a common security problem. There are many reasons to support multiple security implementations, even when one is known to be stronger than the others, but in many cases, as discussed earlier, the reason is to support backward compatibility. Once support for legacy systems is deemed essential, one can expect to see a fair amount of redundancy in protocols and services.

The issue from a security standpoint becomes how to accomplish this backward compatibility without degrading the security of the new systems. Microsoft's naïve solution embodied pretty much the worst of all possibilities: it stored the insecure hash together with the more secure one, and for the benefit of the attacker it transmitted the representations of both hashes over the network, even when not needed!

Remember that *learned helplessness* is the situation where one comes to the conclusion that he is helpless or has no recourse by training rather than from an actual analysis of the situation at hand. In other words, someone tells you that you are helpless and you believe them based on nothing more than their "say so." In engineering work, learned helplessness can be induced by statements from apparent positions of authority, lazy acceptance of backward compatibility (or legacy customer demand), and through cost or funding pressures (perceived or real).

Microsoft believed the legacy systems were important enough to preclude stranding these systems. In doing this they made the decision to keep supporting the LM hash.

But they took a second critical step and chose to deal with the protocol problem of legacy and modern interactions by forcing their new systems to talk to both the current protocol and the legacy one without considering the legacy security issues. Instead, they could have required the legacy systems to patch the handful of functions required to support logins as a final end-of-life upgrade to the legacy systems. Perhaps this solution was rejected because it might set a dangerous precedent of supporting systems that they had claimed had reached their end-of-life. They similarly could have chosen not to send both old and new hashes across the network when both systems could speak the more modern and stronger variant. This would have helped their flagship "New Technology" offering in both actual and perceived security.

Ultimately Microsoft enabled their systems to refrain from transmitting the weaker LANMAN hash representation, due to persistent media and customer complaints about the security weakness, in part prompted by the emergence of attack tools such as L0phtCrack. This shows that the vendor could have chosen a different path to start with and could have enabled the end users to configure the systems to their own security requirements. Instead, they seem to have fallen victim to the belief that when legacy support is required, one must simply graft it onto the new product and allow all systems to negotiate down to the lowest common denominator. This is an example of learned helplessness from the designer and implementer standpoints within a vendor.

NOT MICROSOFT ALONE

Lest the reader think I'm picking on Microsoft, I offer the following equal-opportunity (and potentially offending) observations.

During this time frame (the mid- to late 1990s), Microsoft was taking the stance in marketing and media that its systems were more secure than Unix. The majority of the servers on the Internet were Unix systems, and Microsoft was trying to break into this market. It was well known that numerous security vulnerabilities had been found in the various Unix variants that made up the vast majority of systems on the public Internet. Little research, however, had been performed on the security of Microsoft's Windows NT 4.0 from an Internet perspective. This was due in no small part to the fact that NT 4.0 systems were such a small fraction of the systems on the Net.

Microsoft's stance was, in essence, "we are secure because we are not Unix." But it took until the Vista release of the Windows operating system for Microsoft to really show strong and modern security practices in an initial OS offering. Vista has had its own issues, but less on the security front than other factors. So, when NT 4.0 was novel, Microsoft picked on Unix, citing their long list of security issues at the time. The shoe went on the other foot, and people now cite the litany of Microsoft security issues to date. Now that Microsoft actually offers an operating system with many strong security components, will there be anyone to pick on? Enter Apple.

Apple Computer has seemingly taken a similar marketing tack as Microsoft did historically. Whereas Microsoft essentially claimed that they were secure because they were not Unix, Apple's marketing and user base is stating that its OS X platform is more resistant to attacks and viruses essentially because it is not Windows. Having had a good look around the kernel and userland space of OS X, I can say that there are many security vulnerabilities (both remote and local) still waiting to be pointed out and patched. Apple appears to be in a honeymoon period similar to Microsoft's first NT offering: Apple is less targeted because it has a relatively tiny market share. But both its market share and, predictably, the amount of attack focus it receives seems to be increasing....

Naïveté As the Client Counterpart to Learned Helplessness

As we've seen, the poor security choice made by Microsoft in backward compatibility might have involved a despondent view (justified or not) of their customers' environment, technical abilities, and willingness to change. I attribute another, even larger, security breach in our current networks to a combination of learned helplessness on the part of the vendor and naïveté on the part of the customer. A long trail of audits has made it clear that major manufacturers of network switches have intentionally designed their switches to "fail open" rather than closed. Switches are designed to move packets between systems at the data-link layer. *Failing closed,* in this case, means that a device shuts down and stops functioning or otherwise ceases operation in a "secure" fashion. This would result in data no longer passing through the system in question. Conversely, *failing open* implies that the system stops performing any intelligent functions and just blindly forwards all packets it receives out of all of its ports.‡

In essence, a switch that fails open turns itself into a dumb hub. If you're out to passively sniff network traffic that is not intended for you, a dumb hub is just what you want. A properly functioning switch will attempt to send traffic only to the appropriate destinations.

Many organizations assume that passive network sniffing is not a viable threat because they are running switches. But it is entirely common nowadays to connect a sniffer to a switched LAN and see data that is not destined for you—often to the extreme surprise of the networking group at that organization. They don't realize that the vendor has decided to avoid connectivity disruptions at all costs (probably because it correctly fears the outrage of customer sites whose communications come to a screeching halt), and therefore make its switches revert to a dumb broadcast mode in the event that a switch becomes confused through a bug, a security attack, or the lack of explicit instructions on what to do with certain packets. The vendor, in other words, has quietly made a decision about what is best for its customer.

I would like to believe that the customer would be in a better position to determine what is and what is not in her best interest. While it might be a good idea for a switch to fail open rather than shut down an assembly line, there are situations where switches are used to separate important traffic and segregate internal domains and systems. In such cases it might be in the best interest of the customer if the switch fails closed and sends an alarm. The customer should at least be provided a choice.

Here we have both learned helplessness on the vendor's part and naïveté on the consumer's part. The learned helplessness comes from the vendor's cynicism about its ability to educate the customer and get the customer to appreciate the value of having a choice. This is somewhat similar to the previous discussion of legacy system compatibility solutions. The vendor believes that providing extra configurability of this kind will just confuse the customer, cause the customer to shoot herself in the foot, or generate costly support calls to the vendor.

The naïveté of the client is understandable: she has bought spiffy-looking systems from well-established vendors and at the moment everything seems to be running fine. But the reasonableness of such naïveté doesn't reduce its usefulness to an adversary. *Must a system's security be reduced by an attempt to have it always work in any environment?* Are protocols blinded deliberately to allow legacy version systems to interact at weaker security levels? If a system gets confused, will it revert to acting as a dumb legacy device? These situations can often be traced back to learned helplessness.

‡ This is the opposite of electrical circuits, where failing closed allows current to flow and failing open breaks the circuit.

Confirmation Traps

Hobbit (friend and hacker[§] extraordinaire) and I were having dinner one August (back around 1997) with an executive and a senior engineer[‖] from Microsoft. They wanted to know how we were able to find so many flaws in Microsoft products so readily. I believe, with imperfect memory, that we replied truthfully and said we would input random garbage into the systems. This is a straightforward bug- and security-testing technique, sometimes known as "fuzzing," and has now been documented in major computer science publications. However, fuzzing was not widely practiced by the "hacker" community at the time.

We told the engineer we were surprised how often Windows would go belly-up when confronted with fuzzed input. We followed up by asking what sort of robustness testing they performed, as it would seem that proper QA would include bad input testing and should have identified many of the system and application crashes we were finding.

The engineer's response was that they performed exhaustive usability testing on all of their products, but that this did not include *trying* to crash the products. This response shone a light on the problem. While Microsoft made efforts to ensure a good user experience, they were not considering adversarial users or environments.

As an example, teams that developed Microsoft Word would test their file parsers against various acceptable input formats (Word, Word Perfect, RTF, plain text, etc.). They would not test variations of the expected formats that could be created by hand but could never be generated by a compatible word processor. But a malicious attacker will test these systems with malformed versions of the expected formats, as well as quasi-random garbage.

When we asked the senior Microsoft representatives at dinner why they did not send malicious data or provide malformed files as input to their product's testing, the answer was, "Why would a user want to do that?" Their faces bore looks of shock and dismay that anyone would intentionally interact with a piece of software in such a way as to intentionally try to make it fail.

They never considered that their applications would be deployed in a hostile environment. And this view of a benign world probably sprang from another psychological trait that malicious attackers can exploit: *confirmation traps*.

An Introduction to the Concept

Microsoft's product testing was designed to *confirm* their beliefs about how their software behaved rather than *refute* those beliefs. Software architects and engineers frequently suffer

---

[§] The word "hacker" is being used in the truest and most positive sense here.

[‖] Sometimes it seems it is cheaper to hire a key inventor of a protocol and have him "reinvent" it rather than license the technology. One of the people responsible for Microsoft's "reimplementation" of DCE/RPC into SMB/CIFS was the engineer present at the dinner.

from this blind spot. In a 1968 paper, Peter Wason pointed out that "obtaining the correct solution necessitates a willingness to attempt to falsify the hypothesis, and thus test the intuitive ideas that so often carry the feeling of certitude."[#] He demonstrated confirmation traps through a simple mental test.

Find some people and inform them that you are conducting a little experiment. You will provide the participant with a list of integers conforming to a rule that he is supposed to guess. To determine the rule, he should propose some more data points, and you will tell him whether each of his sets of points conform to the unspoken rule. When the participant thinks he knows what the rule is, he can propose it.

In actuality, the rule is simply *any three ascending numbers*, but you will keep this to yourself.

The initial data points you will provide are the numbers 2, 4, and 6.

At this point, one of the participants might offer the numbers 8, 10, and 12. You should inform her that 8, 10, 12 does indeed conform to the rule. Another participant might suggest 1, 3, and 5. Again, you would confirm that the series 1, 3, and 5 conforms to the rule.

People see the initial series of numbers 2, 4, and 6 and note an obvious relationship: that each number is incremented by two to form the next number. They incorporate this requirement—which is entirely in their own minds, not part of your secret rule—into their attempts to provide matching numbers, and when these sequences conform, the confirmation pushes them further down the path of confirming their preconceived belief rather than attempting to refute it.

Imagine the secret rule now as a software rule for accepting input, and imagine that the participants in your experiment are software testers who believe all users will enter sequences incremented by two. They won't test other sequences, such as 1,14, and 9,087 (not to mention −55, −30, and 0). And the resulting system is almost certain to accept untested inputs, only to break down.

Why do confirmation traps work? The fact is that we all like to be correct rather than incorrect. While rigid logic would dictate trying to test our hypotheses—that all inputs must be even numbers, or must be incremented by two—by proposing a series that does not conform to our hypothesis (such as 10, 9, 8), it is simply human nature to attempt to reinforce our beliefs rather than to contradict them.

"Does a piece of software work as expected?" should be tested not just by using it the way you intend, but also through bizarre, malicious, and random uses. But internal software testing rarely re-creates the actual environments and inputs to which software will be subjected, by regular end users and hostile adversaries alike.

[#] "Reasoning About a Rule," Peter Wason, *The Quarterly Journal of Experimental Psychology*, Vol. 20, No. 3. 1968.

The Analyst Confirmation Trap

Consider an intelligence analyst working at a three-letter agency. The analyst wants to create valid and useful reports in order to progress up the career ladder. The analyst culls information from multiple sources, including the previous reports of analysts in her position. The analyst then presents these reports to her superior. While this might seem straightforward, it entails a potential confirmation trap. Before her superiors were in the position to review her work, it is quite likely that *they* were the prior analysts that created some of the reports the current analyst used as background. In other words, it is not uncommon that the input to a decision was created by the people reviewing that decision.

It should be apparent that the analyst has a proclivity to corroborate the reports that were put together by her boss rather than to attempt to challenge them. She might fall into line quite consciously, particularly if she is trying to make a career in that community or organization, or do it unconsciously as in Wason's example with three ascending numbers. At the very least, the structure and information base of the agency creates a strong potential for a self-reinforcing feedback loop.

I have personally witnessed two cases where people became cognizant of confirmation traps and actively worked to ensure that they did not perpetuate them. Not surprisingly, both cases involved the same people that brought the intelligence analyst scenario to my attention and who confirmed my suspicions regarding how commonly this error is made in intelligence reports.

Stale Threat Modeling

During a previous presidency, I acted as an advisor to a key group of people in the Executive Office. One of my important tasks was to express an opinion about a briefing someone had received about cyber capabilities (both offensive and defensive) and which areas of research in those briefings were valid or had promise. I would often have to point out that the initial briefings were woefully inaccurate in their modeling of adversaries and technologies. The technology, tactics, and capabilities being presented were not even close to representative of the techniques that could be mustered by a well-financed and highly motivated adversary. Many of the techniques and tactics described as being available only to competent nation-state adversaries were currently run-of-the-mill activities for script kiddies and hobbyists of the day.

The briefings did try to understand how cyber threats were evolving, but did so unimaginatively by extrapolating from historical technology. Technology had progressed but the models had not, and had been left far behind reality. So the briefings ended up regurgitating scenarios that were possibly based in accurate generalizations at one point in the past, but were now obsolete and inaccurate. This is endemic of confirmation traps. And as it turned out, the briefings I had been asked to comment on had come about due to situations similar to the aforementioned analyst confirmation trap.

Rationalizing Away Capabilities

As the success of the L0pht in breaking security and releasing such tools as L0phtCrack became well known, the government developed a disturbing interest in our team and wanted to understand what we were capable of. I reluctantly extended an invitation to a group from the White House to visit and get a briefing. Now, mind you, the L0pht guys were not very comfortable having a bunch of spooks and government representatives visiting, but eventually I and another member were able to convince everyone to let the "govvies" come to our "secret" location.

At the end of the night, after a meeting and a dinner together, we walked the government delegation out to the parking lot and said our goodbyes. We watched them as they walked toward their cars, concerned to make sure all of them actually drove away. So our paranoia spiked as we saw them stop and chat with each other.

I briskly walked over to the huddle and interrupted them with an objection along the lines of: "You can't do that! You can tell all the secrets you want once you are back in your offices, but we just let you into our house and extended a lot of trust and faith in doing so. So I want to know what it is you were just talking about!" It's amazing that a little bit of alcohol can provide enough courage to do this, given the people we were dealing with. Or perhaps I just didn't know any better at the time.

I think this stunned them a bit. Everyone in their group of about five high-level staff looked at one member who had not, up to that point, stood out in our minds as the senior person (nice operational security on their part). He gazed directly back at me and said, "We were just talking about what you have managed to put together here."

"What do you mean?" I pressed.

He replied, "All of the briefings we have received state that the sort of setup with the capabilities you have here is not possible without nation-state-type funding." I responded that it was obvious from what we had showed them that we had done it without any money (it should be noted that it is a great oversight to underestimate the capabilities of inquisitive people who are broke). "We were further wondering," he said, "if any governments have approached you or attempted to 'hire' you." So in my typical fashion I responded, "No. Well, at least not that I'm aware of. But if you'd like to be the first, we're willing to entertain offers...."

Even with this poor attempt at humor, we ended up getting along.

But despite the fear on both sides and the communication problems that resulted from our radically different viewpoints, the government team left understanding that our exploits had truly been achieved by a group of hobbyists with spare time and almost no money.

The visitors were the people who received reports and briefings from various three-letter agencies. They were aware of how the career ladder at these agencies could be conducive to confirmation biases. Assured by officials that our achievements required funding on a scale that could only be achieved by specific classes of adversaries, they took the bold step of searching us out so that they might refute some of the basic beliefs they had been taught. They went so far as to visit the dingy L0pht and ended up modifying their incorrect assumptions about how much effort an adversary might really need to pull off some pretty terrifying cyber-acts.

Unfortunately, there are not as many people as one might like who are either able or willing to seek out uncomfortable evidence to challenge assumptions. When testing software and systems, it is important to consider the environment in which engineers, developers, and testers might be working and the preconceived notions they might bring. This is particularly important in regards to what their application might be asked to do or what input might be intentionally or unexpectedly thrust at them.

Functional Fixation

Functional fixation is the inability to see uses for something beyond the use commonly presented for it. This is similar to the notion of first impressions—that the first spin applied to initial information disclosure (e.g., a biased title in a newspaper report or a presentation of a case by a prosecutor) often permanently influences the listener's ongoing perception of the information.

When someone mentions a "hammer," one normally first thinks of a utilitarian tool for construction. Few people think first of a hammer as an offensive weapon. Similarly, a flame-thrower elicits images of a military weapon and only later, if at all, might one think of it as a tool to fight wildfires through prescribed burning tactics that prevent fires from spreading.

Functional fixation goes beyond an understanding of the most common or "default" use of a tool. We call it fixation when it leaves one thinking that one knows the *only* possible use of the tool.

Consider a simple quarter that you find among loose change in your pocket. If someone asks you how to use it, your first response is probably that the coin is used as a medium of exchange. But, of course, people use coins in many other ways:

- A decision-maker
- A screwdriver
- A projectile
- A shim to keep a door open
- An aesthetic and historic collectible

Ignoring these alternative functions can surprise you in many ways, ranging from offers to buy your old coins to a thunk in the head after you give a quarter to a young child.

Vulnerability in Place of Security

Now that you have a general understanding of functional fixation, you might be wondering how it relates to computer and network security.

Many people think of security products such as vulnerability scanners and anti-virus software as tools that increase the security of a system or organization. But if this is the only view you hold, you are suffering from functional fixation. Each of these technologies can be very complex and consist of thousands of lines of code. Introducing them into an environment also introduces a strong possibility of new vulnerabilities and attack surfaces.

As an example, during the early years of vulnerability scanners, I would set up a few special systems on the internal networks of the company that I worked for. These systems were malicious servers designed to exploit client-side vulnerabilities in the most popular vulnerability scanners at the time. Little did I realize that client-side exploitation would become such a common occurrence in malware infection years later.

As one example, the ISS scanner would connect to the finger service on a remote system to collect remote system information. However, the scanning software had a classic problem in one of its security tests: the program did not check the length of the returned information and blindly copied it into a fixed-size buffer. This resulted in a garden-variety buffer overflow on the program's stack. Knowing this about the scanner, and knowing the architecture of the system the scanner was running on, I set up malicious servers to exploit this opportunity.

When the company I was employed by would receive their annual audit, as a part of evaluation the auditors would run network vulnerability scans from laptops they brought in and connected to the internal network. When the scanner would eventually stumble across one of my malicious servers, the scanning system itself would be compromised through vulnerabilities in the scanning software.

This often resulted in humorous situations, as it gave the executives of the company some ammunition in responding to the auditors. Since the compromised auditor system had usually been used for engagements across multiple clients, we could confront them with audit information for other companies that were now exposed by the auditors' systems. The executives could justifiably claim that vulnerabilities found on our internal systems (living behind firewalls and other defensive technologies) were not as severe a risk to the corporation as disclosure of sensitive information to competitors by the auditors themselves—made possible by the "security software" they used. Functional fixation might cause one to forget to check the security of the security-checking software itself.

Modern anti-virus software, unfortunately, has been found to include all sorts of common programming vulnerabilities, such as local buffer overflows, unchecked execution capabilities, and lack of authentication in auto-update activities. This security software, therefore, can also become the opening for attackers rather than the defense it was intended for.

The preceding examples are straightforward examples of functional fixation and can be attributed to the same naïveté I discussed in the section on learned helplessness. However, there are more subtle examples as well.

Sunk Costs Versus Future Profits: An ISP Example

One of the greatest hampers to security springs from negative perceptions of security requirements at a high corporate level. Some of these represent functional fixation.

Several months before the historic Distributed Denial of Service (DDoS) attacks that temporarily shut down major service providers and commercial entities (including eBay, CNN, Yahoo!, and others) on the Internet,[*] I had the opportunity to analyze backbone router configurations for a Tier 1 ISP. The majority of the IP traffic that transited these core routers was TCP traffic, in particular HTTP communications. A much smaller percentage was UDP, and well below that, ICMP. I was surprised to discover that the routers lacked any controls on traffic other than minimal filters to prevent some forms of unauthorized access to the routers themselves. But when I suggested that the core router configurations be modified toward the end of protecting the ISP's customers, the expression of surprise shifted to the company's executives, who immediately told me that this was not an option.

Two schools of thought clashed here. The ISP did not want to risk reducing the throughput of their core routers, which would happen if they put any type of nontrivial packet filtering in place. After all, an ISP is in the business of selling bandwidth, which customers see as throughput. Router behavior and resulting throughput can be negatively impacted when the systems moving packets from point A to point B have to spend any extra time making decisions about how to handle each packet.

Furthermore, neither the ISP nor its customers were suffering any adverse effects at the time. The managers could understand that there might be an attack against their own routers, but were willing to wait and deal with it when it happened. To spend money when there was no problem might be wasteful, and they would probably not have to spend any more money on a future problem than they would have to spend now to proactively keep the problem from happening. Attacks on customers were not their problem.

On my side, in contrast, although there had not been a widespread instance of DDoS at this point in time (in fact, the phrase DDoS had yet to be coined), I was aware of the possibility of network resource starvation attacks against not only the ISP's routers but also the customers behind them. I knew that attacks on customers would be hard to diagnose and difficult to react to quickly, but I entirely failed to convince the ISP. In fact, I had to concede that from a business standpoint, their reasons for not wanting to further secure their systems was somewhat logical.

[*] "Clinton fights hackers, with a hacker," CNN, February 15, 2000 (*http://web.archive.org/web/20070915152644/http://archives.cnn.com/2000/TECH/computing/02/15/hacker.security/*).

(The problem of security as a cost rather than a revenue generator is also examined in Chapter 12, *Oh No, Here Come the Infosecurity Lawyers!*, by Randy V. Sabett.)

Some time after the wide-scale DDoS attacks, I was honored to find myself sitting at the round table in the Oval Office of the White House only a few seats down from President Clinton. The meeting had been called to discuss how government and industry had handled the recent DDoS situation and what should be done going forward.

And once again, I was surprised. The main concern expressed by executives from the commercial sector was that the attacks might prompt the government to come in and regulate their industry. They seemed uninterested in actually understanding or addressing the technical problem at hand.

Then it started to dawn on me that the ISPs were functionally fixated on the notion that government intervention in these sorts of matters is likely to negatively impact revenue. This was the same fixation that I had witnessed when interacting with the large ISPs months earlier in regards to placing packet filters on their core routers: that security costs money and only prevents against future potential damage. They never considered ways that implementing security could *create* revenue.

After the meeting, I reengaged the executive of the large ISP I had previously dealt with. I told him that I understood why he made the security decisions he had and asked him to give me an honest answer to a question that had been on my mind lately. I asked him to suppose I had not approached him from a security standpoint. Instead, suppose I had pointed out that the ISP could negotiate committed access rates, use them to enforce caps on particular types of traffic at particular rates, take these new certainties to better plan utilization, and ultimately serve more customers per critical router. Further, they could use such a scheme to provide different billing and reporting capabilities for new types of services they could sell. The filtering and measurement would prevent inappropriate bandwidth utilization by the client, but any useful traffic the client found to be blocked or slowed down could be satisfied by negotiating a different service level.

But as a side effect, the same filtering would dramatically reduce inappropriate bandwidth utilization by external acts of malice. Would this, I asked, have been a better approach?

The answer was a resounding *yes*, because the company would view this as an opportunity to realize more revenue rather than just as an operational expense associated with security posturing.

I learned from this that I—along with the vast majority of practitioners in my field—suffered from the functional fixation that security was its own entity and could not be viewed as a by-product of a different goal. As so often proves to be the case, architecting for efficiency and well-defined requirements can result in enhanced security as well.

Sunk Costs Versus Future Profits: An Energy Example

Part of my career has involved examining in detail the backend control systems at various electric utilities and, to a somewhat lesser extent, oil company backend systems. I assessed how they were protected and traced their interconnections to other systems and networks. It was surprising how the oil and electric industries, while using such similar systems and protocols, could be operated and run in such widely disparate configurations and security postures.

To put it politely, the electric company networks were a mess. Plant control systems and networks could be reached from the public Internet. General-purpose systems were being shared by multiple tasks, interleaving word processing and other routine work with critical functions that should have been relegated to specialized systems to prevent potential interference or disruption of operations. It appeared in several cases that systems and networks had been put together on a whim and without consideration of optimal or even accurate operations. Implementers moved on to the next job as soon as things worked at all. Many plant control networks, plant information networks, and corporate LANs had no firewalls or chokepoints. From a security standpoint, all this combined to create the potential for malicious interlopers to wreak serious havoc, including manipulating or disrupting the physical components used in the production and transmission of power.

Conversely, the few offshore oil systems that I had looked at, while utilizing similar SCADA systems, were configured and operated in a different fashion. Plant control and information networks were strictly segregated from the corporate LAN. Most critical systems were set correctly to have their results and status handled by a librarian system that then pushed the information out in a diode fashion to higher analysis systems. Concise and efficient network diagrams resulted in crisp and clean implementations of SCADA and DCS systems in the physical world, including restriction of access that resulted in effective security. In many cases the components were custom systems designed and configured to perform only specific functions.[†]

The contrast between the electric and oil organizations intrigued and worried me. As fate would have it, I was in the position to be able to call a meeting about this subject with some high-ranking technical people from electric companies, oil companies, and government (think spook) agencies.

The first salient aspect that surprised me from the meeting was that the people from the electric utilities and their electric utility oversight and clearinghouse organizations did not refute my statements regarding the poor—or completely missing—security on their networks and systems. This surprised me because the electric companies were publicly denying that they had

---

[†] It is important to note that I analyzed only a subset of all the oil and electric systems out there. The differences are put forth here for comparison purposes to help illustrate functional fixation and how it affects corporate views of *security*. The oil industry has its fair share of incorrectly configured systems and environments, as do almost all large industries. Similarly, there are probably some well-configured electric company plant information and control networks...somewhere.

any cyber-system risk. In our meeting they pointed out some examples where security had been implemented correctly—but they acknowledged that these examples were exceptions and not the norm.

My second surprise came when the oil companies stated that they did not go about designing their systems from a security perspective at all, and that although security was important, it was not the business driver for how things were configured. The primary driver was to have an edge against their direct competitors.

If company A could make a critical component operate at 5% greater efficiency than company B, the increased operational capacity or reduction in overhead rewarded company A over time with large sums of money. Examples of how to increase such efficiency included:

- Forced separation and segregation of systems to prevent critical systems from incurring added latency from being queried by management and reporting requests
- Utilizing special-purpose systems designed to accomplish specific tasks in place of general-purpose nonoptimized systems

These efficiencies benefited security as well. The first created strong, clean, and enforceable boundaries in networks and systems. The second produced systems with smaller surface areas to attack.

Enforceable network and system boundaries are an obvious effect, but the case of smaller surface areas deserves a brief examination. Imagine that you have a general-purpose system in its default configuration. The default configuration might have several services already configured and running, as well as many local daemons executing to assist user processing. This allows the system to be deployed in the largest number of settings with minimal reconfiguration required. The systems' vendor prefers such systems with broad capabilities because they make installation easier.

However, this doesn't mean that the default setting is *optimal* for the majority of consumers, just that it is *acceptable*. In the default setting, each of the running services is an attack surface that may be exploited. Similarly, client applications may be compromised through malicious input from compromised or falsified servers. The more services and client applications that are running on the system, the greater the attack surface and the greater the likelihood that the system can be remotely or locally compromised.

Having a large attack surface is not a good thing, but the drawback of generality examined by the oil companies was the systems' suboptimal performance. For each running program, which includes server services as well as local applications, the kernel and CPU devotes processing time. If there are many running applications, the system has to time-slice among them, a kernel activity that in itself eats up resources.

However, if there are few running applications, each one can have a greater number of CPU slices and achieve greater performance. A simple way to slim down the system is to remove superfluous services and applications and optimize the systems to run in the most stripped-down and dedicated fashion possible. Another way is to deploy systems dedicated to specific functions without even the capability of running unrelated routines. These tactics had been used by the oil companies in the offshore rigs I had examined in order to maximize performance and thus profits.

Why hadn't the electric utilities gone through the same exercise as the oil companies? At first, electric companies were regulated monopolies. Where these companies did not need to be competitive, they had no drive to design optimized and strictly structured environments.

One would be tempted to assume that deregulation and exposure of electric companies to a competitive environment would improve their efficiency and (following the same path as oil companies) their security. However, the opposite occurred. When the electric companies were turned loose, so to speak, and realized they needed cost-cutting measures to be competitive, their first steps were to reduce workforce. They ended up assigning fewer people to maintain and work on the same number of local and remote systems (often through remote access technologies), focusing on day-to-day operations rather than looking ahead to long-term needs. This is usually a poor recipe for efficiency or security.

The story of the oil companies confirms the observation I made in the previous section about the ISP. Most organizations think of security as a sunk cost, insofar as they think of it at all. Security approached in this fashion will likely be inadequate or worse. If, however, one focuses on optimizing and streamlining the functionality of the networks and systems for specific business purposes, security can often be realized as a by-product. And once again, security professionals can further their cause by overcoming their functional fixation on security as a noble goal unto itself worth spending large sums on, and instead sometimes looking at sneaking security in as a fortuitous by-product.

Summary

In this chapter, I have offered examples of classic security failures and traced them beyond tools, practices, and individual decisions to fundamental principles of how we think. We can improve security by applying our resources in smarter ways that go against our natural inclinations:

- We can overcome learned helplessness and naïveté by ensuring that initial decisions do not shut off creative thinking.
- We can overcome confirmation traps by seeking inputs from diverse populations and forcing ourselves to try to refute assumptions.
- We can overcome functional fixation by looking for alternative uses for our tools, as well as alternative paths to achieve our goals.

All these ventures require practice. But opportunities to practice them come up every day. If more people work at them, this approach, which I'm so often told is unusual, will become less curious to others.

CHAPTER TWO

Wireless Networking: Fertile Ground for Social Engineering

Jim Stickley

By now, everyone has heard the security concerns about wireless devices. They have been an area of concern for many security professionals since the original Wi-Fi release in 2000. As early as 2001, the standard Wired Equivalent Privacy (WEP) access protocol, designed to keep unwanted users from accessing the device, was discovered to have fundamental flaws that allowed security to be bypassed within a couple of minutes. Although security was greatly increased in 2003 with the release of Wi-Fi Protected Access (WPA), most paranoid system administrators still had their doubts. Sure enough, with time new exploits were discovered in WPA as well. Although it is not nearly as dangerous as WEP, it left many administrators feeling justified in their concerns.

However, while one camp has remained skeptical, others have seen the operational benefits that come with wireless and have embraced the technology. For example, handheld devices carried throughout a department store allow employees to accomplish inventory-related tasks while communicating directly with the organization's servers. This can save a tremendous amount of time and increase customer service satisfaction. Wi-Fi has reinvigorated the use of public spaces from cafés to parks around the world. Unfortunately, several attack scenarios remain largely unknown and could feed an epidemic of corporate and personal identity theft.

This chapter begins with a story of how I, a professional security researcher, probed wireless security flaws in the wild and discovered the outlines of the threat they present. Then I'll return to the state of Wi-Fi and the common ways it undermines organizational security.

Easy Money

Here's an everyday attack scenario. You're on a layover at a major airport in the United States. As you scan the departure monitors checking for your gate, your eyes focus on the words every traveler dreads: "Delayed." Just like that, you have become one of the many refugees who will be spending the next six hours enjoying all the comforts and amenities of the airport.

You head over to your gate and start searching for an electrical plug to boost up your laptop's dying battery. I have done this search many times, slowly walking the whole area trying to spot the plug that might be tucked behind a row of seats or on the backside of a pole. You can always spot the guy searching for this elusive plug as he walks by, staring mainly at what looks to be your feet while trying not to be obvious. I assume it was probably similar to the caveman's quest for fire. Everyone wants it, only a few can find it, and once you have it you become extremely protective of it. In fact, on more than one occasion when others have come near, I have grunted and beaten my chest to show dominance.

Now, assuming you are the alpha male who found the plug, you pop open your laptop, plug it in, and immediately start searching for wireless access. Most airports, hotels, coffee shops, and even parks now offer wireless access service. You simply turn on your laptop, click the wireless access icon, and up pops one or more access points from which to choose. As you scan through the list you see an access point titled "T-Mobile." It turns out this particular airport has partnered with this hotspot service, so you select it without giving it a second thought. A couple of seconds later, you open a web browser. Instead of your home page, you are automatically redirected to the T-Mobile page, where you are given the option to sign in using your existing T-Mobile account or create a new one.

Since you don't have an account, you click to create a new one, only to find that the price is $9.99 for a day. While that's not a horrible price, you did notice there were a couple of other wireless access points available, so you decide to quickly check whether any of them happen to be free. You click on the wireless icon again and see a list of three other wireless access points. Two of them are locked and require the correct key to access them, but one titled WiFly is open. You select WiFly, and this time the page is redirected to the WiFly login page offering access for just $1.99. Pleased that you just saved eight bucks, you pull out your credit card and fill out the online form. You click Submit and, voilà, you are now browsing the Internet.

With nothing else to do, you decide to check your email via the online web interface. You type in the URL to the website and press Enter. Immediately an error message pops up stating there is a problem with the website's security certificate. A security certificate is used when you browse to any site that offers encryption. You will recognize that a site is using an encrypted session because the web link starts with *https://* instead of *http://.*

In addition, you will see the closed lock in the status bar on your web browser that indicates the page is encrypted. However, the pop-up error message indicates that the security certificate was not issued by a trusted certificate authority and that the website you are visiting doses not match the certificate.

You now have the choice to either close the page or continue to the website. You think about it for a second and assume maybe you went to the wrong page, so you choose to close it. You open a new browser and try again, and the same error message pops up. Realizing that you are at the correct page and that something else is wrong, you make the assumption that this probably has something to do with the service provider you are using at the airport, and so you click to continue. The page that comes up looks normal, and so you log in to check your email. You continue to browse over the next several hours, and while that error pops up a few more times, everything else seems to be fine.

Finally your plane arrives, you pack up your laptop, leave your electrical outlet to one of the other cavemen who has waited patiently nearby to make his move, and head off to your final destination.

A few weeks pass and you are back at home paying bills. You open your credit card statement and discover with a shock that your credit card, which previously had a balance of a couple hundred dollars, has now been maxed out. With some concern, you ask your wife if she may have gone on a shopping spree. To your relief, she hasn't, and yet still there are all these charges. Of course, by now you have completely forgotten about that day back at the airport where you chose to submit your credit card information to that cheap wireless access company. Unfortunately for you, it turns out that this cheap wireless access company was really an identity thief.

Setting Up the Attack

As part of my job, I am hired to go out and put security scams to the test. I have performed this particular attack numerous times throughout the United States. In every case I have gained access to credit card information. Although the scam may seem complicated, in fact the ease with which it can be performed is what makes it so worrying.

Before going to the venue where I want to launch my attack, I create a credible, professional-looking login page for a fictional company such as WiFly. It offers a form for people to fill out with their credit card information.

Upon reaching the venue, I open a garden-variety laptop and purchase the real Internet access offered at that location. In locations lacking an Internet provider, I just use my mobile device to gain access via cellular. Even if the speed is slow, it really doesn't matter because by the time the victims are using the access, they will already have been scammed.

Next, I set up a wireless access device connected to my laptop. Depending on the location, I may set up a large antenna to cast a wider net.

Finally, I run software I wrote that passes traffic from the computers of unsuspecting victims through my wireless access device, then through my laptop, and ultimately out to the Internet through the connection I paid for. With everything in place, I am the spider waiting for the fly.

Eventually the victims begin to arrive. They choose to connect to the low-cost wireless access point, hit the web page, submit their credit card information, and in a snap they become (should I so choose) another identity-theft statistic.

A Cornucopia of Personal Data

Obviously, gaining access to the credit card information is useful to an identity thief, but there are even more concerns with this type of attack.

Remember the security warning that popped up about the certificate? The warning popped up because any traffic being encrypted was actually being decrypted at my laptop, not at the final destination as the user assumes. In other words, they're running a secure, encrypted connection just as they want—except the encryption is using my certificate and I can trivially decrypt the data again. As the man in the middle, I can decrypt users' data, record everything, and then reencrypt it and pass it along to its final destination. I could record usernames, passwords, email messages, and other potentially confidential information that the victim assumed was being passed securely to a trusted destination.

Even a small slice of your personal networking traffic can open a chink for serious identity attacks. Say, for example, that I gain access only to your email account. I now start watching all email messages that you receive. Think about all the crazy information that gets passed through email.

If you don't use a web-based email service, you might think there's a safe barrier between your email account and your web accounts. But most websites offer a "forgot your login" option. Simply give them your email address and they will email you your password. By checking someone's incoming email long enough for telltale strings, I can generally gain access to the login name and password for anything, including online banking accounts.

A good identity thief knows that the keys to the kingdom are sometimes spread around. Sometimes you have to collect data from several sources before you have enough. Like a puzzle, each piece of data you obtain can then be used to go after another piece of data. In some tests, I put up a wireless access point without charging anything. In these cases I gave up the opportunity to sniff the user's credit card information right away, but I attracted many more users who probably felt even safer because they didn't have to give me that information. My only goal in these tests was to record all the data that passed through. Within a few hours I recorded everything from login names and passwords to online purchases that included names, addresses, and credit card information.

Often, people who live in apartment buildings will attempt to get on the Internet without buying their own service by jumping on an open wireless device they discover, under the assumption that a neighbor put it up. They think they are getting a free ride, but in reality they are getting scammed day in and day out by the thief who put up that access point for the sole purpose of ripping people off.

Precisely because wireless access points are so prevalent and so much a part of our landscape, most people don't think about where that wireless is coming from. At a shopping mall, you can feel reasonably confident that a fine watch you buy from a jewelry store is real. However, if you were driving down the street and saw a guy selling watches out of the trunk of his car, you're probably not going to make the same assumption. It's fairly easy to see the difference between the two and know what looks safe and what looks like a scam. But with wireless access, you have no idea who is offering the goods. Even if the name says T-Mobile and the login page looks exactly like a real T-Mobile login page, how do you know that this particular site is run by T-Mobile? Anyone can put up a wireless access point and put up any page they like.

A Fundamental Flaw in Web Security: Not Trusting the Trust System

One of the major reasons for the success of my attack revolves around the handling of security certificates by both users and servers. Most people don't pay that much attention to security warnings that show up when browsing the Internet. There are two main reasons for this.

Some people just don't understand what these warnings mean. I like to use the example of my parents. They are intelligent people at the age of retirement who, like the rest of the world, have embraced the Internet experience. However, they have never been trained professionally about the Internet and its risks, nor do they work for a corporation that has engineers dedicated to making sure employees understand what all the security warnings mean. Instead they have felt their way through the process and have just enough knowledge to pay their bills online and check their stock portfolio. Something like a digital certificate makes about as much sense to them as a proton accelerator.

On the other hand, I find technically savvy people who have a comprehensive understanding not only of digital certificates but also of man-in-the-middle attacks. One might think these people would never fall for such a scam, but on the contrary, I have found that even these people are quick to fall victim. The reason is that—unlike my parents, who don't understand anything—the experts understand it so well that they rationalize what is taking place.

For example, when the security alert pops up their first assumption is that the administrator for the WiFly site has dropped the ball and didn't renew her expired certificate. Or they assume that because the site is being offered in a coffee shop or hotel, the person who set it up wasn't well trained technically and simply set up the certificate improperly. In addition, you will often come across intranets where the security certificates have long since expired, but IT tells the employees to just ignore the security warnings and use the site. This type of conditioning teaches average users that the certificates are not important, whereas the more advanced users, while aware of the certificates' importance, simply become desensitized to the point where they just don't pay attention.

When I interview victims after these attacks, a very common answer for their behavior was that they have just stopped paying attention to all the security-warning pop ups. Many seem to be jaded by operating systems (the worst offender in this area being Microsoft's Vista) that present you with so many security warnings every day that they become white noise.

Establishing Wireless Trust

Despite the risks of using wireless access points, they are obviously very convenient and I'm not suggesting everyone stop using them. Society just needs to find ways to reduce the risks without reducing the convenience.

The most obvious thing a user can do to protect himself is to pay attention to security alerts. If you are using a wireless access point and receive a warning that the security certificate has a problem, you need to stop immediately. Although it's true that some website administrators make mistakes and don't update their certificates, the risks of continuing are far greater than bailing out.

Of course, this is also a strong argument for better management of certificates by organizations. The digital certificate is one of the few things a corporation can do to give an end user any sort of confidence in the site's security. If the certificate is not properly maintained, it causes skepticism about the rest of the security.

If the site requires a credit card number, another simple trick you can use to check the authenticity of the site is to submit a bogus credit card number. If the site is legitimate, the site will check the card number and notify you that the transaction failed. If it is a malicious site, it is not going to run the card, and will just accept whatever you give it. There are no guarantees with this trick, but it is better than nothing.

My last recommendation is to avoid using public access points to conduct confidential transactions. The coffee shop might not be the best location for logging in and checking the balance on your bank account. At the airport, logging in to sell some stocks should probably be put on hold. Being a full-time traveler myself, I understand that sometimes you have no choice, and you may be stuck having to pass confidential information to whatever wireless service you can find. If that is the case and you have even the slightest concerns about what you have entered, change your login credentials on any website you visited while using the wireless site immediately upon getting back to a trusted location. Again, it's not a guarantee that you didn't already become a victim, but it can't hurt.

Adapting a Proven Solution

Although being paranoid about your information security can help, it doesn't truly eliminate the risk of these types of attacks. For that to happen, the industry needs to solve the trust relationship. When I open my wireless device software and search for available access points, I need to feel confident that a hub called "T-Mobile" really does belong to T-Mobile.

To do this, the access point and the client need to be able to exchange verifiable information that securely identifies both of them. Although coordinating the implementation of this mutual trust in the different systems may be difficult, the technology itself is rather simple and has been around for years. The same certificate technology that has been used on websites could be put to use on the wireless access devices.

The solution would work something like this. The user opens a wireless client and receives a list of available access points. The client would check the digital certificate assigned to each device. Each certificate would be based on the displayed name, the company name, and a hardware identifier, as well as the certificate authority who signed the certificate. As the devices are displayed via the wireless client, they indicate whether they are valid (see Figure 2-1).

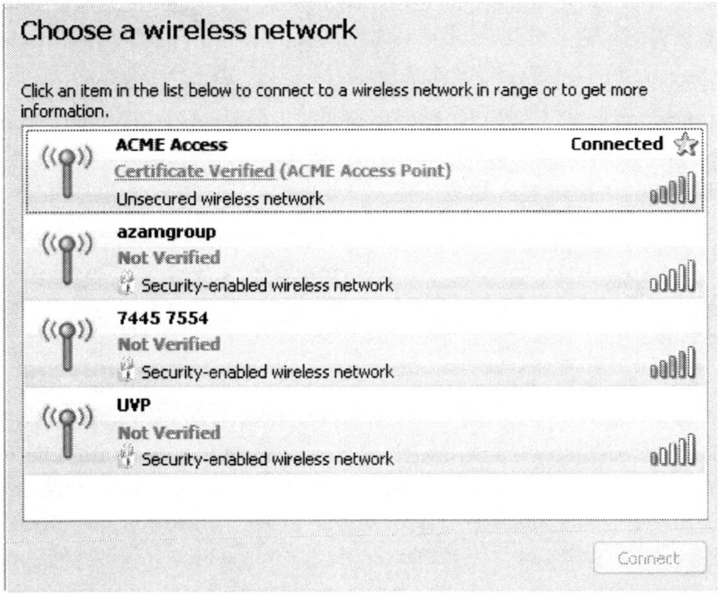

Choose a wireless network

Click an item in the list below to connect to a wireless network in range or to get more information.

((ᵠ))   **ACME Access**   **Connected** ☆
        Certificate Verified (ACME Access Point)
        Unsecured wireless network   ₒₒ◻◻◻

((ᵠ))   **azamgroup**
        Not Verified
        🛡 Security-enabled wireless network   ₒₒ◻◻◻

((ᵠ))   **7445 7554**
        Not Verified
        🛡 Security-enabled wireless network   ₒₒ◻◻◻

((ᵠ))   **UVP**
        Not Verified
        🛡 Security-enabled wireless network   ₒₒ◻◻◻

                                                              [Connect]

FIGURE 2-1. Hypothetical display of certified wireless hubs

While there are numerous ways that the Certificate Authorities could be established, I imagine that the easiest way would be to use the same Certificate Authorities that are trusted for web certificates. Using an already established group would make this particular area of development much easier, and with the infrastructure already in place, the crossover development would be reduced.

I realize that some malicious hubs will post bogus certificates and some users will never pay attention to the difference between a validated and nonvalidated access point. But as people become more educated about the solution, and as the software evolves to help point people in the right direction, the risk of these types of attacks would be greatly reduced.

Wireless Gone Wild

Having charted out the next frontier of wireless attacks and ways to combat them, I'll take a step back to examine the well-known problems with Wi-Fi security and the social conditions of its use that make it an everyday danger.

Network users and administrators who are used to Ethernet-based LANs have trouble grasping the relative uncontrollability of wireless. A LAN uses very insecure protocols (sniffing and altering traffic, masquerading as another system, and carrying out denial-of-service attacks are all trivial), but the physical limitations of the cable are forgiving; it's difficult to tap into the cable and attach a rogue system. Wireless deliberately removes this layer of physical security we so often take for granted, and allows traffic to spill out, even across such physical boundaries as walls and fences.

As I mentioned at the beginning of this chapter, administrators originally used WEP (if they were cautious enough to use any security) to secure access points. The main problem with WEP was that a hacker could simply snoop packets that were in the air and extract the keys to gain access. Numerous tools were created to allow even the most novice hackers to perform these attacks.

WPA was introduced to resolve the security shortcomings of WEP by closing the loophole that allowed the key to be extracted rapidly from snooped packets. For the moment, wireless engineers were happy.

Of course, the joy was short-lived when it was discovered that passphrases used for WPA's Pre-Shared Key (PSK) could still be discovered. WPA starts with an exchange of packets, known as a *handshake*, that verifies the client to the access point. Because data is encrypted, no one can use it to derive the key to break into the system, even by monitoring traffic near the hub and recording the entire handshake. However, the hacker can store that recorded data and perform a password grinding or a brute-force attack on it, which involves taking common words from an extremely large word list and encrypting each one to find which one matches the recorded data.

For a hacker to be successful, a few conditions need to be in place. The most obvious is that the hacker must be able to receive the wireless signal from the access point. I have come across a number of organizations that have thought of this as a primary form of defense. In some cases, the administrator has buried the access point deep inside a facility with the idea that the signal would be too weak to pass its walls. Although it's true that the average laptop using an internal wireless device would not be able to pick up the signal, any determined hacker will own a far more powerful antenna that can pick up a much weaker signal.

Next, the hacker needs to be monitoring the beginning of the session between the client and the wireless access point. Simply monitoring the traffic once the session is already established is of no use. Although this might sound like this requirement greatly reduces the odds of a hacker gaining that initial handshake information, in reality it doesn't help much at all. It turns out that a number of tools have been created that are designed to end a wireless session by faking the client and sending a command to terminate the session. Upon disconnect, the client will generally attempt to reconnect. At this point the hacker will be watching the traffic and now has the initial handshake.

The last major criterion is the strength of the passphrase itself. My tests have turned up access points which such simple phrases as *tootired* or *bicycles*. Password-cracking software can discover these in mere minutes. A WPA passphrase can range from 8 to 63 characters, but I find that most people generally end up using only 8 or 9. Of course, the best possible passphrase someone could deploy would be 63 characters, mixing letters, numbers, and punctuation. So why doesn't every administrator do this?

The main reason is that whatever passphrase you choose for your access point needs to be typed into the wireless client on every computer that will be connecting. The support costs for a really crazy passphrase become a nightmare, as people mistype characters or forget the passphrase altogether. So instead, administrators go to the opposite extreme and make the passphrase as easy as possible. Although there is no perfect solution, my suggestion is to find a happy medium. A passphrase such as "This1was900yearsold!!!" is relatively easy to remember and would be far more difficult to crack than standard dictionary words.

Wireless As a Side Channel

Worrying about bogus wireless access points when you're on the road is one thing, but system administrators tasked with securing their networks have even more to be concerned about.

Some organizations decided long ago that the risk of Internet web use is just too great for their network, and therefore have blocked access to web surfing completely. In the past this solution seemed to work well, but more recently, with the proliferation of open wireless access points popping up everywhere, the threat surfaces anew. Users have discovered that they can bring a USB wireless device to work or use the existing wireless in their laptops and then log on to another, nearby organization's wireless network.

Using others' wireless connections became popular with hackers about five years ago with the advent of *warchalking*. This term referred to the marks left by hackers on the sides of buildings that had open wireless networks. Subsequently arriving hackers could log into these networks from their laptops on the street.

As wireless became more popular, less technically savvy users started putting this technique to use. The problem administrators are now facing is that these users do not understand the potential risk they are placing upon their own organization's network by using this newfound access.

Any user bypassing the main security infrastructure of her own organization to access the Internet through a secondary device is now at the mercy of whatever security the other organization implements. The lack of security already shown at this company in their wireless network is generally not a sign of good things to come. Viruses and worms that might be blocked from entry into your organization have a new avenue through this wireless access point.

Some users set up their laptop or computer so they are plugged into their local company's network and subsequently connect by wireless to the other organization. This design creates a potential conduit between the two networks that directly compromises the entire network security at the more secure organization and negates the majority of its precautions.

Hackers are also aware of how corporate users use open wireless connections to gain Internet access. For that reason, hackers have started setting up bogus wireless access points near sensitive sites, attempting to obtain corporate information.

Their attack is basically simple. Place a wireless access point in a building with Internet access. In most cases, this is extremely easy because most small companies have no real controls on the network and do not know when an employee has installed such a device. Next, boost the signal strength with a modified antenna to reach the largest possible audience. Then, write a small program that watches for any activity on the wireless device. As soon as there is activity, notify the hacker, who begins to attack the computer that has logged onto the wireless network. If the computer is vulnerable, the hacker will allow the user to continue to use the Internet access while the hacker silently gains access. In most cases, spyware and trojans are quickly loaded onto the unsuspecting user's computer.

Once a system is compromised, the sky is the limit regarding the types of information the hacker can obtain. Systems connected to the organization's internal network as well as the hacker's access point are pure gold. Although some routing issues come into play when first attempting to access the user's network, even low-level hackers are able to bypass that problem within a couple of minutes.

What about the corporation's internal network monitoring? Depending on what kind of security has been put into place, they may never know what is happening until long after the damage has been done.

What About the Wireless Access Point Itself?

When I mention TJX, what pops into your mind? Odds are, if you have even casually caught the mainstream news over the past two years, the first thing you think of is the department store credit card numbers that were stolen from this company. It was discovered in December of 2006 that over the past two years, hackers had breached their network and systematically downloaded a minimum of 45.7 million credit card numbers—and there is speculation that the number is probably closer to 200 million. (The TJX breach is covered in detail in Chapter 3, *Beautiful Security Metrics*, by Elizabeth A. Nichols.) While TJX continues to lick its wounds from the fallout and experts are predicting that the total cleanup costs will tip the scales at a billion dollars, it turns out that many more organizations are operating day to day with the exact same security flaws: unprotected wireless access points.

In November 2007, the Motorola AirDefense division, which offers security and compliance monitoring for wireless networks, released a study examining the security of wireless devices at 3,000 stores nationwide. The study revealed that 25% of the devices were not using any encryption at all, and another quarter of the rest were using only the old, vulnerable WEP connection protocol.

It's frightening to still find such sloppy security years after the well-publicized TJX case. One quarter of the stores tested had less security than TJX, while a quarter of the remaining stores mustered only an easily bypassed security matching that of TJX.

Organizations that decide to take advantage of the convenience of wireless need to make sure they not only understand all the risks involved, but also diligently maintain the security necessary to support these devices. TJX, when it first deployed its wireless hubs, had implemented the security available at that time. Unfortunately, that security became quickly outdated. Had the company simply taken the time to upgrade to a properly deployed WPA design, it's probable that most of us would never have heard of TJX.

Still, Wireless Is the Future

From hotels and airports to corporate office buildings and supermarkets, the demand for wireless access continues to grow. Much as with the Internet itself, security risks will continue to be exposed. How organizations, administrators, and even average users respond to these security threats remains the question. Using open wireless access points is risky, and users need to be aware of these risks and respond accordingly. In addition, wireless access points can allow for major security breaches when not properly secured, as TJX discovered the hard way. If you are going to use newer technologies, you must be aware of all potential ramifications.

CHAPTER THREE

Beautiful Security Metrics

Elizabeth A. Nichols

**When you can measure what you are speaking about, and
express it in numbers, you know something about it; but when
you cannot measure it, when you cannot express it in numbers,
your knowledge is a meager and unsatisfactory kind; it may be
the beginning of knowledge, but you have scarcely, in your
thoughts, advanced to the state of science.**

—William Thomson, Lord Kelvin, 1883

**The revolutionary idea that defines the boundary between
modern times and the past is the mastery of risk; the notion that
the future is more than a whim of the gods and that men and
women are not passive before nature. Until human beings
discovered a way across that boundary, the future was a mirror
of the past or the murky domain of oracles and soothsayers who
held a monopoly over knowledge of anticipated events.**

—Peter Bernstein, 1996

THE TWO QUOTES THAT START THIS CHAPTER CAPTURE THE ESSENCE OF BEAUTY in measurement
and its primary deliverable: metrics. Lord Kelvin's message is that there is no science without
metrics. Peter Bernstein's statement is about risk, which is conceptually related to security. Dr.

Bernstein states that metrics free you from the morass of being a prisoner of the past or, even worse, dependent upon fortune tellers—certainly key objectives of science, in general.

For these reasons in themselves, metrics are beautiful—at a conceptual level. What about in practice? In particular, what about the application of metrics for protecting individual, corporate, national, and global interests, especially where those interests rely upon an Information Technology (IT) infrastructure? The purpose of this chapter is to explore the beauty of applied security metrics. I'll start by using the medical field as an analogy. Then I'll turn to the domain covered by this book, computer security, and discuss metrics through examples. To do so, I'll dissect a small collection of highly visible and devastating security incidents. One is in the general area of defending against ATM fraud. Two additional contexts concern well-publicized incidents at two individual public companies: Barings Bank and TJX.

Security Metrics by Analogy: Health

Medical research has used metrics to advance both the science and practice of human health. Health, like security, is intangible. You can feel it but you can't touch it. Health, like security, is all about achieving the *absence* of something—namely the absence of failures in mental or physical well-being for health care, and the absence of failures in confidentiality, integrity, or availability for security. Many security practitioners cite these characteristics—intangibility and "proving a negative"—as reasons why a quantitative, rigorous, analytic approach to IT security is hard or impossible. Medical research is a shining counterexample. Therefore, some observations about metrics as applied to the field of medicine will be useful as a lead-in to our discussion on security metrics by example.

Let's begin by looking at the big questions—stated here as objectives for enlightenment that beautiful security metrics should deliver:

1. How secure am I?
2. Am I better off now than I was this time last year?
3. Am I spending the right amount of dollars, effort, or time?
4. How do I compare with my peers?
5. Could that happen to me?

The "that" in question 5 refers to any recent (usually negative) incident.

The first four questions were initially posed as a challenge for security metrics by Dr. Daniel E. Geer, Jr., a very prominent security "metrician"* whose doctorate is in epidemiology—a cornerstone of metrics used in public health care research. I added the fifth question.

---

* The term *metrician* is not a real word. I, and others, have coined it to refer to someone who performs quantitative analysis to identify requirements, models, and visualizations associated with metrics.

Dr. Geer says that he first heard questions 1–4 from the CFO of a large, public financial services company. In describing the experience, he recounts that there was a fair amount of disdain when answers were not forthcoming—providing yet more evidence that security as a discipline needs metrics to get the respect it deserves.

Mapping the previous security questions to what you might ask your medical doctor requires almost no rewording. Moreover, like security, one's health is a complex function of many factors: threats (such as germs and disease), vulnerabilities (such as genetic or environmental conditions), and the impact of their joint occurrence. Preventive health care, like IT security, aims to identify and implement measures that are designed to reduce the probability that a threat will be able to exploit one or more vulnerabilities. Medicine, like IT security operations, aims to identify treatments that reduce the impact when a threat manages to exploit a vulnerability.

Unreasonable Expectations

In both medicine and IT security, the previous questions are not answerable. In scientific terms, they are (charitably put) ill-formed. The first problem is definitions. What is the definition of being healthy or secure? Is a hangnail enough to render a person unhealthy? Or, analogously, is a single unpatched server enough to render a company's IT infrastructure insecure?

The second problem is context. How did the hangnail get there and is it really a problem? Does the patient have a history or set of characteristics that suggests anything? Does he chew his fingernails? If the hangnail is on the hand of a concert pianist, the impact will be different from the impact of one afflicting a nonmusical office worker. Or, for a vulnerability in an IT asset, the criticality, use, and connectedness (or popularity) of the asset should be considered.

The third problem is uncertainty. A hangnail has some nonzero probability of leading to gangrene and loss of limb or death; or, analogously, a single vulnerability has a nonzero probability of leading to a breach and catastrophic loss or a damaged reputation. Most people know enough about hangnails and their associated risks to treat them appropriately. In contrast, many executives have no idea how to think rationally about vulnerabilities in IT assets. They look to their CISO and CIO who (they perceive) are letting them down.

Why is this? The answer lies in factors that are in part cultural and in part due to lack of scientific rigor. Medical research is currently better at overcoming both factors than is IT security research.

Data Transparency

Let's first look at culture. The medical community has strong and institutionalized data-sharing mechanisms that are critical prerequisites for researchers to learn more and disseminate knowledge. Consider what happens when an emergent health threat is identified with suspected related deaths or illness. Investigators are summoned and inquiries are conducted by experts from organizations with a wide range of specialties: the attending physician, consulting specialists, nurses, orderlies, immunologists from the Centers for Disease Control and Prevention (CDC), the insurer, drug manufacturers, and the hospital. Their findings may well be examined by journalists and politicians. They will also be widely discussed by health care providers and incorporated into medical school courses and other practitioner education to spread awareness quickly and accurately.

In stark contrast, let's look at the behavior of banks that operate 9ATM networks. In the late 1980s, New York banks discovered that printing the customer's full account number on ATM tickets enabled attacks, leading to substantial loss of money for both customers and banks. A thief could stand in an ATM line and obtain a legitimate customer's PIN by observing manual entry. The thief could then use both the PIN and account number (from discarded printed tickets) to steal money. For many years thereafter, non-New York banks continued to print account numbers on ATM tickets—many out of ignorance. As late as 1992, one bank in the UK was pilloried by the press for continuing this practice. While embarrassing, this publicity had the undeniable benefit that the bank immediately discontinued the outdated and insecure practice.

The value of data sharing is well understood by government and regulatory authorities. The Department of Homeland Security (DHS) has mandated Information Sharing and Analysis Centers targeted at industries such as Financial Services, Telecommunication, Power, and Manufacturing. Starting in early 2002 with California SB 1386 and spreading now to over 38 states, state laws require disclosure to a customer when personal data has been breached. This has resulted in a valuable online database called the Data Loss Database (DataLossDB), which security researchers are now beginning to mine for metrics about data loss size and occurrence by industry, type, and source. In particular, the trends regarding breach size and frequency, as well as insider versus externally perpetrated breaches, can now be characterized with metrics computed from accurate and (relatively) complete hard data.

Reasonable Metrics

Medicine's reasonable approach to measuring health gives patients a reasonable guideline for assessing their own health while helping them set reasonable expectations. Although patients do ask, "How healthy am I?" they know that it is essentially an unanswerable question, and most medical practitioners give a somewhat circumspect response like, "Everything looks good today." If pressed, the doctor may embellish this with "Your vital signs are normal. All your test results are normal. You are not overweight, but you should stop smoking"—or something similar. They give a summary that captures a list of unweighted positive and negative facts, all directly or indirectly derived from metrics. In some cases, they use medical terms such as cholesterol and osteopenia and are prepared to provide layman's definitions, if requested.

The point is that doctors don't attempt to give one a patient an all-encompassing score. Often, the list is organized into organ systems: cardiovascular, lungs, skin, nervous system, etc. Each of these systems has its associated specialists that the patient can be referred to for focused, in-depth testing and diagnosis.

And, equally importantly, patients find such answers acceptable. Unlike the CFO in Dr. Geer's meeting, they don't expect a quick, deterministic score.

Moreover, the field of medicine has also developed an impressive collection of metrics that security metricians can learn from.

First, medical research calls for collecting "patient history," "vital signs," and "basic biometrics" to frame a discussion about health. Patient history provides extensive general context that is typically represented as a collection of yes or no answers, like a survey: "Have you ever had measles?" or "Did your mother, father, sister, or brothers have high blood pressure?"

Medical vital signs for most people include temperature, blood pressure, pulse, and respiratory rate. Basic biometrics are height, weight, and pain. For newborns, a special set of vital signs called the Apgar score was designed. This metric was devised in 1952 by Virginia Apgar, a pediatric anesthesiologist, as a simple, somewhat repeatable method to quickly and accurately assess the health of a newborn child immediately after birth. A baby is evaluated at one minute and at five minutes after birth on five criteria: appearance, pulse, irritability reflex, activity, and respiration. The Apgar score is obtained by assigning a value of 0, 1, or 2 to each of the five criteria and computing the total. A perfect score is 10. Along with guidance about assigning values for each criterion, there is also guidance on how to interpret the final score. A score over 7 is viewed as normal. Scores below 3 are critically low.

Second, medical research endorses relative as opposed to absolute measurements. The "pain" biometric mentioned earlier is a great example. Interestingly, pain is measured on a scale of 0 to 5 or a scale of 0 to 10, where a 0 means no pain and a 5 or 10 means the most pain the patient has ever felt. It is considered good practice for the physician to allow the patient to pick which scale (0–5 or 0–10) to use. Equally important is that this metric is measured relative to the patient's prior experience. There is no absolute scale. Since a given patient can't have experienced the pain of others, this approach is the only sensible option.

Third, medical research embraces the concept of "good enough." Positive vital signs and biometrics are probably neither necessary nor sufficient for someone to be healthy. A person can be sick with good scores or, conversely, be well with bad scores. But the latter situation is unusual and, in the spirit of "good enough," measuring vital signs and biometrics is still viewed as a "best practice." Moreover, through statistical analysis, medical research has produced levels of confidence that tell how likely it is that an exception will occur.

Finally, and probably most significantly, metrical researchers base their guidance on vast repositories of patient data, collected over decades. The values for medical vital signs have been empirically determined and validated by analyzing this data. This data is available because (1) patients readily agree to being measured and (2) patients agree to share those measurements. Analysis of freely shared patient data allows researchers to identify normal values with distributions that describe the likelihood that an individual will exhibit values different from the norm and how to interpret the differences. Also, they can determine values for different populations, such as newborns, children, teenagers, adults, and the elderly. Analysis can identify other influences on normal values, such as gender, nationality, race, recent activity or lifestyle, whether the person is overweight, and more. Note that individual patient data is never revealed to either the doctors or patients during consultations, just the derived metrics: namely averages, percentile ranges, highs, lows, and standard deviations.

Culturally, the security profession needs to change in ways that emulate the medical profession. Security must develop a system of vital signs and generally accepted metrics that it understands and are "good enough." These metrics need not be deterministic nor absolute. They can be relative, perhaps even subjective at times. They can have a nonzero chance, but acceptably low and measurable, probability of being false negatives or false positives. IT security practitioners must embrace not only being regularly measured but also sharing data instead of perpetuating the cloak of secrecy that dominates their current behavior. If they don't change, mandatory fiats, such as the California SB 1386 mandate, will force them to share.

With these changes, security researchers can apply rigorous science to back up their analysis. Only then can they free themselves from being viewed with a level of credibility normally ascribed to soothsayers and fortune tellers.

Security Metrics by Example

Metrics have clearly helped medical practitioners by providing both a framework for quantifying the health of an individual or population and a collection of guidelines to communicate that state to nonexperts. Can metrics do the same for the security of an enterprise? As mentioned earlier, voluntary data sharing in this field is rare, but sometimes, when the consequences are sufficiently dire, information cannot be suppressed and the results of the ensuing investigations become public. In this section, we analyze two situations where catastrophic security incidents occurred and discuss how an effective security metrics program might have alleviated or even eliminated suffering and loss.

Barings Bank: Insider Breach

Let us first look at a breach with the most dire of consequences: bankruptcy. The breach was actually a succession of breaches perpetrated by one individual, Nick Leeson, over a period of four years that resulted in the collapse of Barings Bank and its ultimate sale to the ING Group for one pound sterling in 1995.

The players

Barings Bank was Britain's oldest merchant bank, founded in 1762. It had a long and distinguished history, helping to finance the Louisiana Purchase, the Napoleonic Wars, the Canadian Pacific Railway, and the Erie Canal. The British government used Barings to liquidate assets in the United States and elsewhere to finance the war effort during World War II. Princess Diana was the great-granddaughter of one of the Barings family. Barings was Queen Elizabeth's personal bank.

Born in 1967 as a working class son of a plasterer, Nick Leeson's life is a tale of rags to riches to rags, and possibly back to somewhat lesser riches. He failed his final math exam and left school with few qualifications. Despite this, he managed to land a job as a bank clerk, which led to a succession of additional jobs with other banks, ending up with Barings in the early 1990s. At Barings and earlier, Leeson worked in back office operations, but shortly after joining Barings, he applied for and received a transfer to the Far East to help straighten out a back-office problem in Jakarta. His work there was visible and successful. In 1992, he was appointed to the position of general manager of Barings Securities (Singapore) Limited (BSS) with the authority to hire both traders and back-office staff to start up a futures trading operation on the SIMEX (today's Singapore Exchange). Although it was not his job to trade but, rather, to manage, he quickly took the necessary exam, passed it, and began trading on SIMEX along with his team of traders. Consequently, at the time of the breaches, he held three roles: general manager, trader, and de facto head of back-office operations (due to his extensive past experience). Separation of duties is a fundamental tenet of any trading operation, yet it was absent at the BSS operating unit of Barings for four years, only to be discovered too late.

How it happened

Leeson and his team of traders had the authority to perform two types of trades: futures and option orders for external clients and for other Barings business units, and price arbitrage to leverage price differences between futures traded on SIMEX and Japan's Osaka Securities Exchange (OSE).

Officially, Barings (and Leeson as its designated representative) adopted a trading strategy called a "short straddle." This involves selling (going short) both a call option and a put option on some stock, interest rate, index, or other underlying instrument—in Leeson's case, the Nikkei 255 index (among others). For this discussion let's assume that some number of shares of a publicly traded stock is the underlying instrument.

If you are not familiar with options trading, a few definitions are in order. There are two basic types of options: *puts* and *calls*. Both puts and calls are contracts between two parties—a seller and a buyer.

Put options provide a right to sell. A buyer of a put has the option, at her sole discretion, to sell a certain number of shares of stock (N) for a strike price (S) at a time T in the future. The seller of a put option is making a commitment to buy a certain number of shares of stock (N) for a strike price (S) at a time (T) in the future. For one put option, the values of N, S, and T are the same for both the buyer and seller of the put option. The price of the option ($Qput$) is what the buyer pays to the seller for the contract (i.e., the option).

Calls are essentially a mirror of puts. Call options provide a right to buy. The buyer of a call has the option, at his sole discretion, to purchase a certain number of shares of stock for a strike price at a time in the future. The seller of a call option is making a commitment to sell a certain number of shares of stock for a strike price at a time in the future. As with put options, the parameters N, S, and T all apply and are the same for one contract between the buyer and seller of a call. The price of the option ($Qcall$) is what the buyer pays to the seller.

A *short straddle* is a trading strategy in which a trader—say, Nick Leeson—**sells** matching put and call options. Note that a *long straddle* is a strategy in which the trader **buys** matching put and call options. For both of these trading strategies, one can build a model that projects trading profits (Y) as a function of N, S, T, and the current stock price per share (X). Since Nick was authorized to follow a short straddle strategy, let's look at short straddles in detail.

On day one, Nick sells two options: a put and a call for N shares, strike price S, and expiration date T. Nick receives:

Q = Qcall + Qput

from the buyers of his two options. So Nick is starting out with a profit equal to Q. As you will see from our analysis, this is the best Nick can do. At time day 1 plus T, when the two options expire, there are three possible cases:

Case 1: X = S (the current stock price X is equal to the strike price S at time T)
> If the current price and strike price are the same, then neither option will be exercised and Nick will not have to buy or sell any stock. He keeps his profit Q and enjoys the fleeting taste of victory.

Case 2: S < X (the current stock price X is greater than the strike price S at time T)
> In this case, the holder of the call option, who has a right to buy at S (a lower price), will do so. The holder of the put option, with the right to sell at S, will not exercise this option because she can sell at the higher current price. Thus, Nick has to purchase N shares at X and sell N shares at S, yielding an overall profit equal to:
> > Q – N * (X – S)
>
> This is OK as long as $N*(X-S)$ is less than Q. It is easy to imagine a circumstance where this would *not* be the case. Large N or large ($X-S$) will put Nick in the hole.

Case 3: X < S (the current stock price X is less than the strike price S at time T)
> In this case, the holder of the put option, who has a right to sell at S (a higher price), will do so. The holder of the call option, with the right to buy at S, will not exercise this option, because he can buy at a lower current price. Thus, Nick has to purchase N shares at S and sell N shares at X, yielding an overall profit equal to:
> > Q – N * (S – X)
>
> This is OK as long as $N*(S-X)$ is less than Q. It is easy to imagine a circumstance where this would *not* be the case. Large N or large ($S-X$) will put Nick in the hole.

We can compute the break-even value for the current stock price X at time T by solving the equations shown earlier with the profit set to zero:

$$0 = Q - N * (S - X) \text{ where } S > X$$
$$0 = Q - N * (X - S) \text{ where } X > S$$

This yields:

$$X = S - Q/N \text{ for } X < S$$
$$X = S + Q/N \text{ for } X > S$$

To summarize, the model for short straddles can be expressed as a graph as shown in Figure 3-1. This graph shows how profit on the y-axis varies in response to changes in the current stock price as reflected on the x-axis.

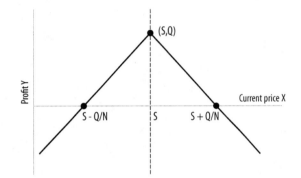

FIGURE 3-1. Short straddle profit model: profit Y is expressed as a function of current stock price X at option expiration

This is not a pretty picture at all. To be sure, it is a strategy that will yield (limited) profits in a nonvolatile market but potentially huge losses if the market becomes volatile. As Figure 3-1 shows, for large values of N or for large differences between X and S (high price volatility), the profits become increasingly negative.

Almost immediately after beginning to trade, Leeson began taking unauthorized and speculative positions in Nikkei 255 futures, Nikkei stock options, and Japanese Government Bonds. Using his influence over the back-office staff, he reported his profits from the authorized straddles in the proper accounts while hiding his unauthorized activities and losses in an old error account (Account #88888) that was an artifact of his previous back-office project in Jakarta. Table 3-1† shows some financial metrics that characterize the situation. All values are in millions of Great Britain Pounds (GBP).

† Source: Report of the Board of Banking Supervision Inquiry into the Circumstances of the Collapse of Barings, Ordered by the House of Commons, Her Majesty's Stationery Office, 1995.

TABLE 3-1. Barings Bank: some financial metrics

Year	Reported	Actual	Cumulative
End 1993	+8.83 M	−21 M	−23 M
End 1994	+28.529 M	−185 M	−208 M
End 1995	+18.567 M	−619 M	−827 M

Up until January of 1995, Leeson was primarily unskilled and unscrupulous. But on January 17, 1995, he became monumentally unlucky as well. A major earthquake in Kobe, Japan caused the Nikkei 225 average to plunge. Extreme volatility continued for over a month. Whereas a prudent trader would have taken his losses, Leeson did the opposite: he started an aggressive buying campaign of futures in the Nikkei 225 index, as shown in Figure 3-2.[‡]

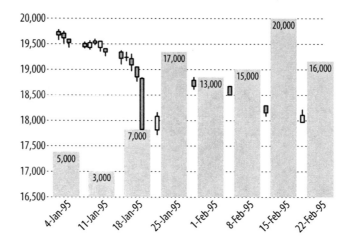

FIGURE 3-2. Purchases by Leeson during crisis

The x-axis reflects time, beginning just before the Kobe earthquake on January 17, 1995, and continuing until just before Barings went into receivership on February 27, 1995. The lefthand y-axis and the bars with whiskers show the Nikkei 225 high, low, and closing averages on the OSE. Before the earthquake, the Nikkei 225 index was trading at a price between 19,000 and 19,500. After the Kobe earthquake, that price plummeted and then wildly swung between as low as 17,400 and as high as 18,800. This translates to high differences between X and S in the short straddle model.

The gray bars in Figure 3-2 are plotted on a scale of Millions of U.S. Dollars ($M) that represent the long futures positions of Barings' traded by Leeson. This scale ranges from a low of about

[‡] See *http://www.asiafunclub.com/japan/finance/stock_market/nikkei_1995.shtml* and Zang, Peter G., "Barings bankruptcy and financial derivatives," 1995, *World Scientific*, p. 137.

$3B to a high of more than $20B, as opposed to the scale represented in the left y-axis that represents the Nikkei index, ranging from a low of 16,500 to 20,000. Numbers are provided for each bar to indicate the associated value in $M. So, the height of each bar reflects Leeson's commitment to purchase Nikkei index shares at a future date for a specific price. Leeson's maximum commitment during this period was $20 billion—more than 32 times Baring's then-reported capital of approximately $615 million. This translates to high values for N in the short straddle model.

The end was swift, painful, and very public.

To be sure, the numbers and charts in this section reflect financial metrics, not security metrics. A key characteristic of beautiful security metrics is that they are linked somehow to financial metrics, or at least some meaningful measure of the performance of a business. What are some security metrics that might have provided the red flags needed to catch the problem before the situation became unsalvageable? We first analyze what when wrong and then look at a "what-if" scenario that assumes Barings had a metrics program.

What went wrong

In reviewing the context and sequence of events described, we can make the following observations:

- Leeson did not have a clearly defined role with targeted system privileges. In fact, he simultaneously was wearing three hats: trader, back-office manager, and general manager.
- Separation of duties between those who define, enforce, and follow policies was absent.
- There was no formal process for reviewing Leeson's access and entitlements for performing back-office and trading functions—specifically gaining access to IT applications.
- No controls were in place to ensure that reviews were performed when Leeson's responsibilities and functions changed.

An important role to which security metrics are well suited is monitoring and performance measurement for controls. In the Barings case, many critical controls were absent. In the next section, we leverage some inspiration from medical research to show how security metrics can be used for both detecting an absence of critical controls and monitoring ongoing effectiveness and efficiency.

Barings: "What if..."

As discussed earlier, medical research has defined a collection of facts that a physician can collect to evaluate a person that she is meeting for the first time and of whom she has no prior knowledge. The first step is to take a history—we have all done that many times. This history is a series of simple questions that provide an overview of patient status. Turning to companies in general and Barings in particular, what would be an appropriate analogy to taking a medical history? The answer is a "security history." This is a series of high-level questions that provide a general characterization of the organization's implementation of controls that protect the security of IT assets. Here are some sample questions:

- Does the organization have formally documented information security policies and procedures?

- Are employees required to follow these policies and procedures?

- Does the organization have an identity and access management process that governs the management of user access and entitlements?

- Is a separation of duties enforced between individuals that authorize access and those that enable such access to IT assets?

- Is a formal review process conducted whenever an employee's job or responsibilities change?

- Is system and application activity instrumented via mechanisms such as logfiles?

- Are activity logs regularly analyzed?

The number of questions in a security history may number in the hundreds. Unlike a patient history, it may take days or even weeks for an organization to complete it, but the principle is the same. It highlights the top-level issues and is intended to give the big picture as well as provide a road map for further investigation and ultimately the collection of more targeted metrics.

The IT security market, as of 2008, is starting to develop guidelines for security histories. Unlike the medical profession, where recommended medical history questions are available, there is little organization or structure in the IT security space. But this is changing. Some organizations are emerging to provide requirements:

- The Payment Card Industry (PCI) has issued a set of requirements required from its members to trust that a company will appropriately protect customer credit card data.

- The Santa Fe Group in partnership with BITS has created the Financial Institution Shared Assessments Program to boost the effectiveness and efficiency of assessing a company's IT security posture.

- Companies such as the Unified Compliance Framework (*http://www.unifiedcompliance .com*) are developing specifications that harmonize requirements as adumbrated by regulations, standards, best practices, and more.

These efforts have high potential for generating a level of consensus "security history" similar to that which the medical profession currently enjoys for medical history.

Barings' answers to these sample (admittedly targeted) questions, had anyone asked, would have been telling. However, it is reasonable to conjecture that the Barings senior management in the U.K. did not realize how bad things were at BSS operations in the Far East. In fact, had they asked, it is certainly possible that Leeson would have lied in filling out his answers to a questionnaire. A subjective questionnaire that reflects what people *say or think* needs to be backed up with *hard facts and data*. Thus, like a medical history, this type of security history must be augmented with metrics. The history is merely a quick and somewhat subjective precursor that can point to areas where more in-depth investigation should begin.

Consider the following what-if scenario: What if a present-day Barings had decided to obtain a Shared Assessments security rating? Or what if a present-day Barings had undergone a mandatory PCI audit as required for maintaining a good-standing status with payment card companies such as Visa and American Express?

Right away, Barings' lax controls for access to trading and back-office IT systems would likely have been determined. Auditors might have discovered a lack of centralized controls. They might have discovered that there were no regular reviews of employee entitlements—especially when employees changed jobs. In light of these findings, Barings would be faced with a low Shared Assessments rating, which in turn would impact their reputation, or they would potentially lose their ability to process payment card data, thereby losing significant revenue.

These last two business impacts would likely have gotten the attention of senior Barings management. Perhaps this would have prompted them to initiate a project to treat the problem. But how much should they commit to spend, and what should they adopt as realistic objectives or measures of success? It is easy to imagine them asking:

- "How did our competitors do?"
- "How sophisticated are their identity and access management controls?"

Unlike health care, the IT security profession has no help to offer here. Individuals whose medical data is used for research have similar risks that can materialize in several forms—higher insurance costs or no insurance coverage, difficulty finding employment, credit problems, and possibly litigation if they infect others. But individuals do, despite these risks, share their data. Why? One reason may be a general confidence that their data is appropriately anonymized prior to its release to researchers. Addressing this concern in relation to corporate security, the Center for Internet Security (CIS)[§] has announced a cross-enterprise benchmark metrics project. Associated with this project, my company PlexLogic is launching a service, called MetricsCenter, that can anonymously collect the data needed to compute the CIS benchmark metrics. The MetricsCenter technology leverages research in anonymization, much of which was motivated by the privacy requirements for medical research.[∥]

Of course, like Barings in the early 1990s, many companies may not be collecting metrics, so there are none to report. This is like an individual choosing never to visit a physician: not prudent.

[§] See *http://www.cisecurity.org* for more information.

[∥] See *http://www.plexlogic.com* and *http://www.metricscenter.org* for more information.

As a result, the Barings executives cannot use metrics (others or their own) to define the scale and scope of their "treatment." Since they have no choice (they need and want a good security rating), Barings must launch an internal project to "treat" their "sick" identity and access management controls based upon intuition. Let's assume that, this time, they decide to implement a metrics program along with the treatment program.

The good news is that Barings' project can benefit greatly from metrics, and their implementation is entirely within the control of internal captive resources. In particular, there is no reliance upon others to collect and share data.

Barings: Some security metrics

So, in our what-if scenario, let's assume that Barings is well along in their project to institute improved controls for identity and access management. Let's further assume that they have embraced security metrics and are busy collecting, analyzing, and reporting results. Note that while the access management improvements are slowly advancing toward the BSS business unit in Singapore, it is certainly possible for Leeson to be blissfully trading away. But his days are numbered. Let's take a look at some generic metrics that will have a high likelihood of exposing his transgressions:

Coverage metrics

These characterize how far a solution has been implemented, as well as inconsistencies in deployment. Here are some examples, in the context of the Barings scenario:

- Percentage of applications or basic services—such as email, websites, or shared storage—whose access is managed by an authoritative system. The closer this value is to 100%, the more complete control has been concentrated in one or a few well-managed places, thereby facilitating accountability. To calculate this metric, one would compare two lists: one from the authoritative systems and one compiled from configuration files and activity logs for the target application or service. The percentage of overlap of these two lists is what this metric measures. In Leeson's case, the metric would expose the existence of secret accounts that the applications recognized for the purpose of granting access but were not officially managed by an authoritative system.

- Percentage of login accounts that are explicitly linked to a valid employee or contractor. Any deviation of this metric from 100% should be examined carefully and ultimately justified. A large class of accounts that are not linkable to current employees or contractors would be terminated employees—some of whom may have less than positive attitudes toward their former employer and would almost certainly have "inside" information. Again, this metric is calculated by comparing two lists: the first from an authoritative access control system and the second from the corporation's human resources or employee roster. The amount of overlap of these two lists is what this metric measures. It would expose that Leeson was using a former employee's account or a bogus account to gain unauthorized access.

- Percentage of accounts or of employees whose access and entitlements are formally reviewed at least once per year, reviewed once per quarter, or have never been reviewed. The percentage of accounts or employees never reviewed should be as close to zero as possible. This metric is often derived from service ticketing systems that keep records of reviews conducted. The result is calculated by dividing the number of conducted reviews by the total number of active accounts. Leeson and his accounts likely were never reviewed, with the worst possible consequences. Leeson was promoted after his first project in Singapore, but his access credentials were never reviewed. As with the other metrics, his existence as an unreviewed employee would prevent this metric from reaching its target.

- Percentage of group overlap. In access control systems, it is common practice to define groups of accounts that share the same entitlements. For example, a group called Options Traders could be defined to possess all of the entitlements needed to grant access to a set of trading applications, or another group called Trade Administration could be defined to possess all of the entitlements needed to account for the exchange of money between buyers, sellers, exchanges, and other parties. The percentage of group overlap between the Options Traders and the Trade Administration group should ideally be zero. It may be less of a red flag if all of the accounts in that intersection have recently been reviewed (e.g., within one quarter). In Leeson's case, his account would have been in that group intersection with no record of any review for over 12 quarters.

Like measuring temperature or pulse rate, none of these metrics are difficult to understand, and none require advanced mathematical computations. Also, they are probably not definitive. It is, after all, unrealistic for any company to achieve 100% perfection in these metrics, just as a person with less than perfect temperature or pulse rate may have a good reason for the deviation (e.g., they just ran up 10 flights of stairs). Also, these metrics are values derived at a single point in time, which gives only a snapshot of an organization's status. When regularly and repeatedly computed, the time series of measurements can form a valuable data set that will support further, potentially more sophisticated analysis.

Time-series metrics are based on a set of values obtained at regular or irregular time intervals. Dynamic changes in a system over time, as reflected by a time series, show whether system state is improving or degrading—and how rapidly. As examples, consider what we would see if we collected all of the previously described metrics monthly or quarterly. Metrics derived from one business unit within a single organization such as Barings could potentially be used to forecast how rapidly other business units could reasonably be expected to roll out new controls. Perhaps we could even project how long it would take to discover and end Leeson's unauthorized access to back-office functions.

Investment metrics

Similarly, if one were tracking the costs associated with a program to improve access controls, one could derive a cost per unit of improvement for any or all of the previous metrics. If the rate of spending is constant and the rate with which a metric approaches its target (e.g., 100%) is slowing, the cost per unit of improvement is increasing. Using forecasting models, one can project how much it will cost to achieve alternate control targets (say, 95%, 96%, etc.). Of course, in Leeson's case, it would be (with the advantage of hindsight) easy to justify any expenditure to get BSS's identity and access management systems under control.

Treatment effect metrics

To derive treatment effect metrics, run a time-series metric to compare performance before and after a "treatment" is applied. Using basic statistical analysis, one can test the null hypothesis, which in this case would say that any detected change is due merely to chance and that the "treatment" made no difference.

As an example, suppose that before initiating the access control project for a designated business unit, Barings decided to collect some metrics about access-related security incidents. Metrics such as the Mean Time Between Security Incidents (MTBSI) or Mean Time to Repair Security Incidents (MTTRSI) would characterize the frequency and impact of observed access security incidents. These baseline values (the "before" time series) could later be compared with the same measures taken after access control was deployed (the "after" time series). Was there improvement? Was it significant (not just by chance)? A statistically significant result would give you confidence that the improvement can be attributed to the deployment of access control.

With "before" and "after" time series data, Barings would have hard facts with which to assess the effectiveness of its treatment. Additionally, it would have hard data to present to auditors and thus either pass an initial audit or clear a negative finding. As more results are gathered in the fullness of time, the statistically derived levels of confidence and quantification of the treatment effects will improve. Finally (this can be only a conjecture in the absence of data), they might have been able to avoid the big access control incident that ended it all.

It is well and good to collect measurements, compute metrics, and analyze results, but these activities are of little value unless one also communicates the findings to the right audience at the right time for driving better decisions. For Barings, it is safe to say that senior executives would not be likely to read detailed reports about access control incidents or, for that matter, any of the detailed technical metrics that we just described. What they might look at is a dashboard with a list of general areas and associated color codes: say, red (bad), yellow (caution), or green (OK). The managers in charge of each area would assign the color codes based upon their interpretation of metrics such as those I just described.

The managers have a tightrope to walk when they are responsible for tracking and reporting security vulnerabilities. Reporting a problem simultaneously brings both the potential benefit of evoking the funding to resolve the problem and the reputational damage for allowing it to happen in the first place. This reputational downside is actually similar to some (but not all) health care situations. Metrics bypass the dilemma by forcing managers to share information with their bosses, who can then evaluate their performance in isolation or as compared with their peers. It's ironic that these same bosses often refuse to share information outside of their department or outside of their company because they fear being evaluated against their peers as members of the same market ecosystem.

Certainly, Nick Leeson's account and its contribution to metrics such as those described would have merited at least a yellow rating for access management controls in the BSS business unit or in the Far East location. The presence of a persistent yellow rating, with no improvement, would hopefully have precipitated an executive decision to commission some type of investigation, if for no other reason than to be able to annotate the yellow with statements that the accounts had been reviewed and no problems were discovered.

It is a safe bet that any sort of review would have curtailed or ended Leeson's unauthorized activities. And, again, it is interesting to note that no understanding of complex derivatives, arbitrage, or higher mathematics would have been necessary.

TJX: Outsider Breach

The second example for security metrics in this chapter looks at the biggest case of payment card theft ever recorded (as of 2008). This is a very recent breach. In fact, events and information about it are still coming to light as this chapter is being written in October 2008. Because of the currency of this case, it is often difficult to assert what is proven and what is yet to be proven. Some of the following narrative is based upon unverified allegations from law enforcement and others close to the case. However, this does not diminish the value of the lessons I draw, because I am using the case to illustrate the value of security metrics.

The breach (or really, breaches) is believed to have started in July 2005 in a parking lot outside a Marshalls discount clothing store near St. Paul, Minnesota. Breaches continued for 18 months until December 2006, when TJX took action. TJX was actually not the first to detect the massive egress of credit card and other customer personal data from their network. Rather, it was credit card holders and issuers who began to see strange transactions on their credit card bills as early as November 2005. It wasn't until December 2006 that TJX became suspicious enough to hire forensics experts and launch an investigation. Although TJX has survived the breach, it may cost the company as much as $1 billion over five years to cover all of their expenses, such as consultants, IT security upgrades, legal fees, and potential liability to payment card companies and banks. Costs to affected individuals and partners doing business with TJX will take a long time to determine.

The players

TJX Companies, Inc., with 2007 revenues of over $17 billion, is the largest off-price apparel and home fashions retail store chain. The company is parent to eight businesses, 2,500 stores, and 130,000 employees. TJX businesses in the U.S. currently consist of T.J. Maxx, Marshalls, HomeGoods, and A.J. Wright.

As of summer 2008, 11 men have been charged with not only the T.J. Maxx and Marshalls thefts, but also hitting an additional eight retailers in the U.S.: Office Max, Barnes & Noble, Sports Authority, Boston Market, DSW Shoe Warehouse, Dave & Buster's, Forever 21, and B.J.'s Wholesale Club. Ten are in custody; one is at large. The accused ringleader is Albert Gonzalez, age 27, of Miami, Florida. The others come from Estonia, the Ukraine, China, and Belarus, as well as the U.S.

At the time of his arrest, Gonzalez had in his possession a Glock 27 firearm, a 2006 BMW, a condominium in Florida, and $1.65 million in cash. He had a high school education, was single, and lived with his parents. In 2003, Gonzalez was arrested on fraud charges in New Jersey and was subsequently recruited by the Secret Service to help an investigation into a major computer hacking operation. In 2004, he was credited with helping to take down a message-board operation that was used as a clearinghouse to buy and sell credit card numbers and other personal information. He was subsequently assigned to the TJX case. His assignment was to be an informant and pass information learned about the hackers to the Secret Service. However, the Secret Service now alleges that he was a double agent, passing information he learned from the Secret Service investigators to the hackers. Gonzalez's Secret Service consulting position allegedly paid him $6,000 per month.

How it happened

Let us first look at how events unfolded from the public perspective. The following time line was published by the *Boston Globe* on October 25, 2007:[#]

> **2007 Jan. 17:** TJX Cos. says it suffered an unauthorized intrusion into its computer systems, potentially compromising customer credit and debit card data as far back as 2003. The company said it knows of no misuse of data.

> **2007 Jan. 18:** Credit card companies, banks, and customers begin to report fraudulent use of credit and debit card numbers that had been stored in the TJX system. Thousands of cards are canceled.

> **2007 Feb. 21:** TJX reports that hackers may have gained access to its computers in 2005, a year earlier than it previously thought.

> **2007 March 28:** TJX puts the number of credit and debit card numbers stolen by hackers at 45.7 million, but says about 75 percent of those were expired or had their data masked.

> **2007 July:** Florida police obtain guilty pleas from several individuals in Florida for using credit card numbers taken from TJX to purchase $8 million in gift cards and electronics at Wal-Mart and Sam's Club.

> **2007 Aug. 14:** In a corporate filing, TJX puts the total cost of the data breach at $256 million.

[#] See *http://www.boston.com/business/globe/articles/2007/10/25/tjx_timeline*.

2007 Sept. 21: TJX reaches a tentative settlement with customers affected by the breach, offering store vouchers to those affected and planning to hold a three-day "customer appreciation" sale. The settlement is later amended to offer affected customers the choice of vouchers or cash.

2007 Sept. 25: Canadian privacy officials fault TJX for failing to adopt adequate safeguards to protect customer information.

2007 Oct. 23: Court filings in a case brought by banks against TJX say the number of accounts affected by the thefts topped 94 million.

This time line shows the progression of escalating revelations regarding the impact of the breach, both in terms of numbers affected and ensuing litigation (all interesting metrics in their own right). As of October 2007, the criminals had not been caught, but there was an active investigation involving multiple law enforcement organizations in multiple states and countries. Almost a year later, in August 2008, arrests and indictments were announced.

Here is a time line based upon a technology perspective:

1999: Wireless LANs born: IEEE 802.11b completed and approved.

2001: Hack to crack WEP protection of wireless communication demonstrated.

2002 April: IEEE 802.1X ratified to address port-level security using Extensible Authentication Protocol (EAP), which works with RADIUS servers, already in wide commercial use. It was intended to standardize security for wired network ports, but was found to be applicable to wireless networking as well.

2002 July: Widespread publication of IEEE 802.11b security weaknesses with detailed recommendations to obtain enterprise-class strength.

2004 June: IEEE 802.11i ratified as an amendment to the wireless IEEE 802.11 standard to provide a standard specification for security mechanisms and to supersede the previous security specification.

2005 June: TJX use of WEP protection still prevalent at retail stores.

It is now alleged by law enforcement that Gonzalez and others practiced a popular and low-budget technique called *wardriving* to uncover open wireless networks. Wardriving involves cruising public areas (in this case, the parking lots of malls and retail stores) in cars equipped with PCs and a good antenna. The antenna discovers wireless networks. The PC runs wireless client software that attempts a connection if the network has open access, or records transmitted packet streams if the network has implemented some form of access security. If the access security is weak, the packet streams can be analyzed using readily available software to extract all the information needed to break in. Once in, the hackers can access network-connected customer databases and begin collecting credit card numbers and other personal information.

To understand how this works in a bit more detail, let us look at a few key facts about wireless networks. We will also provide Consensus Good Practices, recommendations that have been developed by various industry groups and standards organizations:

- The IEEE 802.11b standard specifies a Service Set Identifier (SSID) that differentiates wireless access points (independent networks). As an example, a hotel called the Good Night's Rest might name its WAP GoodNR for convenience. WAPs operating in default mode broadcast the SSID every few seconds in what are known as "Beacon Frames." While this makes it easy for authorized users to discover and connect to a network, it also makes the same thing easy for unauthorized users.

  CONSENSUS GOOD PRACTICE: A company should set the value of all SSIDs to something obscure. A setting such as "TJX-Miami" is not a good choice. Additionally, it is best to turn off SSID broadcasts.

- To authenticate a user who wishes to connect to a network, IEEE 802b specifies a protocol called Wireless Equivalent Privacy (WEP). Most WAPs ship with a default setting for open authentication, which means that WEP is disabled and there is no authentication for clients who wish to connect.

  CONSENSUS GOOD PRACTICE: A company should change the default setting for authentication to disallow open access for all clients.

- When WEP is enabled, each individual client is configured with a secret key that is shared with its associated WAP. A prospective network client begins by sending an association request to the WAP, whereupon the WAP replies by sending a string of challenge text to the client. The client then applies an algorithm called RC4 to encrypt the challenge text and then sends it back to the WAP. The WAP authenticates that the client of the challenge text was encrypted correctly.

  CONSENSUS GOOD PRACTICE: Key management for WEP is a nightmare. To change the shared key, the configurations for each and every WAP and client must be updated.

- The WEP protocol allows an unauthorized listener to capture two of the three variables in the authentication equation: the challenge text and the RC4-encrypted response. With enough sample pairs, a hacker can discover the shared key using well-known mathematics embodied in freely downloadable software.

  CONSENSUS GOOD PRACTICE: WEP is not adequate protection for a wireless network. Good practices for achieving strong wireless security include the following:
  — Turn off WEP
  — Select obscure SSIDs
  — Isolate wireless subnets with routers and firewalls
  — Use 802.1X for key management

Apparently TJX, as well as other breached retailers, did not follow guidelines issued as early as July 2002. The hackers leveraged this fact to gain access to the company network. As a result, they could acquire customer information in transit within a store's network, as well as wirelessly transmitted employee credentials. Using the employee credentials, the hackers gained access to both in-store servers and servers at TJX headquarters in Massachusetts, which stored repositories of customer data.

What went wrong

Unlike the Barings Bank failure, which was an internal breach attributable to an egregious lapse in access management processes, the TJX failure was a breach perpetrated by outside attackers that succeeded due to lapses in network and system management processes. People close to the ongoing investigation allege that the outside attackers found WAPs with default configurations, WAPs with self-evident SSIDs and open access, and WAPs configured to use WEP. These WAPs were the low-hanging fruit that let the hackers gather enormous quantities of valuable data with an incredibly small investment.

So, given our perfect 20/20 hindsight, what did TJX do wrong? The technical lapses are easy to list:

- Inadequate network configuration control
- Inadequate network usage surveillance
- Inadequate server configuration and usage monitoring
- Inadequate data protection, particularly data egress

At a deeper level, of course, the technical failures were symptoms of mismanagement:

- Ignorance of or indifference to basic security practices, such as password protection
- Ignorance about wireless network operation, compounded by failure to follow industry alerts and news about common vulnerabilities
- Lack of unified policies and lack of communication with remote sites about recommended policies
- Refusal to pursue evidence of trouble when reported
- Lack of concern in general for security at all times: during installation, during staff training, and during ongoing use when monitoring should have been taking place

The wireless standards committees and manufacturers also have to shoulder some of the blame for the problem, but that is a wider discussion that I can't attempt in this article.

> ### NOTE
> It's not just TJX that is guilty. Nine other retail companies were hit by the same thieves using the same hacking techniques and exploiting the same holes in their IT systems' security.

TJX: "What if..."

What if TJX had sophisticated sensors that could continually monitor the millions of transactions and the (likely) terabytes of data both stored and in transit within their IT infrastructure? What if they could regularly summarize the telemetry (no human can read it all) and embody it in a collection of metrics, covering a spectrum of aggregation criteria, for regular review? Medical research has produced sophisticated sensors that yield vast quantities of data that can be made available to both researchers and practitioners. It is certainly possible.

The key to successfully creating "smart sensors" in medicine (along with data sharing) is that medical practitioners who deal directly with patients work closely with researchers who, in turn, work closely with vendors that manufacture sensors. As a result, when a medical diagnostic tool is released, it not only can sense data but can also summarize it and provide very specific guidance as to how to interpret results.

As an example, consider equipment that performs bone density or DEXA scans for osteopenia. First, the manufacturer provides information about what the equipment does, how to operate it, when it should be used, and how to interpret results. In addition, medical researchers provide information about risk factors for osteopenia, various treatments (e.g., diet, medication), current research (including medical trials), support groups, references, and additional products. DEXA scan results are often presented as a color-coded picture of a patient's skeleton, where color represents bone density. It is a complete package.

With the current state of security products, one gets software and a set of manuals that are all about the technology and how to operate it. Papers covering recommended usage and the significance of events, which would be the main vehicle for delivering a diagnosis and interpretation, are, for many security vendors (and their investors), the least interesting part of the product. Indeed, system administrators in the field also have a poor record of reading and understanding such documents. The patented gizmo that lies deep within a sensor or software platform, and which end users will never understand, seems to be what is valued most highly—especially in startups, where a lot of the innovation resides. Security vendors, in general, lack the domain expertise to deliver a complete solution, thereby leaving a gap between what their products deliver and what end users can effectively use.

Security metrics have the potential to bridge some of this gap. By providing definitions that specify both sources of raw (sensor) data as well as how to interpret results, metrics can significantly add to the value of the existing wealth of security management products. The Security Metrics Catalog project, jointly sponsored by SecurityMetrics.org and MetricsCenter.org, is designed to provide a centralized, searchable repository of metrics definitions.[*]

Let's look at a few security metrics that TJX would have found useful.

---

[*] See *http://www.securitymetrics.org* and *http://www.metricscenter.org* for more information.

TJX: Some security metrics

The problem of data breaches, unlike other computer security issues, gives us the unique opportunity to look at some public metrics, on both global and local levels. Global metrics capture industry-wide experience, whereas local metrics capture the experience of a single enterprise.

Global metrics.   Global metrics need global data to drive them. California's SB 1386 mandate and similar legislation require the reporting, starting in July 2003, of public breaches that affect individual personally identifiable information. The Open Software Foundation, a group of volunteers, tracks publicly reported security incidents, using press accounts as their primary source of information. Their results are posted at the Attrition website[†] in the form of the Data Loss Data Base (DataLossDB) repository, which physically is a comma-delimited file that is easily ingested by most statistics software. As of July 15, 2008, the Open Security Foundation has assumed hosting responsibilities from Attrition.org for the DataLossDB. Maintenance of the DataLossDB will be a community-driven project at a new location, *http://datalossdb.org.*

Using the DataLossDB as a source, one can derive a simple metric, "Number of Events per Quarter," and generate the time-series plot shown in Figure 3-3.

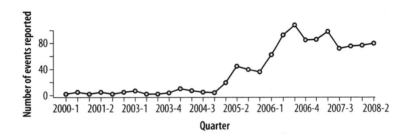

FIGURE 3-3. Incidence of data breaches over first years of mandated reports

The scope and scale of the mandate to report breaches has grown from just California in mid-2003 to an increasing number of states over the past five years. Clearly, the trend in the number of breaches reported is up, but it does seem to be flattening out. No doubt some of the early growth during 2005 can be attributed to new mandates in more jurisdictions. People who otherwise might not have disclosed an event are now required to do so by law. In Figure 3-4 we'll "zoom in" to view monthly data, starting in 2005.

The monthly data shows a fair amount of volatility. If we fit a line (using a least-squares model) to the observations, we can see that the trend is increasing slightly. One can use such a line to make projections into the future, but precision is not the goal. The metrics diagrammed (namely the slope and intercept of the dotted line) paint a clear picture that incidents are

† See *http://datalossdb.com* and the DataLossDB database.

increasing in frequency and therefore it is fair to say that the situation is getting worse, not better.

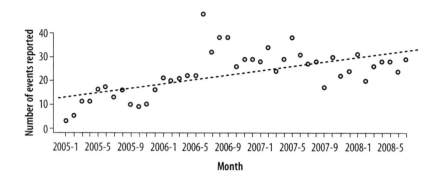

FIGURE 3-4. Incidence of data breaches over recent years

The TJX breach was perpetrated by outsiders. It is widely believed that insider breaches are increasing faster than outsider breaches. The DataLossDB data allows us to investigate this question with hard facts and data. Since DataLossDB tags each breach with an "insider" or "outsider" label, we can create a new plot, similar to the previous one but breaking event frequency down into these two subsets. This calculation produces the graph in Figure 3-5, again starting in 2005.

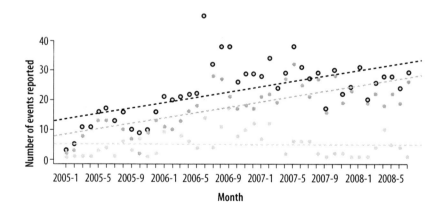

FIGURE 3-5. Breakdown of data breaches

The solid dark gray dots represent the number of insider breaches, and the solid light gray dots represent the number of outsider breaches. The black donuts just replicate the total of the two, as plotted in the earlier trend graph. The dark gray, light gray, and black dotted lines are least-squares fits for the outside, inside, and total frequencies, respectively. It is easy to see that outside breaches are increasing, whereas the incidence of inside breaches are essentially flat, so the increase in total breach frequency is due entirely to the increase in outside breach frequency—at least according to the data in the DataLossDB.

Another aspect of a breach is impact. How far-reaching is the amount of data compromised by each incident? It turns out that the Attrition volunteers record data about each breach that provides a good measure of impact: the total number of individuals affected by the breach. The name for this value is *TotalAffected*. Of course, for most events this is just the best estimate that the breached company can provide, but it is much better than nothing. Again, we are not necessarily pursuing precision here. So Figure 3-6 shows a box plot that reflects the several "distribution" metrics for *TotalAffected* on the $\log_{10}$ y-axis, scaled across all breaches for each year starting in 2005 and going through August 11, 2008. In truth, since 2008 is not complete at the time of this writing, one could debate whether we should include 2008 in the graph. Our rationale is that the current year is always of great interest. But it is important to note that the data shown reflects only 7.5 months.

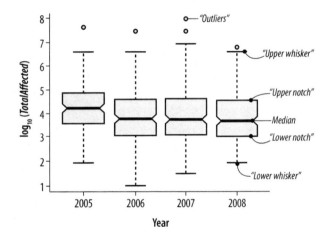

FIGURE 3-6. Compared severity of data breaches

The median is the value of $\log_{10}(TotalAffected)$ for which half of the years' observations are either higher (or lower). The upper and lower notches approximate the third and first quadrant observations, respectively. The upper and lower whiskers reflect values that encompass a 95% confidence interval around the medians of two distributions. In this case, a distribution covers one year of reported breaches, so Figure 3-6 characterizes four distributions, one each for 2005, 2006, 2007, and 2008 (only 7.5 months). The high degree of overlap in all the distributions indicates that the number of individuals affected per breach varies by two orders of magnitude (two notches on the $\log_{10}$ vertical axis), from about 5,000 on the low end to 100,000 on the high end.

It would be interesting to determine the sensitivity of the *TotalAffected* value to the length of time it takes for a breach to be discovered. In the TJX case, that length of time was approximately 18 months. According to the DataLossDB, the *TotalAffected* value for the TJX breach is 94 million. Note that the callout labeled "Outlier" points to the bubble that represents TJX's breach.‡ Unfortunately, the DataLossDB does not track a value for breach time to discover.

Local metrics. Before leaving the topic of TJX, let us very briefly identify local metrics worth tracking, with a focus on internal operations. Perhaps a regular review of these metrics would have inspired TJX IT security operations first to detect and then to protect some of the holes that enabled the breach we have discussed.

Within the TJX IT infrastructure, vulnerability, patch management, and configuration management systems are examples of proactive security systems whose objective is to ensure that certain classes of weaknesses are discovered and repaired before hackers have a chance to exploit them. In performing their work, these systems create vast quantities of data that can be used to derive metrics that characterize how well they are meeting objectives. Two sample classes of metrics include:

Scan coverage
How much of the corporate network is actually being reviewed? Typically, this metric is expressed as a percentage, and is often broken down by location, owning business unit, type of device, type of vulnerability, or severity. Clearly, the goal is to achieve measurements as close as possible to 100%—i.e., total coverage.

It appears that coverage metrics for TJX WAPs were almost or totally lacking. TJX neglected to review the configuration of any of their wireless access points.

Available tools also complicate monitoring. Often, due to specialization, security management products cover only one type of target, such as routers, WAPs, servers, or even servers running a specific operating system. As is often the case, in 2002, wireless access points were delivered to market well in advance of the enterprise-class scanners capable of discovering vulnerabilities in their configuration. It is certainly possible that TJX was a victim of that gap. This is not to say that they shouldn't have known better.

Mean Time to Repair (MTTR)
How long (on average) does it take to remove a flaw that has been discovered (broadly defined) in the IT infrastructure? This metric is expressed in some unit of time: hours, days, weeks, etc. In general, the lower the value of this metric, the less time hackers will have to exploit vulnerabilities.

Although this metric is clearly valuable as a leading indicator of risk, it requires several prerequisites.

---

‡ $\log_{10}(94,000,000)$ is approximately 7.97.

First, sensors need to be installed to detect faults such as vulnerabilities, bad configurations, unpatched software, etc. Second, when a vulnerability is found, records must be kept that track the time it was discovered and the time it was validated as fixed. It is not clear that TJX had any mechanism in place to detect deployed wireless access points, much less poorly configured ones. So they were never fixed. MTTR equaled infinity.

If one can't prevent a breach, the next best strategy is to detect it quickly. It took TJX 18 months and hundreds of thousands of credit card numbers to become suspicious. What are some detection metrics that could have helped?

The thieves who stole the credit card numbers left numerous artifacts of their work:

Sensitive data (e.g., credit card numbers or SSNs) in outbound network traffic
This is easily detected and can be blocked within minutes by existing commercially available tools generically called data usage monitors.

Unexplained account activity
Having intercepted account credentials from authorized users, the hackers logged into accounts, searched databases, extracted data, created files, and performed file transfers to move their ill-gotten gains off to servers that they controlled. All of this activity is detectable via database management tools and, often, application logs.

Metrics that aggregate quantities based upon the data collected by data usage monitors, database management systems, and application logs would reflect the magnitude of activity that was required for the hackers to marshal and export their stolen materials. These numbers would stand out in any time series.

More Public Data Sources

Finally, it is worth noting that there are an increasing number of additional public sources for global threat information. This is progress that should not go unacknowledged:

Symantec DeepSight Threat Management Service[§]
Provides views of the global security threat landscape by capturing and processing security log data from routers, firewalls, IDSs, and other devices. Limited metrics are available, aggregated by dimensions such as location, severity, and type. A sample report for July 2008 is available at *http://eval.symantec.com/mktginfo/enterprise/white_papers/b -whitepaper_internet_security_threat_report_xiii_04-2008.en-us.pdf*.

iDefense Labs (http://labs.idefense.com/)
A subsidiary of VeriSign, iDefense Labs monitors threat as well as hacker activity and reports the results of its analyses to subscribers and the public.

[§] *http://www.symantec.com/business/services/overview.jsp?pcid=hosted_services&pvid=deepsight _early_warning_services*

SANS Internet Storm Center (http://isc.sans.org/)
> This is a free and open service that uses a platform called DShield to allow users of firewalls to share intrusion information. The Internet Storm website extracts simple metrics and publishes reports that identify top ports attacked, top sources of attacks, country reports, and others.

Additional sources of interest are:[||]

- *http://www.gocsi.com* for industry survey results
- *http://antiphishing.org* for phishing, malware, and data-theft data and statistics
- *http://nvd.nist.gov* for vulnerability data and statistics
- *http://www.commtouch.com/Site/ResearchLab/statistics.asp* for spam data and statistics
- *http://www.postini.com/stats* for spam data and statistics
- Symantec Internet Security Threat Reports (ISTR), issued annually
- *http://www.webroot.com* for spyware data and statistics
- *http://www.counterpane.com* for polity violations (e.g., IDS, IPS, etc.)
- *http://www.qualys.com/research/rnd/vulnlaws* for interesting analysis on vulnerability prevalence, persistence, and "half-life"

Summary

Security metrics are a critical prerequisite for turning IT security into a science instead of an art. The major ideas I have discussed in this chapter can be summarized as follows:

Metrics can make a difference
> Metrics can and do facilitate better awareness and better decision-making. They force a structure around the analysis of complex situations and shine a light on broken processes or anomalous activity. Once executives and managers know about something, they are usually capable of identifying a solution and monitoring its effects when enacted. In the cases of Barings and TJX, major failures might have been averted or significantly mitigated if only a metrics program were in place to provide critical transparency.

One size does not fit all
> Metrics that matter must address situations of critical interest as well as reflect a high degree of domain knowledge about the situations that they measure. In the discussion in "Security Metrics by Example" on page 38, we spent as much time discussing the business context as we did the metrics that might have demonstrated their beauty by helping to avert disaster.

[||] Many thanks to Dr. D. E. Geer, Jr. for providing pointers to these sources.

You get what you give

If companies do not begin sharing more data about their security successes and failures, IT security management will be doomed to a morass of soothsaying, oracles, and lack of credibility. In the discussion in "Security Metrics by Example" on page 38, there was little data available for us to actually compute and present internal metrics. The DataLossDB data is far better than nothing, but, as a project staffed by volunteers, one can't expect it to expand its scope and scale without a corresponding increase in investment.

If, on the other hand, a security data-sharing culture takes hold, the IT security management discipline can grow up, become a science, and deliver quantitative metrics to help decision-makers invest in the infrastructure that is the foundation of our increasingly digital world.

Security metrics is an interdisciplinary pursuit

There is much to be learned from other disciplines, such as medical research. Security metricians must also be knowledgeable in IT security, in mathematics and statistics, in the visualization of quantitative information, in scalable software implementation, and in the business that the metrics will serve.

Security metrics is in its infancy and, in my opinion, has been stuck there for too many years. This chapter is about what I believe is required to give it a kick start. Toward that end, we first looked to the relative success of a more mature discipline with a lot of similarities, and then we applied what we learned to some noteworthy IT security failures.

CHAPTER FOUR

The Underground Economy of Security Breaches

Chenxi Wang

THE LATEST STATISTIC FROM NETCRAFT PUTS TODAY'S INTERNET at 185,497,213 sites. Though the absolute number suffered some loss lately due to the late economic downturn, the Internet growth at mid-2008 was measured at over 130,000 sites per day! It is estimated that the worldwide Internet user population will reach 500 million some time soon. The Internet is fast becoming one of the most significant markets in our modern economy.

Not surprisingly, just like its physical counterpart, the Internet is fostering one of the biggest underground economies.

As one might expect, this cyber underground has one main goal: *money*. The actors in this economy employ a wide array of digital ammunitions—including malware, botnets, and spam—to help them achieve this goal.

Unlike the physical world, where behavior can be held in check in most places by laws and regulations, the laws that govern the digital universe are, for all intents and purposes, ill-defined and poorly enforced. As a result, the cyber underground flourishes. In recent years, cyber attacks have graduated from the ad hoc, script-kiddie attacks to large-scale, organized crimes.

The 2007 CSI/FBI Study offers these statistics:

- The average annual loss due to computer crime jumped from $168,000 in 2004 to $350,424 in 2006. This figure represents a three-year high since 2004.

- For the first time in history, financial fraud overtook virus attacks as the largest cyber source for financial losses.

The cyber underground is, without a doubt, a global, thriving economy whose actors can reap handsome benefits from their activities and investments. The increasingly organized nature of the market and its growing sophistication mark a move toward automation and optimization, ultimately yielding higher financial gains for the criminals.

So how does this underground economy work? How do the various actors interact with each other and conduct illicit activities? This chapter presents high-level results of my investigation into these topics.

I'll end this article with some suggestions for ways we could disrupt the cyber underground or mitigate its destructive effects. But I'm not a law enforcement professional, so finding solutions is not my role. Rather, I hope to initiate an open discussion that will spur a community effort to combat the rise of this underground economy.

The Makeup and Infrastructure of the Cyber Underground

Perverse as it may sound, the cyber underground is a thriving community, with all kinds of collaboration and trading taking place every minute. The members of that community rarely work alone; it is a common practice for different parties to exchange assets (e.g., data and malware) to achieve mutually beneficial goals or shorten the time to launch an attack.

The cyber underground breaks down into an assortment of different actors, which I loosely classify as follows:

Malware producers
> Much of the malware for purchase today is of production quality: highly functional, easy to use, and effective. A professional malware writer goes through production cycles similar to those of a legitimate software producer, including testing, release, and frequent updates once out in the field.

Resource dealers
> These actors profit by selling computing or human resources. Computing resources often come from a botnet comprised of infected machines that can execute commands given remotely as part of an attack. Human resources represent actual hackers, residing in all corners of the world, waiting to be mobilized. A resource dealer's existence depends on the ability to tap into the massive botnet pool, and as such they are constantly on the lookout to amass more botnet resources. Their main mission is the creation, maintenance, and expansion of botnets.

Information dealers
> An information dealer sells valuable information—such as customer data, bank accounts, and security vulnerabilities—for a profit. Their main goal, therefore, is to gather more information of that nature. An information dealer is sometimes the customer of malware

producers, paying for information-stealing malware. In February 2008, the security firm Finjan reported that a database of information containing more than 8,700 FTP user accounts was up for sale. In the wrong hands, this information can result in a massive compromise of trusted domains. A person with valuable credit card information is called a "carder."

Criminals, fraudsters, and attack launchers

These are the final consumers of the underground economy. They pay for resources, malware, and information to launch attacks such as financial frauds, distributed denial-of-service (DDoS), and other crimes.

Cashiers

This player in the cyber underground holds legitimate bank accounts but acts on behalf of fraudsters to route and accept money through those accounts. The cashier is the party that cashes out an account and sends the money (often via Western Union) to the fraudster. A cashier typically receives handsome financial rewards.

As the descriptions show, these categories of cyber criminal often play interlocking roles, each being a client or supplier for other categories. In addition, a single party often plays multiple roles: a malware producer may sell valuable information that he reaped from unleashing the malware, and a resource dealer may produce malware to perpetuate the reach of a botnet. When necessary, the different actors may trade their respective assets for mutual gains.

An interesting development in this underground economy is the adoption of traditional business tactics. Many form long-term business relationships with their vendors and consumers. A malware producer, for instance, will thoroughly test her code before release and will often issue updates and patches to keep her customers happy. The cyber underground is, for all intents and purposes, a serious industry. As we'll see later, cyber criminals even carry out their own variant of demographically targeted advertising!

The Underground Communication Infrastructure

Internet Relay Chat (IRC) networks are a classic and well-understood method for communication in the cyber underground. A proliferation of cheap hosting services worldwide is making it extremely easy to set up professionally managed IRC networks. If one network starts to be monitored by law enforcement, criminals can move to different networks with relative ease. When one notorious network called Shadowcrew was taken down by the Secret Service, it had approximately 4,000 members and was conducting a booming business of trading stolen personal data.

IRC members often take measures to conceal their identities. On sites like Shadowcrew and BoA Factory, members often use anonymizing proxies or virtual private networks (VPNs) to avoid being traced.

The underground market and its members are also avid users of social networking. Public forums represent a well-exercised way to vet potential business partners. Many members trade on reputation; a fraudulent transaction may result in some level of complaints against the person in the open trading channel, and the negative reputation will severely impede this person's further trading activities.

The Attack Infrastructure

The different actors in the cyber underground use a variety of tools and mechanisms to obtain information, garner resources, and launch attacks. In addition to one-off exploits and attacks targeting a particular vulnerability or a particular system, which we explore in depth in later sections, many attacks often involve the use of a botnet.

Attackers create a botnet by luring unsuspecting users to download malicious code, which turns the user's computer into one of the "bots" under the command of the bot server. After installation, the infected bot machine contacts the bot server to download additional components or obtain the latest commands, such as denial-of-service attacks or spam to send out.

With this dynamic control and command infrastructure, the botnet owner can mobilize a massive amount of computing resources from one corner of the Internet to another within a matter of minutes. It should be noted that the control server itself might not be static. Botnets have evolved from a static control infrastructure to a peer-to-peer structure for the purposes of fault tolerance and evading detection. When one server is detected and blocked, other servers can step in and take over. It is also common for the control server to run on a compromised machine or by proxy, so that the botnet's owner is unlikely to be identified.

Botnets commonly communicate through the same method as their creators' public IRC servers. Recently, however, we have seen botnets branch out to P2P, HTTPS, SMTP, and other protocols. Using this real-time communication infrastructure, the bot server pushes out instructions, exploits, or code modifications to the bots. The botnet, therefore, can be instructed to launch spam, DDoS, data-theft, phishing, and click fraud attacks. As such, botnets have become one of the most versatile attack vehicles of computer crime.

The Payoff

According to The Aegenis Group (*http://www.aegenis.com/*), the black market value of a payment card account number was estimated to be between $4 and $6 in the 2007–2008 period. Magnetic stripe data for a payment card carries a price tag between $25 and $35, depending upon the credit limit and type of card. Full information sufficient to open a bank account, including birthday, address, and Social Security number, goes for approximately $200 to $300.

Other personal data, such as driver license numbers, Social Security cards, and PayPal or eBay accounts, are often seen for sale on the black market. Drivers' licenses and birth certificates go for about $100. A PayPal or eBay account goes for $5 to $10.

Thus, a piece of malware that exploits an unpatched vulnerability can fetch anywhere between $20,000 and $40,000 a pop, depending on the consequences. Bot army building software (e.g., the exploits and bot agent code) goes for approximately $5,000–$10,000 on the black market.

The rising black market value of personal data and data-stealing malware has created a cottage industry of criminals (the information dealers mentioned earlier) that focus on trading financial information. The incidents at TJX and Hannaford Brothers illustrate just the tip of the iceberg; the magnitude of the problem is not yet well understood by the general public. In the next few sections, we explore the data-gathering game of the cyber underground and how they've turned it into a massively profitable business.

The Data Exchange

The following is a fragment of a captured IRC conversation between an information dealer and a consumer:

> <A> selling adminpassword of online store with hundreds of cvv2 and Bank account # and Routing #. I receive the payment 1st (WU/E-Gold). Also trade cvv2 for *[WEBSITE]* account.

This information dealer obtained credit card and checking account information by hacking an online store, or more likely bought the information from somebody who actually hacked the store. Buying and selling financial information remains the number one activity in the underground market. Compromised information is often dealt multiple times before the information is put to use.

It's alarming how much "full" personal information is out there for sale. A package of such information includes almost every vital aspect of one's identity: everything you'd need to apply for an account, pass simple web authentication, and buy goods online. The following is a captured advertisement (actual details obfuscated) from one of the underground trading channels:

```
<A> Full info for sale
<A> Name: John Smith
<A> Address 1: XXX S Middlefield Road.
<A> City: XXX
<A> State: CA
<A> Zip: XXXXX
<A> Country: usa
<A> Date Of Birth: 04/07/19XX
<A> Social Security Number: XXX-XX-5398
<A> Mothers Maiden Name: Jones
<A> Drivers License Number: XXXX24766
<A> Drivers License State: CA
<A> Credit Card Number: XXXXXXXXXXXX2134
<A> Credit Card Brand: Visa
```

```
<A> EXP Date: 10/2010
<A> CVV Number: 178
<A> Card Bank Name: Citibank
<A> Secret Question 1: What is the model and make of your first car?
<A> Secret Question 1 Answer: Geo, Prism
<A> Secret Question 2: What is your first Pet's name?
<A> Secret Question 2 Answer: Sabrina
```

As you can see, whoever possesses this information can easily assume the identity of the person to whom this information belongs. Mechanisms such as knowledge-based authentication (KBA) using secret questions are useless against this wealth of stolen information.

Information Sources

So where do the information dealers get this data? From a number of sources, including:

Financial institutions

> These are attractive targets because they house all the information a fraudster needs to commit financial crimes. For that reason, online banking sites are constantly under attack; criminals are looking for "way-in" loopholes to take them through the web server to the backend customer data.

Merchant stores

> Many retailers, whether online or physical, have poor security and data privacy practices, and thus remain a popular source for those with a prying eye for private financial data. The data breaches at both TJX and Hannaford Brothers were due to insufficient security procedures.

Individual cardholders

> Spyware, key loggers, and pharmware on a user's desktop are other conduits through which private data is gathered.

Phishing

> Phishing sites masquerading as legitimate businesses can lure users into giving up private information such as login IDs and passwords. Phishing is still a widespread threat, especially for less computer-savvy users.

Attack Vectors

The cyber underground players of today use many attack methods for data gathering. I'll list a few prominent ones here. But many other, more esoteric methods have been observed in the wild that are beyond the scope of this study.

Exploiting website vulnerabilities

A vulnerable website, particularly that of a financial institution or an online e-commerce site, is often the most direct route to valuable data. Because the web server runs software that issues SQL commands to retrieve and modify the internal database (e.g., sensitive customer information), a successful SQL injection attack that fools the web server into passing arbitrary SQL commands to the database can fetch whatever data it chooses.

A well-known women's clothing store was recently informed by their web application firewall vendor that an SQL injection error in their web application could lead to the compromise of their entire customer database, including credit card numbers, PINs, and addresses.

It is almost routine now for security vendors who engage in web application scanning to discover not one, not two, but many SQL injection attack vulnerabilities in existing web applications. With the advent of Web 2.0 and its still-esoteric secure code development practices, we should not be surprised that many web applications are vulnerable to data theft attacks.

Organized crime groups have long realized that digital data theft represents a gold mine for them. It is known that some of these groups have both automated and manual means to scan the Internet continuously, looking for vulnerable sites.

Malware

Many Internet crimes today can be traced back to some form of malware. For example, spyware, installed on a user's machine, can steal private information on the hard disk, such as Social Security numbers, credit card information, and bank account information. Injected iFrames, a form of malware that typically lives on the server, can capture user login information and other proprietary communications between the browser and the server. Bot-building malware, once installed on a user's machine, wakes up once every so often to participate in botnet activities unbeknownst to the user.

The most popular means of malware distribution today is via the Web. Users browsing the Web who come in contact with a malware distribution or hosting site may subject their computers to a malware infection. Many such infections produce no visual clues and therefore are not easily identifiable without special detection tools.

A disturbing trend is that we are seeing more and more legitimate websites unwittingly participating in malware distribution. Malware injected on the website (e.g., the injected iFrames mentioned earlier) can transparently redirect a user's browser to a third-party site that hosts malware. Google reports that 6,000 out of the top one million ranked websites (according to Google's page rank algorithm) have been listed as "malicious" at some point. Many are legitimate sites that are compromised at one point or another. Social networking sites and high-volume e-commerce sites have all been hot targets for malware distribution.

Symantec reports that in 2007, 1,950 new malware instances were discovered every day! Figure 4-1 shows the normalized growth of new malware from 2005 to 2007, according to the numbers reported by Sophos, Symantec, and Panda Labs. In this figure, the most conservative of the three vendors, Sophos, reported a greater than 100% growth in new malware for the last two years. Panda Labs reported a whopping 800% increase in malware from 2006 to 2007.

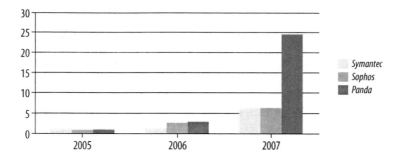

FIGURE 4-1. Estimated (normalized) growth of malware programs

Much of the increase springs from increasing variations of the same malware; that is, polymorphic malware that is written once but can take on many forms to evade signature detection. Indeed, the rate at which malware producers today release malware and the way in which malware morphs itself has rendered signature-based detection all but useless.

Phishing, facilitated by social-engineering spam

Email spam propels more phishing threats on the Web. Instead of carrying actual malware, spam today tends to promote phishing or malware-laden websites.

Another visible trend is the increase in targeted spam attacks that deliver specially engineered spam messages to a special interest group of recipients; for instance, it is not uncommon to see prescription drug savings messages targeting senior citizens and hot stock tip messages targeting active traders. Such targeted spam has a much higher success rate, which helps to sustain phishing as a viable attack method.

Antispam technologies have seen significant advances in the past a few years. However, the absolute volume of spam on the Internet has almost doubled since 2005. This has significantly strained the limit of many antispam systems.

The Money-Laundering Game

A significant step toward greater viability by the cyber underground economy is the ability to turn financial frauds into actual, usable *cash*. This is a nontrivial step that involves extracting cash from legitimate financial institutions.

One of the most valuable assets in the cyber underground is so-called "drop" accounts where money can be routed and withdrawn safely. These are often legitimate accounts owned by parties that are willing to play the cashier role discussed earlier in exchange for a cut of the take.

Let's say Johnny the hacker has full account information for 20 Bank of America customers. Johnny could set up a bank transfer from these compromised accounts (to which he has access) to another Bank of America account owned by Betty, the cashier acting on his behalf. Betty then goes to her local bank and cashes out her entire account. She wires 50% of Johnny's deposit to a predetermined location, which will be picked up by Johnny, and keeps the remaining 50%.

Being a cashier carries a nontrivial level of risk. Experienced cashiers rarely stay put, often having at their disposal a number of different accounts opened with fraudulent credentials. A good cashier can often demand a market premium. Without the drop accounts and the cashiers, the underground economy would be nothing more than an academic study.

How Can We Combat This Growing Underground Economy?

Are companies doing enough to protect their data from computer crime? Some would argue not. In economic terms, the cost associated with a data breach includes both *private* costs, i.e., those internal to a firm, and *external* costs, i.e., those that other entities are forced to pay due to the breach. The problem is that traditional cost models, such as total cost of ownership (TCO), rarely take into account any external costs. As such, the investment in protection technologies rarely matches the true cost of a data breach. It is time for us as a community to face up to these costs and look for alternative solutions, perhaps even ones that are traditionally deemed too cost prohibitive. Some thoughts on alternative directions follow.

Devalue Data

One reason that fraudsters target data is that data carries value. What if we devalue the data, hence reducing the incentive for data theft?

One way to devalue data is to restrict what you can do with it. Take the case of credit cards. If issuing banks reduced general credit limits and made it difficult to obtain cards with high limits, they would significantly curb the appetite for stolen cards and as a result reduce the volume of data theft incidents.

Clearly, this approach goes against the *modus operandi* of those who are in the lending business. But if the recent credit market crash taught us anything, it is to exercise caution before extending credit. As data theft incidents become more common and the cost of protecting data rises further, financial institutions will, at some point, reevaluate the true value behind data. Why not do it now?

Separate Permission from Information

One common pitfall in most security systems is to confuse the granting of *permission* (authentication and authorization to do something, such as make a purchase) with the possession of *information* that uniquely identifies a client. Names and birth dates are personal information that identify a person and can be used for identity theft. Credit card numbers have a similar value to criminals, even though they provide little information beyond some credit history. Authentication and authorization should not require the actual possession of sensitive identifying information.

Imagine a payment card whose number is a one-way hash of the spatial geometry of a person's face and a PIN of some sort. A transaction is authorized only when a facial scan and the PIN verify the card number; the card is otherwise useless. If we design truly hard-to-bypass authentication procedures, we can even publish everyone's identifiers and not think twice about it.

Institute an Incentive/Reward Structure

Today, compliance is a big driver in the adoption of security technologies. Several other authors discuss it in this book. However, compliance is centered on penalties: if you are not compliant, there will be a price to pay. There is very little incentive structure to reward *good* behavior.

The impact of reward structure on improving performance is well understood. It is perhaps time for the information security community to stop relying solely on compliance and start investigating how we can improve overall data protection competency by rewarding good behavior. This should include rewards for internal behavior within an organization as well as across organizations in society.

Establish a Social Metric and Reputation System for Data Responsibility

Just as "greenness" measures a company's commitment to the environment, we need an analogous metric that measures the company's maturity in its data-handling operations. And just as greenness can help a company achieve social goodwill, a good data security reputation should result in customer royalty and heightened trust from business partners. Perhaps such a metric and reputation framework would make firms more inclined to internalize some of the external cost, if it will help them garner a more favorable reputation.

Clearly, implementing these proposals would require a shift in thinking and, in some cases, a complete overhaul of infrastructures, which can be an expensive undertaking. But if we do not drastically change the way we approach the problem, count on it: we will not have seen the last of security disasters like those involving Hannaford Brothers and TJX.

Summary

In the physical world, no one organization or company would be expected to fight organized crime single-handedly. It should be fairly obvious that the same logic applies in the virtual world. Eliminating the underground cyber economy is not the job of one group, one organization, or even one country. It requires the collaboration of many entities and many organizations, including users, researchers, security operations, law enforcement agencies, and task forces organized by commercial consortia and governments.

CHAPTER FIVE

Beautiful Trade: Rethinking E-Commerce Security

Ed Bellis

INFORMATION SECURITY HAS ALWAYS BEEN ONE OF THE LARGEST BARRIERS to e-commerce. Those of us who spend most of our waking moments thinking of new and different ways to secure these systems and applications know it starts with the data. After all, it's information that we are trying to protect.

One of the primary challenges in e-commerce security is coming up with practical ways to secure payment transaction data. This term means a lot of different things to a lot of different applications, but for the purpose of this writing, let's focus on credit card data such as account numbers, security and CV2 codes, PIN numbers, magnetic stripe data, and expiration and issue dates. We will also include extra data we deem necessary to make this process more secure, such as to authenticate or authorize a transaction.

Let's look at the possible points of failure for credit card information. When a consumer makes a purchase using his credit or debit account where a card is not involved, whether online or offline in a scenario such as a phone purchase, he supplies this data to the merchant in order to prove he has the resources or credit to pay for the merchandise. This data passes through various systems within and beyond the merchant environment through payment gateways, back-office applications, acquiring banking networks and systems, issuing banks, and card association networks.

Some of these merchants (affiliates) may resell items on behalf of other merchants, while other merchants (packagers) bundle merchandise and services from various providers and resellers. This currently means that the data must pass through all of the service providers and secondary merchant systems as well, increasing many times over the number of places where sensitive payment data is housed (see Figure 5-1). Finally, degrading safety further, many of these networks and systems contain legacy applications and operating systems that make it difficult to secure the payment data.

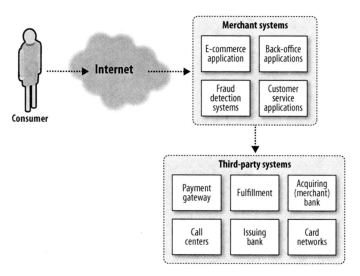

FIGURE 5-1. Credit card data proliferation

But what if we took another approach? What happens when we throw out a lot of today's assumptions around electronic payments and e-commerce and assume that the merchant shouldn't have to store the data at all? What if we never even handed this sensitive information over to the merchant in the first place? As we can see, one of the primary difficulties in securing this data is identifying all the places to which it travels. But what if this no longer mattered? Or at least mattered significantly less?

Deconstructing Commerce

In order to rethink e-commerce security, we must first examine what is in place today. The current security model contains fundamental flaws and suffers from assumptions that are overly broad and ultimately unnecessary. A series of patches and Band-Aids have been billed as best practices and part of an in-depth security strategy. And although these security practices are helpful in protecting data in a generic sense, they do not focus on the real issues of our payment systems.

As an industry, we have spent a great deal of time and money tracking this data, transforming this data through encryption, and protecting it in storage and transmission—all to make up for a lacking security model.

An entire industry has been created around the Payment Card Industry's Data Security Standard requirements for merchants and service providers. But why? This data has become the crown jewels to many security professionals (and those who work against them) in the e-commerce and retail industries.

Analyzing the Security Context

The fundamental problem is that cardholder data becomes a *shared secret*. As we've seen, this secret often needs to be shared amongst a lot of parties in order to fulfill even a single transaction. Because security relies on the least common denominator of security controls amongst these parties, a leak is almost inevitable during the life of an account.

Visa, Inc. stated, in its earnings report for the third quarter of 2008, that the total transactions on Visa's brands—Visa, Interlink, Plus, and Electron—grew 11% from $8.65 billion a year to $9.59 billion. This gives us some perspective when analyzing breach data. Visa is the largest of the card brands, but it is only one of many. And each transaction probably passed through multiple merchant systems, payment gateways, service providers, fulfillment systems, bank networks, and card networks. That's an awful lot of shared secrets!

To compound the issues and complexities of these shared secrets, a merchant or service provider has several reasons to store information such as account numbers after finishing the initial transaction:

Recurring charges
> Many merchants offer services that require regular payments on a weekly, monthly, quarterly, or annual basis. In order to continue to charge the same account on a regular basis, the merchant needs to store sensitive payment information as long as the consumer remains a customer.

Chargebacks
> To issue a refund, the merchant must store the account number that its service or merchandise was charged to. As a measure of fraud prevention, many acquiring banks require the merchants and service providers to refund the exact card account that was originally charged.

Consumer convenience
> Consumers often elect to store their account information with a merchant where they make frequent purchases. This aligns with our discussion later around consumer incentives. For many people, convenience outweighs the risks.

Weak Amelioration Attempts

To address the problems associated with shared secrets among large groups of people, the card associations came up with the concept of a security code (CV2), a three- or four-digit number printed on the card. This is used as a pseudo-second factor for authentication, attempting to prove the purchaser has the card in her possession.

There are two weaknesses in this patch to the system. First, the security code becomes an additional shared secret. There are specific rules around handling security codes for merchants and service providers, but again we rely on the weakest link in the purchase path. Second, not all banks currently support this code, nor is it required in all cases. This means there is little incentive for the merchant or acquirer to reject a purchase based on a failed check of this code. Thus, the security code offers minimal improvement to the anti-fraud system.

While CV2 attempts to authenticate the consumer, we still lack authentication for the merchant. How does the purchaser know the merchant is legitimate? What prevents consumers from being socially engineered or phished out of their payment data?

The card associations and third-party payment providers have created additional security programs to authenticate and authorize payments in card-not-present situations. Let's analyze a few of the more common processes in place today in order to assess what is working and any areas that may be flawed.

3-D Secure

3-D Secure is an XML-based protocol created by Visa to authenticate the consumer to the card. Visa, MasterCard, and JCB International have adopted the protocol under the names Verified by Visa, MasterCard SecureCode, and J/Secure, respectively.

3-D Secure transactions

The name 3-D Secure refers to the three domains involved in the security model. The first domain, the *acquirer*, is essentially the e-commerce merchant or acquiring bank. A merchant, using compliant software, makes a call to the issuing bank (the second domain, or *issuer*) to verify that the account holder (the third domain) is enrolled in the 3-D Secure card program. If the cardholder is enrolled, the issuing bank collects a PIN or password directly from the account holder via a frame on the merchant's web page. This authentication protocol is transmitted in an XML document over Secure Sockets Layer (SSL). The SSL ensures confidentiality of the account holder's PIN or password and the authenticity of both the host and client. At the same time, the PIN or password is not available to the merchant or acquiring bank, keeping this data confidential to only the account holder and her issuing bank. The procedure, while complex to describe, is a familiar third-party trust scenario:

1. The shopper connects to a merchant's site, makes a purchase selection, and enters card details.

2. The Merchant Server Plug-in (MPI) sends the Primary Account Number (PAN) to the Directory Server.

3. The Directory Server queries the appropriate Access Control Server (ACS) to determine whether authentication (or proof of an authentication attempt) is available for the Primary Account Number.

   If no appropriate Access Control Server is available, the Directory Server creates a response for the MPI and processing continues with step 5.

4. The Access Control Server responds to the Directory Server.

5. The Directory Server forwards the Access Control Server response (or its own) to the MPI.

   If neither authentication nor a proof of authentication attempt is available, 3-D Secure processing ends, and the merchant, acquirer, or payment processor may submit a traditional authorization request, if desired.

6. The MPI sends a Payer Authentication Request (PAR) to the Access Control Server.

7. The Access Control Server receives the Payer Authentication Request.

8. The Access Control Server authenticates the shopper using processes applicable to the Primary Account Number (PAN), which may involve a password, chip, PIN, etc. Alternatively, the Access Control Server may produce a proof of authentication attempt.

9. The Access Control Server then formats the Payer Authentication Response message with appropriate values and signs it.

10. The Access Control Server returns the Payer Authentication Response to the MPI in order to cache the response for use in further transactions.

    The Access Control Server can send selected data to an Authentication History Server (AHS).

11. The MPI receives the Payer Authentication Response.

12. The MPI validates the Payer Authentication Response signature (either by performing the validation itself or by passing the message to a separate Validation Server).

13. The merchant proceeds with an authorization exchange with the acquirer.

Following step 13, the acquirer processes the authorization with the issuer via an authorization system such as VisaNet, and then returns the results to the merchant.

Evaluation of 3-D Secure

3-D Secure has some nice features for authenticating the user to the account, as well as due diligence on the merchant side to ensure it is registered with the card brands; uses compliant payment software; and maintains an active, legitimate merchant account with an acquiring bank. But it has proven unwieldy in practice.

Phishing concerns have been a persistent issue with 3-D Secure. On the one hand, some phishers mimic its behavior. On the other hand, some users reject authentic 3-D Secure transactions as phishing attempts. This has to do with the somewhat out-of-band nature of the PIN authentication, since the request is coming from a different domain than the merchant, and the fact that the issuing bank and the DNS name may not be recognized by the consumer.

A more fundamental security problem in 3-D Secure is that, just like the CV2 number described in the previous section, it is not mandatory for all transactions. So the customer's account number is still a valuable shared secret. All of the same precautions must go into protecting the Primary Account Number as it makes its way through the various merchant, payment, and supplier systems.

Precertification requires a notable overhead in setting up the protocol between the merchant, the bank, and the consumer. Although the overhead is significantly less than what we will see in our analysis of the SET protocol in the next section, it's still not ideal.

Beyond the phishing complaint of some 3-D Secure consumers lies a liability issue. The card brands that support 3-D Secure have stated they will not hold merchants liable for fraudulent transactions run through 3-D Secure. This is a great incentive for the merchant to implement 3-D Secure, but moves the requirement of proof of a fraudulent transaction to the consumer, an area where the consumer previously had little liability. Since 3-D Secure is not foolproof, this may not go over very well with cardholders. It essentially places blame for a successful phishing attack on the victim.

Secure Electronic Transaction

Secure Electronic Transaction (SET) is a protocol Visa and MasterCard developed in 1996 for securing credit card transactions over insecure networks such as the Internet. SET utilizes X.509 certificates and extensions, along with public key cryptography to identify each party within the e-commerce transaction and transmit the data while maintaining confidentiality. SET's unique binding algorithm substitutes a temporary certificate for the consumer's account number, so that the online merchant never needs access to this sensitive information. Each party is required to preregister with the certificate authority (CA), allowing the card issuer to perform due diligence before it allows the merchant to perform e-commerce transactions, and then authenticating all parties in the transaction.

On the consumer end, SET creates a hash value of the order information together with the payment information. The payment information is sent to the bank along with the signed hash of the order information. The consumer-side software also sends the order information to the merchant with the signed hash of the payment information. Both the cardholder and the merchant create equivalent hashes, compared when they are received by the bank or payment gateway.

This protocol offers a number of different protections for the transaction:

- It authenticates all parties in the initial transaction at time of registration with the CA.

- It performs additional authentication at transaction time through the exchange of certificates with the consumer, merchant, and payment gateway.

- Sensitive data such as the account number is shared only between the consumer and the bank and kept on a "need to know" basis, freeing the merchant from the need to store or transmit this information.

SET transactions

The sequence of events required for a transaction follow:

1. The customer obtains a credit card account with a bank that supports electronic payment and SET.

2. The customer receives an X.509 v3 digital certificate signed by the bank.

3. The customer places an order.

4. Each merchant has its own certificate, which it sends to the customer so his software can verify that it's a valid store.

5. The order and payment are sent.

6. The merchant requests payment authorization from the issuing bank.

7. The merchant confirms the order.

8. The merchant ships the goods or provides the service to the customer.

9. The merchant requests payment.

Evaluation of SET

Unfortunately, due to the amount of overhead involved in the massive Public Key Infrastructure (PKI) and registration process required by SET, it will never be widely adopted. The complexities with managing it become unbearable given the size of the e-commerce market.

Single-Use and Multiple-Use Virtual Cards

A recent trend in cardholder security comes via *virtual cards*. Companies such as PayPal, MBNA, and Citi are among some of the larger competitors in this space.

A virtual card is used in card-not-present transactions just like a regular credit card, and it is processed by the merchant in exactly the same manner. In fact, the merchant is not even aware that this card is virtual, and thus treats it with the same care as the other card account numbers going through the merchant systems.

How virtual cards work

Each supplier differs slightly in its implementation of virtual cards, but there are essentially two variants: single-use and multiple-use virtual cards. Both types are usually generated "on the fly" via a cardholder request. An existing card account holder requests a virtual card from her virtual card provider for use on a particular e-commerce site. The provider supplies the account holder with a virtual card number, including an expiration date and CV2 security code.

A single-use card can be used for a single transaction involving a limited payment. These cards typically expire in a matter of weeks or less and can be used only with the merchant designated during the cardholder's request. Thus, lost or stolen information rapidly becomes invalid and worthless to the attacker.

Multiple-use virtual cards are also available through many virtual card providers. These allow for use cases where recurring charges apply, such as paying a monthly bill. Multiple-use cards still carry with them many of the security features of their single-use equivalents, such as being valid with a single merchant and containing limited monthly charge caps. If a multiple-use virtual card is lost or stolen, an attacker could use the card only at that merchant and only for the authorized amount of the recurring charge. This mitigates a great deal of fraud.

Broken Incentives

A common economic issue in information security involves broken incentives. Incentives are a critical factor in any system dealing with multiple parties, particularly where that system depends on people with free choice doing the "right thing." If the proper incentives are not in place, breakdowns typically occur. To adjust for these external pressures that lead to breakdowns (market failures), financial systems adopt two methods:

Regulation
> Governments or industry consortia put rules in place to address market failures such as monopolies, pollution, lack of alignment with the "greater good," or in this case a lack of information security. Forms of regulation in this area include the Health Insurance Portability and Accountability Act (HIPAA), the Gramm-Leach-Bliley Financial Services Modernization Act (GLBA), the Sarbanes-Oxley Act (SOX), etc.

Liability
> This legal framework enforces damages (often financial) on those judged liable for damages of commission or omission. In the case of information security, a person or company may be found liable if they do not take reasonable precautions to protect information.

Let's look now at why the credit card "security market" experiences market failures. Following our financial model, we must examine the current incentives of the primary participants in this market: consumer, merchant, service provider, acquiring bank, issuing bank, and card associations.

Consumer

It's often assumed that consumers guard their credit card information with care because they have the most to lose when it's abused, but because of existing regulation to control some of these externalities, this is not actually the case. In the United States, a consumer is liable only for the first $50 of any fraud committed against his account. Typically, the issuing bank will also waive the $50 requirement in order to keep its customer base happy.

Therefore, while most consumers express a desire to protect their account numbers, security codes, and expiration dates, in the heat of a purchase there is actually very little incentive for the consumer to hold back the information. The incentives that do exist are not financial as much as saving the time and hassle associated with a compromised card.

As a point of comparison, there is a greater consumer incentive to protect a debit card, because the consumer is not protected by the same regulations as with credit cards. Also, debit cards are often tied directly to consumer checking and savings accounts, causing an immediate financial hit to the consumer upon a debit card security compromise.

Merchant and service provider

In the existing model, the merchant actually has quite a bit to lose in case of a breach. A compromise of cardholder data can lead to consequences related to both regulations and liability. The merchants are regulated by the card associations via the Payment Card Industry, which imposes a security standard that merchants must adhere to when handling data, along with the systems and networks that contains and transmit it. A merchant found in breach of this standard suffers both financial and operational penalties, enforced by the card associations. Financial penalties are often assessed against the acquiring bank, which in turn passes those fines on to the merchant. Merchants can also be found liable and sued by the issuing banks, indemnifying the banks for any costs associated with a breach, including the cost of reissuing cards.

Merchants also bear the financial responsibility of accepting fraudulent cards used to make purchases within their environment (except when using 3-D Secure). A merchant must put a number of fraud-detection systems in place in order to ensure that the card being used is valid and is wielded by the assigned cardholder. If a merchant ends up accepting a fraudulent card, the issuing bank issues a chargeback, refunding the consumer's account. If the merchant has already processed the transaction and provided the product or service, it has to absorb the loss associated with that transaction.

Although the merchants have a lot of incentive to protect this information, they do not control enough of the purchase process to do so effectively. As noted earlier, this data must pass through multiple systems, including systems outside the merchant's direct control. We also saw that many merchants hold on to some of this data long after the transaction, adding further risk.

Service providers are also regulated by the PCI Data Security Standard (DSS). According to the PCI Security Council, the definition of a service provider is a:

> ...business entity that is not a payment card brand member or a merchant directly involved in the processing, storage, transmission, and switching of transaction data and cardholder information or both. This also includes companies that provide services to merchants, services providers or members that control or could impact the security of cardholder data. Examples include managed service providers that provide managed firewalls, IDS and other services as well as hosting providers and other entities. Entities such as telecommunications companies that only provide communication links without access to the application layer of the communication link are excluded.

Many of the same rules that apply to merchants also apply to service providers, who have similar penalties and liabilities. Their incentives are not quite the same, however, as they do not have direct interaction with the consumer. That said, brand damage could still be a large factor within the business-to-business space.

Acquiring and issuing banks

The acquiring (merchant) bank and issuing banks are heavily regulated entities whose requirements for information protection go well beyond the Payment Card Industry. The issuing bank has an added incentive of representing the consumer in this transaction. This usually means it not only looks to protect this data, but often serves as an advocate to its customer. The merchant bank, while regulated by many of the financial laws and exchanges, usually serves as a middleman or pass-through and is therefore implicated in the penalties associated with merchants and service providers. When a merchant or one of its service providers is believed to have been breached, the acquiring bank will pass on any fines assessed by the card associations to these groups, since they directly manage the relationship with the merchant.

Card association

The card association's primary incentive to prevent fraud is brand protection. Simply stated, excessive breaches of a given brand could taint the image and lower the use of its network. The financial consequences of a breach to the card associations are not necessarily tangible. The card associations mainly want consumers to feel safe when shopping with their card. The PCI DSS was formed by several card brands that combined their security programs in an attempt to self-regulate and protect their brand.

He who controls the spice

Overall, each player within a transaction carries some incentive to protect this data (ironically, the consumer has the least). But significantly, the incentives do not directly align with who has control. That is, no single player can completely control the protection of the data, nor do the parties have incentives commensurate with their control over the protection of the shared secret as it travels through the various environments.

The current system simply has too many parties that require knowledge of this shared secret with inadequate incentives to expect the information to remain confidential throughout its life. Multiply the generic diagram of a single transaction in Figure 5-1 by the number of transactions throughout the life of a card, and you'll see that thousands of data handlers are often handed care of a single shared secret.

E-Commerce Redone: A New Security Model

By reviewing the current security model for e-commerce transactions, we now have a good feel for both its strengths and its weak points. Now I would like to propose a more elegant way to look at e-commerce security that renders the value of card account information useless to attackers and brings assurance to consumers.

When conducting a credit or debit transaction in a card-not-present use case, there are essentially seven base requirements that will ensure the transaction is secure while keeping the system usable for both consumers and merchants.

Requirement 1: The Consumer Must Be Authenticated

The first requirement is to authenticate consumers to ensure they are who they say they are. If consumer John is tied to credit account John123, we must first know this is indeed consumer John. So who is the best party and what is the best method to perform this authentication?

The best party is the manager of the cardholder's account, which is the issuing bank in most cases. This is for several reasons: the issuer already has the information, so storing it with them does not add another point of failure to the system; also, they have the most resources to invest in the expertise and processes to do authentication properly; finally, there are much fewer issuers than there are other actors.

This authentication may be handled through a combination of any of the three classic factors of authentication:

- Something the consumer *knows*, such as a password.
- Something the consumer *has*, such as a token or certificate.
- Something the consumer *is*, such as biometric data.

As we will see later, the latter two may add complexities to mass distribution and management.

Requirement 2: The Merchant Must Be Authenticated

The second requirement is to authenticate the merchant. This gives the consumer assurance that the merchant is legitimate and is providing the goods and services ordered by the consumer. Similar to the first requirement, the optimal party for authenticating the merchant is the manager of the merchant's account—in most cases, the acquiring bank.

OK, so we have authenticated both the consumer and the merchant, but now we hit a challenge. The issuer and the acquirer have performed authentication, but the transaction is being initiated between the consumer and merchant. How do we share this authentication so that the two primary actors in this use case have verification of each other's authenticity? We need the issuer and the acquirer to communicate this verification in a secure manner. I will go into more detail on this topic when I lay out the proposed process.

Requirement 3: The Transaction Must Be Authorized

This brings us to the third requirement: the transaction itself must be authorized. So far we have determined that consumer John is indeed consumer John and tied to consumer John's account. We have verified that merchant Vencer Corp is a legitimate merchant tied to an acquiring bank. We now need to know that consumer John is authorized to make this purchase.

The third requirement, luckily, has not raised problems in e-commerce, provided the consumer is properly authenticated. The issuing bank can confirm the appropriate approvals for this transaction based on all the existing systems in place for account status, credit limits, etc. Thus, fraud from an intruder (often called "hostile fraud") can be prevented if requirement 1 is perfected (easier said than done).

Admittedly, e-commerce systems can suffer from what is called (in a contradiction of terms) "friendly fraud," which means fraud from the very person with whom the merchant wants to transact. Friendly fraud occurs when a consumer experiences a change of heart after the purchase or simply refutes legitimate charges. Detecting friendly fraud pre-transaction is more difficult than detecting hostile fraud. There may be ways to bring friendly fraud down to a more acceptable volume through digital signatures, but that's beyond the scope of this chapter.

Requirement 4: Authentication Data Should Not Be Shared Outside of Authenticator and Authenticated

Our fourth requirement for a secure e-commerce transaction is not to share authentication data outside of the party being authenticated (in our case, either the consumer or the merchant) and the party responsible for the authentication. In a typical card-not-present transaction, these are four different entities. A consumer (1) should be authenticated by an issuing bank (2), while a merchant (3) is authenticated by its acquiring bank (4). The real trick here is sharing the verification of a successful or unsuccessful authentication among all of these parties without sharing the actual credentials.

Unlike today's model with its (widely) shared secret, our new model must be able to share the consumer's and merchant's authentication status without sharing their credentials. If we accomplish this, breach of data at the merchant about the consumer's authentication status has no impact on the consumer's credit account. Consumers could then rely on the security of the issuing bank's system, not the security of every merchant from which they have ever made a purchase.

Merchants are typically authenticated by this kind of single provider system, where the provider is the acquiring bank. Since the acquiring bank authenticates the merchant, my model shares this authentication status with the consumer prior to that transaction. As we will see later, I propose this should be handled between the acquirer and the issuer across the card networks.

Requirement 5: The Process Must Not Rely Solely on Shared Secrets

The fifth requirement simply repeats the central message of this chapter. The new model must not break if a merchant or service provider is compromised. Virtual card account numbers, discussed earlier, are a good way to meet this requirement—but it must become universal. When provided with nothing but one-time or limited-use accounts, a compromise at a single merchant or service provider will not break the overall e-commerce authentication model.

Requirement 6: Authentication Should Be Portable (Not Tied to Hardware or Protocols)

Portability is a must because there is simply too much infrastructure and too many systems currently in place to expect a massive redeployment or overhaul. We must build a model that allows for consumer and merchant authentication within the existing payment frameworks and networks.

Although SET provided a robust set of security controls and met most of the requirements mentioned so far, this area is where it fell short. Adding the extra overhead of a PKI infrastructure and process proved to be too much for the current payment process.

Requirement 7: The Confidentiality and Integrity of Data and Transactions Must Be Maintained

Our seventh and final requirement—to maintain confidentiality and integrity of data and transactions—is a no-brainer and a must for our new model to be taken seriously. This includes all authentication data, transaction and order data, and any data maintaining the state of any of these. This requirement must be adhered to as this data is transmitted across networks and stored throughout these systems.

The New Model

Considering the requirements in the previous sections, I would like to propose the following payment model for card-not-present transactions. Let's begin by walking through an example e-commerce transaction within the new model at a high level:

1. A consumer sends order information to both the merchant and the issuing bank in a common format.
2. When the merchant receives the order information from the consumer, the merchant authenticates with its acquiring bank and sends order information to the bank in a one-way hash.
3. Upon successful authentication, the acquiring bank signs the hashed value of the order information and sends this value to the issuing bank over the card network.
4. The issuing bank verifies the signature of the acquiring bank and creates a one-way hash of the order information sent by the consumer. It then compares the hashes, which should match, in order to verify the order.
5. If the issuing bank successfully verifies both the acquirer's signature and the consumer order information, the issuing bank sends a virtual card number to the consumer with a limit equal to the amount of the consumer order info.
6. The consumer submits payment information to the merchant using a virtual card account.

The steps are illustrated in Figure 5-2.

This fairly simple six-step process meets all of our requirements and will prevent a single compromise of any of the numerous systems that process the transaction from compromising the overall consumer account. Although none of these security concepts are new to us in the field of information security, they have not been used together effectively to secure modern e-commerce transactions. I believe the simplicity of this approach is what makes it beautiful and at the same time scalable to today's environment. By melding a series of existing security features and processes, we can fundamentally change the overall model, creating a hybrid that is simple, secure, and beautiful.

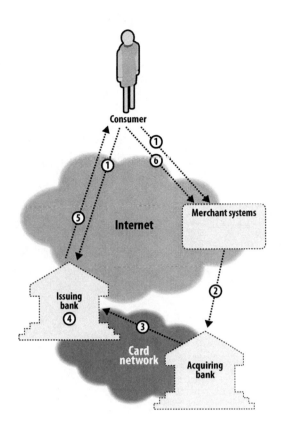

FIGURE 5-2. New model for credit transactions

CHAPTER SIX

Securing Online Advertising: Rustlers and Sheriffs in the New Wild West

Benjamin Edelman

READ THE NEWS OF RECENT COMPUTER SECURITY GUFFAWS, AND IT'S STRIKING how many problems stem from online advertising. Advertising is the bedrock of websites that are provided without charge to end users, so advertising is everywhere. But advertising security gaps are equally widespread: from "malvertisement" banner ads pushing rogue anti-spyware software, to click fraud, to spyware and adware, the security lapses of online advertising are striking.

During the past five years, I have uncovered hundreds of online advertising scams defrauding thousands of users—not to mention all the Web's top merchants. This chapter summarizes some of what I've found, and what users and advertisers can do to protect themselves.

Attacks on Users

Users are the first victims—and typically the most direct ones—of online advertising attacks. From deceptive pop-up ads to full-fledged browser exploits, users suffer the direct costs of cleanup. This section looks at some of the culprits.

Exploit-Laden Banner Ads

In March 2004, spam-king-turned-spyware-pusher Sanford Wallace found a way to install software on users' computers without users' permission. Wallace turned to security vulnerabilities—defects in Windows, Internet Explorer, or other software on a user's computer —that let Wallace take control of a user's computer without the user granting consent. Earlier intruders had to persuade users to click on an executable file or open a virus-infected document —something users were learning to avoid. But Wallace's new exploit took total control when the user merely visited a website—something we all do dozens of times a day.

Wallace emailed a collaborator to report the achievement:[*]

> From: Sanford Wallace, *masterwebfanclub@aol.com*
>
> To: Jared Lansky, *jared@optintrade.com*
>
> Subject: I DID IT
>
> Date: March 6, 2004
>
> I figured out a way to install an exe without any user interaction. This is the time to make the $$$ while we can.

Once Wallace got control of a user's computer via this exploit, he could install any software he chose. A variety of vendors paid Wallace to install their software on users' computers. So Wallace filled users' PCs with programs that tracked user behavior, showed pop-up ads, and cluttered browsers with extra toolbars.

But Wallace still had a problem: to take over a user's computer via a security exploit, Wallace first needed to make the user visit his exploit loader. How? Jared Lansky had an answer: he'd buy advertisements from banner ad networks. Merely by viewing an ad within an ordinary website, a user could get infected with Wallace's barrage of unwanted software.

Still, buying the advertisement traffic presented major challenges. Few websites sold ads directly to advertisers; instead, most sites sold their ad space through ad networks. But once an ad network realized what was going on, it would be furious. After all, exploits would damage an ad network's reputation with its affiliated websites.

Wallace and Lansky devised a two-part plan to avoid detection. First, they'd run exploits on the weekend when ad networks were less likely to notice:

> From: Sanford Wallace, *masterwebfanclub@aol.com*
>
> To: Jared Lansky, *jared@optintrade.com*
>
> Subject: strategy
>
> I do my sneaky shit…today through Sunday—everyone's off anyway…

Second, if an ad network noticed, Lansky would deny any knowledge of what had happened. For instance, Lansky replied to a complaint from Bob Regular, VP of ad network Cydoor:

---

[*] These emails were uncovered during FTC litigation, cited in *FTC v. Seismic Entertainment, Inc., et al.* No. 04-377-JD, 2004 U.S. Dist. LEXIS 22788 (D.N.H. 2004).

From: Jared Lansky, *jared@optintrade.com*

To: Bob Regular, *bob@cydoor.com*

Subject: RE: Please Terminate OptinTrade Online Pharmacy - Violated Agreement

Hi Bob - The pharmacy campaign was a new advertiser with a new code set. When tested it didn't launch pops or change my homepage so I approved it to run with you. I have no idea how this is happening...

Through this scheme, Wallace and Lansky infected thousands of computers, if not one to two orders of magnitude more. (Litigation documents do not reveal the specifics.) But the Federal Trade Commission (FTC) ultimately caught on, bringing suit and demanding repayment of more than $4 million of ill-gotten gains.[†] Unfortunately, Wallace and Lansky's strategy was just the tip of the iceberg.

Later in 2004, British IT news site *The Register*[‡] was hit by an exploit that installed malware on users' computers, showed pop ups, tracked user behavior in great detail, and even converted users' computers into spam-spewing "zombies." I happened to test that exploit, and found that it installed at least a dozen different programs, totaling hundreds of files and thousands of registry keys.[§] Other such exploits, seen throughout 2005 and 2006, used similar tactics to drop ever-larger payloads.[‖]

Visiting even a familiar and respected site could turn a user's computer into a bot, without the user ever realizing that the trusted site had become a malware factory.

There's no defending exploit-based software installation: the FTC has repeatedly prohibited nonconsensual installations,[#] and consumer class-action litigation confirmed that nonconsensual installations are a "trespass to chattels": an interference with a consumer's use of his private property (here, a computer).[*] So how do exploit-based installers get away with it? For one, they continue the sneakiness of Wallace's early weekend-only exploits: I've seen exploits running only outside business hours, or only for users in certain regions (typically, far from the ad networks that could investigate and take action).

[†] *FTC v. Seismic Entertainment, Inc., et al.* No. 04-377-JD, 2004 U.S. Dist. LEXIS 22788 (D.N.H. 2004).

[‡] "Bofra Exploit Hits Our Ad Serving Supplier." *The Register.* November 21, 2004. *http://www.theregister.co.uk/2004/11/21/register_adserver_attack/.*

[§] Edelman, Benjamin. "Who Profits from Security Holes?" November 18, 2004. *http://www.benedelman.org/news/111804-1.html.*

[‖] Edelman, Benjamin. "Spyware Installation Methods." *http://www.benedelman.org/spyware/installations/.*

[#] See *FTC v. Seismic Entertainment, Inc., et al.* See also *In the Matter of Zango, Inc. f/k/a 180Solutions, Inc., et al.* FTC File No. 052 3130. See also *In the Matter of DirectRevenue LLC, et al.* FTC File No. 052 3131.

[*] *Sotelo v. Direct Revenue.* 384 F.Supp.2d 1219 (N.D. Ill. 2005).

More generally, many exploit-based installers use intermediaries to try to avoid responsibility. Building on Wallace's partnership with Lansky, these intermediary relationships invoke an often-lengthy series of companies, partners, and affiliates. One conspirator might buy the banner, another runs the exploit, another develops the software, and yet another finds ways to make money from the software. If pressured, each partner would blame another. For example, the company that bought the banner would point out that it didn't run the exploit, while the company that built the software would produce a contract wherein its distributors promised to get user consent. With so much finger-pointing, conspirators hope to prevent ad networks, regulators, or consumer protection lawyers from figuring out whom to blame.

These attacks are ongoing, but noticeably reduced. What changed? Windows XP Service Pack 2 offers users significantly better protection from exploit-based installs, particularly when combined with post-SP2 patches to Internet Explorer. Also, the financial incentive to run exploits has begun to dry up: regulators and consumers sued the "adware" makers who had funded so many exploit-based installs, and advertisers came to hesitate to advertise through such unpopular pop ups.

For sophisticated readers, it's possible to uncover these exploits for yourself. Using VMware Workstation, create a fresh virtual machine, and install a vulnerable operating system—for instance, factory-fresh Windows XP with no service packs. Browse the Web and watch for unusual disk or network behavior. Better yet, run a packet sniffer (such as the free Wireshark) and one or more change-trackers. (I like InCtrl for full scans, and HijackThis for quick analysis.) If your computer hits an exploit, examine the packet sniffer logs to figure out what happened and how. Then contact sites, ad networks, and other intermediaries to help get the exploits stopped. I find that I tend to hit exploits most often on entertainment sites—games, song lyrics, links to BitTorrent downloads—but in principle, exploits can occur anywhere. Best of all, after you infect a virtual machine, you can use VMware's "restore" function to restore the VM's clean, pre-infection state.

Malvertisements

Unlucky users sometimes encounter banner ads that literally pop out of a web page. In some respects these ads look similar to pop ups, opening a new web browser in addition to the browser the user already opened. But these so-called "malvertisement" ads pop open without the underlying website authorizing any such thing; to the contrary, the website intends to sell an ordinary banner, not a pop up. Furthermore, after these malvertisements pop out of a web page, they typically fill the user's entire screen, whereas standard pop ups are usually somewhat smaller. Worse, sometimes these malvertisements redirect the user's entire web browser, entirely *replacing* the page the user requested and leaving the user with only the unrequested advertisement.

As Figure 6-1 shows, malvertisements typically promote rogue anti-spyware software with claims that a user's computer is infected with spyware, despite lacking specific evidence that the user's computer is anything other than normal. For example, the screenshot claims to be "scanning filevw80.ocx"—even though no such file exists on my test PC. Indeed, the pop-up web page is *just a web page*—not a bona fide scanner, and hence incapable of scanning anything at all. Furthermore, the "now scanning" box is merely part of the advertisement, and even the realistic-looking buttons and icons are all a ruse. But by combining the pop-out interruption with the realistic user interface and the overstated "warning" of infection, these ads can be remarkably effective at getting users' attention and convincing them to make a purchase.

FIGURE 6-1. Fake scanning ad

Malvertisements work hard to avoid detection by websites and ad networks. When viewed in its innocuous state, a malvertisement typically looks like an ordinary Flash ad: a banner, perhaps with limited animation. But when the time is right, the malvertisement uses Flash ActionScript to pop out of the ad frame. How? ActionScript often sports obfuscated code, using a stub procedure to assemble commands decoded from a block of what is, to casual inspection, gibberish. Other ActionScript programs check in with a web server that can consult a user's IP address and decide how the ad should behave. These systems even detect auditors testing the ad's behavior by employing remote proxies to adopt a faraway address. Specifically, ActionScript lets an ad obtain the time according to the clock on the user's PC. If the user's PC says it's one time but it's actually another time at the location associated with the user's apparent IP address, the ad server can infer that the "user" is a tester connecting by proxy— and the ad server can revert to its innocuous banner mode.

The best defense against these attacks is to fully secure client devices. In the context of typical banner ads, Flash is supposed to show only pictures, animation, and perhaps an occasional video. Why allow such rich code for what is supposed to be just an ad? By default, an ad should have limited permissions, but Flash tends to give ads surprisingly free reign. Unfortunately, a new security model would require fundamental changes to the Flash architecture, meaning action by Adobe, which to date has shown little interest in such defenses.

Fortunately, decentralized development offers two possible ways forward. First, Flash's `"AllowScriptAccess"` tag lets ad networks disable ad scripts to defend against concealed hostile ads.[†] An ad network need only place this attribute in the `PARAM` or `EMBED` tag that places a Flash banner within a page. With this attribute in place, the ad can't invoke outside code, so attacks are greatly reduced. Some advertisers may insist that their rich media requires external scripting. But advertisers who have proven their trustworthiness through their reputation and responsible behavior can persuade ad networks to let their ads run scripts, while standard or little-known advertisers get limited permissions to match their limited reputations.

Alternatively, ad networks can test ads to uncover bad actors. The best-known product in this vein is Right Media's Media Guard, which uses automated systems to examine ads using a variety of computers in a variety of locations. It's hard work—serious automation technology that Right Media built at significant expense. But this system lets Right Media feel confident in the behavior of its ads, which becomes crucial as more ad networks exchange inventory through Right Media's platform. Google now has similar testing, which flags exploits both on advertisers' pages and in organic search results. But other ad networks, especially small networks, still lack effective tools to catch malicious ads or to ferret them out. That's too bad for the users who end up caught in the mess created by these networks' inability to meaningfully assess their advertisers.

Deceptive Advertisements

Thirty years ago, Encyclopædia Britannica sold its wares via door-to-door salesmen who were pushy at best. Knowing that consumers would reject solicitations, Britannica's salesmen resorted to trickery to get consumers' attention. In subsequent litigation, a judge described these tactics:

---

† "Using AllowScriptAccess to Control Outbound Scripting from Macromedia Flash." *http://kb.adobe.com/ selfservice/viewContent.do?externalId=tn_16494.*

One ploy used to gain entrance into prospects' homes is the Advertising Research Analysis questionnaire. This form questionnaire is designed to enable the salesman to disguise his role as a salesman and appear as a surveyor engaged in advertising research. [Britannica] fortifies the deception created by the questionnaire with a form letter from its Director of Advertising for use with those prospects who may question the survey role. These questionnaires are thrown away by salesmen without being analyzed for any purpose whatsoever.

The FTC successfully challenged Britannica's practices,[‡] despite Britannica's appeals all the way to the Supreme Court.[§] The FTC thus established the prohibition on "deceptive door openers" under the principle that once a seller creates a false impression through her initial statements to consumers, the deception may be so serious that subsequent clarifications cannot restore the customer's capacity for detached judgment. Applying this rule to Britannica's strategy, the salesman's claim that he is a research surveyor eviscerates any subsequent consumer "agreement" to buy the encyclopedias—even if the salesman ultimately admits his true role.

Fast-forward to the present, and it's easy to find online banner ads that are remarkably similar to the FTC's 1976 *Britannica* case. One group of sleazy ads asks consumers to answer a shallow survey question ("Do you like George Bush?"), as in Figure 6-2, or to identify a celebrity ("Whose lips are these?"), as in Figure 6-3. Despite the questions, the advertiser doesn't actually care what users prefer or who users recognize, because the advertiser isn't really conducting market research. Instead, just as Britannica's salesmen claimed to conduct "research" simply to get a consumer's attention, these ads simply want a user to click on a choice so that the advertiser can present users with an entirely unrelated marketing offer.

FIGURE 6-2. Eye-catching survey question

FIGURE 6-3. Eye-catching quiz

But "deceptive door opener" ads go beyond survey-type banners. Plenty of other ads make false claims as well. "Get free ringtones," an ad might promise, even though the ringtones cost

[‡] *Encyclopædia Britannica, Inc.* 87 F.T.C. 421 (1976).

[§] *Encyclopædia Britannica, Inc.* 445 U.S. 934 (1980).

$9.99/month—the very opposite of "free" (see Figures 6-4 and 6-5). Or consider an ad promising a "free credit report"—even though the touted service is actually neither free nor a credit report. Other bogus ads try to sell software that's widely available without charge. Search for "Firefox," "Skype," or "Winzip," and you may stumble into ads attempting to charge for these popular but *free* programs (see Figure 6-6).

These scams fly in the face of decades of consumer protection law. For one thing, not every clause in an agreement is legally enforceable. In particular, material terms must be clear and conspicuous, not buried in fine print.[||] (For example, the FTC successfully challenged deceptive ads that promised ice cream was "98% fat free" when a footnote admitted the products were not low in fat.[#]) Yet online marketers often think they can promise "free ringtones" or a "free iPod" with a small-type text admitting "details apply."

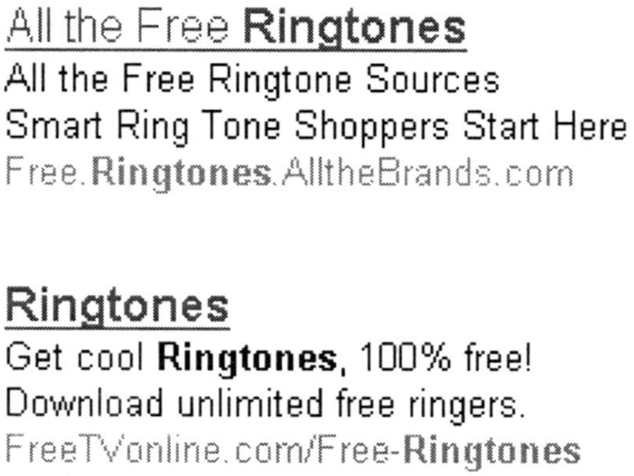

All the Free **Ringtones**
All the Free Ringtone Sources
Smart Ring Tone Shoppers Start Here
Free.**Ringtones**.AlltheBrands.com

Ringtones
Get cool **Ringtones**, 100% free!
Download unlimited free ringers.
FreeTVonline.com/Free-**Ringtones**

FIGURE 6-4. "Free" ringtones that aren't

Unlimited Free **Ringtones**
Unlimited **Ringtones** & Screen Savers
Color Phone & Net Access Required
www.freeringers.net

FIGURE 6-5. "Unlimited Free" ringtones that actually cost $7.99

[||] "FTC Advertising Enforcement: Disclosures in Advertising." *http://www.ftc.gov/bcp/workshops/ disclosures/cases/index.html.*

[#] *Häagen-Dazs Co.* 119 F.T.C. 762 (1995).

Ringtones
Get cool **Ringtones**, 100% free!
Download unlimited free ringers.
FreeTVonline.com/Free-**Ringtones**

Free Calls- 2007 Download
Talk Anywhere for Free
Great Quality- Latest Version
Skype-Free-Calls.com

Download **WinZip** ™ 10.0
Download **WinZip** ™ 2007 Software.
Latest Version - 100% Guaranteed!
Winzip.Download-all-4-Free.com

FIGURE 6-6. Charging for Skype and Winzip

Fortunately, regulators are beginning to notice. For example, the FTC challenged ValueClick's deceptive banners and pop ups, which touted claims like "free PS3 for survey" and "select your free plasma TV." The FTC found that receiving the promised merchandise required a convoluted and nearly impossible maze of sign-ups and trials. On this basis, the FTC ultimately required ValueClick to pay a $2.9 million fine and to cease such practices.[*] The attorney general of Florida took a similarly negative view of deceptive ringtone ads, including holding ad networks responsible for deceptive ads presented through their systems.[†] Private attorneys are also lending a hand—for example, suing Google for the false ads Google displays with abandon.[‡] And in July 2008, the EU Consumer Commissioner reported that more than 80% of ringtone sites had inaccurate pricing, misleading offers, or improper contact information, all bases for legal action.[§] New scam advertisements arise day in and day out, and forward-thinking users should be on the lookout, constantly asking themselves whether an offer is too good to be true. Once suspicious, a user could run a quick web search on a site's name, perhaps uncovering complaints from others. Or check Whois; scam sites often use privacy protection or far-flung addresses. For automatic assistance, users could look to McAfee SiteAdvisor,[‖] which specifically attempts to detect and flag scams.[#]

[*] *ValueClick, Inc.* Case No. CV08-01711 MMM (RZx) (C. Dist. Cal. 2008).

[†] "CyberFraud Task Force." Office of the Attorney General of Florida. *http://myfloridalegal.com/.*

[‡] *Goddard v. Google, Inc.* Case No. 108CV111658 (Cal. Super. Ct. 2008).

[§] "EU Crackdown of Ringtone Scams." EUROPA Memo/08/516. July 17, 2008.

[‖] "SiteAdvisor FAQs." *http://www.siteadvisor.com/press/faqs.html.*

[#] Disclosure: I am an advisor to McAfee SiteAdvisor. John Viega, editor of this volume, previously led SiteAdvisor's data team.

Are deceptive ads really a matter of "computer security"? While security experts can address some of these shenanigans, consumer protection lawyers can do at least as much to help. But to a user who falls for such tricks, the difference is of limited import. And the same good judgment that protects users from many security threats can also help limit harm from deceptive ads.

Advertisers As Victims

It's tempting to blame advertisers for all that goes wrong with online advertising. After all, advertisers' money puts the system in motion. Plus, by designing and buying ads more carefully, advertisers could do much to reduce the harm caused by unsavory advertising practices.

But in some instances, I'm convinced that advertisers end up as victims: they are overcharged by ad networks and get results significantly worse than what they contracted to receive.

False Impressions

In 2006 I examined an online advertising broker called Hula Direct. Hula's Global-store, Inqwire, and Venus123 sites were striking for their volume of ads: they typically presented at least half a dozen different ad banners on a single page, and sometimes more. Furthermore, Hula often stacked some banners in front of others. As a result, many of the "back" banners would be invisible, covered by an ad further forward in the stack. Users might forgive this barrage of advertising if Hula's sites interspersed banners among valuable content. But, in fact, Hula's sites had little real material, just ad after ad. Advertising professionals call these pages "banner farms": like a farm growing a single crop with nothing else as far as the eye can see, banner farms are effectively just ads.

Industry reports indicated that Hula's advertisers typically bought ads on a Cost Per Thousand Impressions (CPM) basis. That is, they paid a fee (albeit a small fee, typically a fraction of a cent) for each user who purportedly saw an ad. This payment structure exposes advertisers to a clear risk: if a website like Hula presents their ads en masse, advertisers may end up paying for ads that users were unlikely to notice, click on, or buy from. After all, a page with nothing but banners is unlikely to hold a user's attention, so an ad there has little hope of getting noticed. An ad at the back of the stack, largely covered by another ad, has no hope at all of being effective (see Figure 6-7).

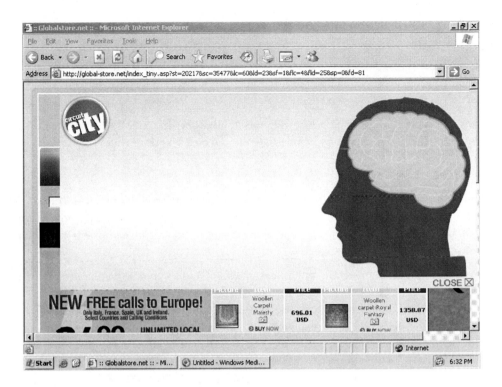

FIGURE 6-7. False impressions in action: a large Circuit City pop up covers even more banner ads

Hula's banner farms revealed two further ways to overcharge advertisers. First, Hula loaded ads in pop unders that users never requested. So not only could Hula claim to show many ads, but it could show these ads in low-cost pop-up windows Hula bought from spyware, adware, or low-quality websites. Second, Hula designed its ads to reload themselves as often as every nine seconds. As a result, an advertiser that intended to buy an appearance on a bona fide web page for as long as the user viewed that page would instead get just nine seconds in a Hula-delivered banner farm.* Meanwhile, other scammers developed further innovations on the banner farm scam, including loading banners in windows as small as 1×1 pixel each, so that the scammers could get paid even though no ads were actually visible. No wonder advertisers widely view CPM as prone to fraud and hence, all else equal, less desirable than alternative payment metrics.

---

* Edelman, Benjamin. "Banner Farms in the Crosshairs." June 12, 2006. *http://www.benedelman.org/news/061206-1.html.*

Escaping Fraud-Prone CPM Advertising

For an advertiser dissatisfied with CPM, online advertising vendors offer two basic alternatives. First, advertisers could pay CPC (cost per click), with fees due only if a user clicks an ad. Alternatively, advertisers could pay CPA (cost per action), where fees are due only if the advertiser actually makes a sale.

At first glance, both these approaches seem less fraud-prone than CPM. Perhaps they're somewhat better—but experience shows they too can be the basis of troubling scams.

Gaming CPC advertising

CPC advertising is the bedrock of search engines and the source of substantially all of Google's profit. At its best, CPC lets advertisers reach customers when they're considering what to buy—potentially an exceptionally effective marketing strategy. But CPC ad campaigns can suffer from striking overcharges.

Consider an independent website publisher that enters into a *syndication* relationship with a CPC vendor. In such a contract, the CPC vendor pays the publisher a fee—typically a predetermined percentage of the advertiser's payment—for each advertisement click occurring within the publisher's site. This creates a natural incentive for the publisher to report extra clicks. How? Some publishers tell their users to click the ads. ("Support my site: Visit one of these advertisers.") Other publishers use JavaScript to make a user's browser "click" an ad, regardless of whether the user wants to visit the advertiser.[†] The most sophisticated rogue publishers turn to botnet-type code that causes infected PCs to load a variety of CPC ads—all without a user requesting the ads or, often, even seeing the advertisers' sites.[‡]

CPC advertising is vulnerable to these attacks because its underlying tracking method is easy to trick. Just as a CPM ad network cannot easily determine whether a user actually *saw* an ad, a CPC vendor often can't tell whether an ad "click" came from an actual user moving her mouse to an ad and pressing the button, or from some kind of code that faked the click. After all, the CPC vendor tracks clicks based on specially coded HTTP requests sent to the search engine's web server, bearing the publisher's ID. But rogue publishers can easily fake these requests without a user actually clicking anything. And in developing countries, there are low-cost services where contractors click ads all day in exchange for payments from the corresponding sites.[§]

For a concerned CPC network, one easy response would be to refuse syndication partnerships, and instead only show ads on its own sites. For example, through mid-2008, Microsoft showed

---

[†] Edelman, Benjamin. "The Spyware – Click-Fraud Connection – and Yahoo's Role Revisited." April 4, 2006. *http://www.benedelman.org/news/040406-1.html.*

[‡] Daswani, Neil and Stoppelman, Michael. "The Anatomy of Clickbot.A." *Proceedings of the First Workshop on Hot Topics in Understanding Botnets.* 2007.

[§] Vidyasagar, N. "India's Secret Army of Online Ad 'Clickers.'" *The Times of India.* May 3, 2004.

ads only at Live.com, on Microsoft sites, and at sites run by trusted top-tier partners. But this strategy limits the CPC network's reach, reducing the traffic the network can provide to its advertisers. In contrast, Google chose the opposite tack: in the second quarter of 2008, Google paid its partners fully $1.47 billion to buy ad placements on their sites.[ll] This large payment lets Google increase its reach, making its service that much more attractive to prospective advertisers. No wonder Microsoft announced plans in July 2008 to open its syndication more broadly.[#]

CPC vendors claim they have robust methods to identify invalid clicks, including the monitoring of IP addresses, duplicates, and other patterns.[*] But it's hard to feel confident in their approach. How can CPC vendors know what they don't catch? And how can CPC vendors defend against a savvy botnet that clicks only a few ads per month per PC, mixes click fraud traffic with genuine traffic, fakes all the right HTTP headers, and even browses a few pages on each advertiser's site? These fake clicks would easily blend in with bona fide clicks, letting the syndicator claim extra fees with impunity.

In 2005–2006, a series of class actions claimed that top search engines Google, Yahoo!, and others were doing too little to prevent click fraud on credit advertisers' accounts. The nominal value of settlements passed $100 million, though the real value to advertisers was arguably far less. (If an advertiser didn't file a claim, its share of the settlement disappeared.) Meanwhile, search engines commissioned self-serving reports denying that click fraud was a major problem.[†] But the fundamental security flaws remained unchanged.

In hopes of protecting themselves from click fraud, advertisers sometimes hire third-party click-fraud detection services to review their web server logfiles in search of suspicious activity.[‡] In a widely circulated response, Google mocks some of these services for analytical errors.[§] (Predictably, Google glosses over the extent to which the services' shortcomings stem from the limited data Google provides to them.) Furthermore, it's unclear whether a click-fraud detection service could detect botnet-originating click fraud that includes post-click browsing. But whatever the constraints of click-fraud detection services, they at least impose a partial check on overcharges by search engines through success in identifying some clear-cut cases of click fraud.

[ll] Google Form 10-Q, Q2 2008.

[#] Microsoft adCenter Publisher Program (*http://advertising.microsoft.com/publisher*).

[*] See, for example, "How Does Google Detect Invalid Clicks?" *https://adwords.google.com/support/bin/answer.py?answer=6114&topic=10625.*

[†] See, for example, Tuzhilin, Alexander. "The Lane's Gifts v. Google Report." June 21, 2006. *http://googleblog.blogspot.com/pdf/Tuzhilin_Report.pdf.*

[‡] See, for example, Click Defense (*http://www.clickdefense.com*) and Click Forensics (*http://www.clickforensics.com*).

[§] "How Fictitious Clicks Occur in Third-Party Click Fraud Audit Reports." August 8, 2006. *http://www.google.com/adwords/ReportonThird-PartyClickFraudAuditing.pdf.*

Inflating CPA costs

Purportedly most resistant to fraud, cost-per-action (CPA) advertising charges an advertiser only if a user makes a purchase from that advertiser's site. In an important sense, CPA lowers an advertiser's risk: an advertiser need not pay if no users see the ad, no users click the ad, or no users make a purchase after clicking the ad. So affiliate networks such as LinkShare and Commission Junction tout CPA as a low-risk alternative to other kinds of online advertising.[||]

But CPA is far from immune to fraud. Suppose a merchant were known to pay commissions instantly—say, the same day an order occurs. A co-conspirator could make purchases through an attacker's CPA link and then return the merchandise for a full refund, yielding instant payment to the attacker, who would keep the commissions even after the return. Alternatively, if declined credit cards or chargebacks take a few days to be noticed, the attacker might be able to abscond with commissions before the merchant notices what happened. This may seem too hard to perpetrate on a large scale, but in fact such scams have turned up (less now than in the past).

In a more sophisticated scheme, an attacker designs a web page or banner ad to invoke CPA links automatically, without a user taking any action to click the link. If the user later happens to make a purchase from the corresponding merchant, the attacker gets paid a commission. Applied to the Web's largest merchants—Amazon, eBay, and kin—these "stuffed cookies" can quickly yield high commission payouts because many users make purchases from top merchants even without any advertising encouragement.[#] By all indications, the amounts at issue are substantial. For example, eBay considers such fraud serious enough to merit federal litigation, as in eBay's August 2008 suit against Digital Point Systems and others. In that litigation, eBay claims defendants forced the placement of eBay tracking cookies onto users' computers, thereby claiming commissions from eBay without providing a bona fide marketing service or, indeed, promoting eBay in any way at all.[*]

In an especially complicated CPA scheme, an attacker first puts tracking software on a user's computer—spyware or, politely, "adware." This tracking software then monitors a user's browsing activity and invokes CPA links to maximize payouts. Suppose an attacker notices that a user is browsing for laptops at Dell's website. The attacker might then open a CPA link to Dell, so that if the user makes a purchase from Dell, the attacker gets a 2% commission. (After all, where better to find a Dell customer than a user already examining new Dells?) To Dell, things look good: by all indications, a user clicked a CPA link and made a purchase. What Dell doesn't realize is that the user never actually *clicked* the link; instead, spyware opened the link. And Dell fails to consider that the user would have purchased the laptop anyway, meaning

---

[||] See, for example, "pay affiliates only when a sale…is completed" within "LinkShare – Affiliate Information." *http://www.linkshare.com/affiliates/affiliates.shtml.*

[#] See, for example, Edelman, Benjamin. "CPA Advertising Fraud: Forced Clicks and Invisible Windows." *http://www.benedelman.org/news/100708-1.html.* October 7, 2008.

[*] *eBay, Inc. v. Digital Point Solutions,* No. 5:08-cv-04052-PVT (N.D. Cal. complaint filed Aug. 25, 2008).

that the 2% commission payout is entirely unnecessary and completely wasted. Unfortunately, Dell cannot know what really happened, because Dell's tracking systems tell Dell nothing about what was happening on the user's computer. Dell cannot identify that the "click" came from spyware rather than a user, and Dell cannot figure out that the user would have made the purchase anyway, without payment of the CPA commission.

During the past four years, I've uncovered literally hundreds of bogus CPA affiliates using these tactics.[†] The volume of cheaters ultimately exceeded my capacity to document these incidents manually, so last year I built an automated system to uncover them autonomously. My software browses the Web on a set of spyware-infected virtual machines, watching for any unexpected CPA "click" events, and preserving its findings in packet logs and screen-capture videos.[‡] I often now find several new cheaters each day, and I'm not the only one to notice. For example, in class action litigation against ValueClick, merchants are seeking recovery of CPA commissions they shouldn't have been required to pay.[§] A recently announced settlement creates a $1 million fund for refunds to merchants and to legitimate affiliates whose commissions were lost after attackers overwrote their commission cookies.

Why Don't Advertisers Fight Harder?

From years of auditing online ad placements, I get the sense that many advertisers don't view fraud as a priority. Of course, there are exceptions: many small- to medium-sized advertisers cannot tolerate losses to fraud, and some big companies have pervasive commitments to fair and ethical practices. That said, big companies suffer greatly from these practices, yet they tend not to complain.

Marketers often write off advertising fraud as an unavoidable cost of doing business. To me, that puts the cart before the horse. Who's to say what fraud deserves action and what is just a cost of doing business? By improving the effectiveness of responses to fraud—through finding low-cost ways to identify and prevent it—merchants can transform "unavoidable" losses into a bigger bottom line and a real competitive advantage. Nonetheless, that hasn't happened often, I believe largely due to the skewed incentives facing advertisers' staff.

Within companies buying online advertising, individual staff incentives can hinder efforts to protect the company from advertising fraud. Consider an advertising buyer who realizes one of the company's suppliers has overcharged the company by many thousands of dollars. The

---

[†] See Edelman, Benjamin. "Auditing Spyware Advertising Fraud: Wasted Spending at VistaPrint." *http://www.benedelman.org/news/093008-1.html*. September 30, 2008. See also "Spyware Still Cheating Merchants and Legitimate Affiliates." *http://www.benedelman.org/news/052107-1.html*. May 21, 2007. See also "How Affiliate Programs Fund Spyware." September 14, 2005. *http://www.benedelman.org/news/091405-1.html*.

[‡] Edelman, Benjamin. "Introducing the Automatic Spyware Advertising Tester." *http://www.benedelman.org/news/052107-2.html*. May 21, 2007. U.S. patent pending.

[§] *Settlement Recovery Center v. ValueClick*. Cen. Dis. Calif. No. 2:07-cv-02638-FMC-CTx.

company would be best served by the buyer immediately pursuing this matter, probably by bringing it to the attention of in-house counsel or other managers. But in approaching higher-ups, the ad buyer would inevitably be admitting his own historic failure—the fact that he paid the supplier for (say) several months before uncovering the fraud. My discussions with ad buyers convince me that these embarrassment effects are real. Advertising buyers wish they had caught on faster, and they instinctively blame themselves or, in any event, attempt to conceal what went wrong.

Equally seriously, some advertisers compensate ad buyers in ways that discourage ad buyers from rooting out fraud. Consider an ad buyer who is paid 10% of the company's total online advertising spending. Such an ad buyer has little incentive to reject ads from a bogus source; for every dollar the company spends there, the buyer gets another 10 cents of payment. Such compensation is more widespread than outsiders might expect; many advertisers compensate their outside ad agencies in exactly this way.

For internal ad buyers, incentives can be even more pronounced. For example, a CPA program manager ("affiliate manager") might be paid $50,000 plus 20% of year-over-year CPA program growth. Expand a program from $500,000 to $800,000 of gross sales, and the manager could earn a nice $60,000 bonus. But if the manager uncovers $50,000 of fraud, that's effectively a $10,000 reduction in the bonus—tough medicine for even the most dedicated employee. No wonder so many affiliate programs have failed to reject even the most notorious perpetrators.

Similar incentive issues plague the ad networks in their supervision of partners, affiliates, and syndicators. If an ad network admitted that a portion of its traffic was fraudulent, it would need to remove associated charges from its bills to merchants. In contrast, by hiding or denying the problem, the network can keep its fees that much higher. Big problems can't be hidden forever, but by delaying or downplaying the fraud, ad networks can increase short-term profits.

Lessons from Other Procurement Contexts: The Special Challenges of Online Procurement

When leading companies buy supplies, they typically establish procurement departments with robust internal controls. Consider oversight in the supply chains of top manufacturers: departments of carefully trained staff who evaluate would-be vendors to confirm legitimacy and integrity. In online advertising, firms have developed even larger supply networks—for example, at least hundreds of thousands of sites selling advertising inventory to Google's AdSense service. Yet advertisers and advertising networks lack any comparable rigor for evaluating publishers.

Indeed, two aspects of online advertising make online advertising procurement harder than procurement in other contexts. First, advertising intermediaries tend to be secretive about where they place ads. Worried that competitors might poach their top partners, networks tend to keep their publisher lists confidential. But as a result, an advertiser buying from (for example) Google AdSense or ValueClick Media cannot know which sites participate. The advertiser thus cannot hand-check partners' sites to confirm their propriety and legitimacy.

Furthermore, even if a publisher gets caught violating applicable rules, there is typically little to prevent the publisher from reapplying under a new name and URL. Thus, online advertisers have limited ability to block even those wrongdoers they manage to detect. In my paper "Deterring Online Advertising Fraud Through Optimal Payment in Arrears,"[||] I suggest an alternative approach: delaying payment by two to four months so that a publisher faces a financial detriment when its bad acts are revealed. But to date, most advertisers still pay faster than that, letting publishers cheat with little risk of punishment. And advertisers still treat fast payment as a virtue, not realizing that paying too quickly leaves them powerless when fraud is uncovered.

Creating Accountability in Online Advertising

Online advertising remains a "Wild West" where users are faced with ads they ought not to believe and where firms overpay for ads without getting what they were promised in return. But it doesn't have to be this way. Enforcement by public agencies is starting to remind advertisers and ad networks that long-standing consumer protection rules still apply online. And as advertisers become more sophisticated, they're less likely to tolerate opaque charges for services they can't confirm they received.

Meanwhile, the online advertising economy offers exciting opportunities for those with interdisciplinary interests, combining the creativity of a software engineer with the nose-to-the-ground determination of a detective and the public-spiritedness of a civil servant. Do well by doing good—catching bad guys in the process!

[||] Edelman, Benjamin. "Deterring Online Advertising Fraud Through Optimal Payment in Arrears." February 19, 2008. *http://ssrn.com/abstract=1095262*.

CHAPTER SEVEN

The Evolution of PGP's Web of Trust

Phil Zimmermann
Jon Callas

WHEN *PRETTY GOOD PRIVACY* (PGP) FIRST ARRIVED IN 1991, it was the first time ordinary people could use strong encryption that was previously available only to major governments.

PGP led to new opportunities for human rights organizations and other users concerned with privacy around the world, along with some oft-misunderstood legal issues that we'll touch on later.

One of the most influential aspects of PGP is its solution to the problem of connecting people who have never met and therefore never had a chance to exchange secure keys. This solution quickly earned the moniker "Web of Trust," which describes the way the system operates about as accurately as any phrase.

The trust mechanism in PGP has evolved a lot since the early releases. It's worth examining the reasons for the trust model and the way PGP has evolved to provide more robustness.

The Web of Trust also offers an interesting historical angle because it was an early peer-to-peer design, and arguably one of the first social networks.

Much has been written about PGP and practical public key cryptography, but to our dismay, we've found that much of what is written contains substantial inaccuracies. It is our goal in this chapter to describe the PGP trust model, as well as its implementation, standardization, and use. We also will put it in its historic and political context.

PGP and OpenPGP

PGP is software; *OpenPGP* is a standard and a protocol. PGP is also a registered trademark presently owned by PGP Corporation (as are the related terms "Pretty Good Privacy" and "Pretty Good").

Before PGP was a protocol, it was merely software. This is important because nowadays we use the term "PGP" to refer to the software made by PGP Corporation, which implements a number of standards and protocols, among them OpenPGP. Additionally, PGP is one implementation of many implementations of the OpenPGP standard. But much of the PGP story predates the OpenPGP standard, and there is no defined term to separate the pre-OpenPGP software from the pre-OpenPGP protocol.

The core OpenPGP protocol is defined in the IETF RFC 4880 and RFC 3156. The early PGP protocol is defined in RFC 1991. Consequently, we will use *PGP* to refer primarily to this early software, and *RFC 1991* to refer to the early protocol.

Trust, Validity, and Authority

Trust is a broad concept. It means many things in many contexts. In this discussion we will use a narrow, strict definition: the mechanism that is used to decide whether a key is valid. A key is *valid* if it is actually owned by the person who claims to own it. In other words, if the descriptive information traveling with the key is accurate, then the key is valid. You tell PGP whom you trust to introduce keys; in return, PGP tells you which keys are valid.

Thus, if a key says it is owned by the same person who owns the email address "Alice" <alice@example.com> and that information is correct, that key is valid (or accurate). If Bob believes the key is valid because Charlie signed that key, then Bob considers Alice's key valid because he trusts Charlie.[*]

Let us start with this definition:

> A key is *valid* if it is actually owned by the person who claims to own it.

We can then move on to define trust:

> *Trust* is the mechanism we use to decide that a key is valid.

Most people confuse trust and validity. Even those of us who know the Web of Trust best sometimes make mistakes. Validity is only a score and can be used only to determine whether the name on a key is accurate. Trust is a *relationship* that helps us determine validity.

You tell PGP whom you trust to sign keys, and in return PGP tells you which keys are valid. It does this by tallying up a score for each key depending on who signed the key and how much

---

[*] For a discourse both amusing and instructional on the use of these names, see the entry for John Gordon in "References" on page 129.

you trust the person who signed it. (PGP calls the signer an *introducer*, for reasons we'll explain later.)

For instance, if Bob believes that keys signed by Charlie are valid, Charlie can sign Alice's key and Bob will trust the key because he trusts Charlie.

A *trust model* is a general scheme that formalizes trust so a computer can automate the trust calculations. Let's look the basics of trust models.

Direct Trust

Direct trust is the most straightforward type of trust. In direct trust, Bob trusts that a certificate is Alice's because Alice gave it to him. It is the best trust model there is, and so simple that we described it without giving it a name. It is not only the simplest trust model, but at the end of the day it is the most, well, trustworthy!

People use direct trust all the time by doing things like putting an OpenPGP key fingerprint (which is itself a hash of an OpenPGP key) on their emails or business card. Even simpler, if I mail you my key, we're using direct trust. You trust that the key is valid because I am only hurting myself if that is wrong.

Often in a direct trust system, a certificate that holds the key is signed by that certificate itself. In other words, it is self-signed. Self-signing is useful because it provides a consistency check. We know that a self-signed certificate is either wholly accurate or wholly inaccurate.

The only problem with direct trust is that it doesn't scale very well to something the size of the Internet. That doesn't mean it's not useful; it just means it doesn't scale.

Hierarchical Trust

Hierarchical trust is also straightforward. In hierarchical trust, you trust that a certificate is valid because it was signed by someone whom you believe to be accurate, as in the example mentioned earlier. Bob considers Alice's certificate to be valid because Charlie signed it, and Bob trusts Charlie to be an authority on accurate signing.

There are a good number of companies that make it their business to be Charlies. GoDaddy and VeriSign, to name two, are widely trusted Certificate Authorities (CAs), and they are trusted because of the practices they follow in creating certificates. Part of these practices are that they have a relatively few number of keys that extend this trust. These keys are themselves held in *root certificates* (which are self-signed certificates). The key in this root certificate signs a key in another certificate. This can extend some number of times before we get to the actual certificate we're interested in.

To verify that certificate, we trace a chain of certificates. Alice's certificate is signed by a certificate that is signed by a certificate that is signed by the certificate that Jack built. Many large corporations, governments, and so on have their own hierarchies that they create and maintain.

X.509 certificates of the sort that we use for SSL connections on the Web use hierarchical trust. If you go to Amazon.com, that web server has a certificate that was signed in a hierarchy that traces up to a root certificate that we trust. For these commercial Certificate Authorities, they typically use a depth of two or three.

Ah, now we hear you ask, "But how do we trust that root certificate?" The answer is: direct trust. Built into your web browser is a set of root certificates. You consider them valid because they are part of the software you installed. This is an important point: hierarchical trust ultimately derives from direct trust.

Hierarchical trust is straightforward, but has an obvious risk. If the authority makes a mistake, the effect of that mistake is great. In a notorious example of this problem, Microsoft uses a hierarchical trust system for its code-signing system, Authenticode. That hierarchy is maintained by VeriSign. A few years ago, some miscreants convinced VeriSign that they were Microsoft employees, but they were not. VeriSign issued Microsoft code-signing certificates to people who were not Microsoft. Fortunately, the scam was caught quickly. Had they gotten away with the improperly issued certificates, whoever ended up with those certificates would have been able to sign software with a Microsoft key, and from the system's viewpoint, that bogus software would have been Microsoft software.

Cumulative Trust

The drawback of hierarchical trust—that a hierarchy is brittle—leads us to the last major trust model, that of cumulative trust. Cumulative trust takes a number of factors into consideration and uses these factors to decide whether a certificate is valid.

Cumulative trust comes from an examination of the limitations of the hierarchy. In an idealized world, when everything goes right, hierarchical trust works best. We use hierarchical trust in the real world all the time. Passports, visas, driver's licenses, national identity systems, credit cards, and even an employer's credentials are all done through a hierarchical trust system.

However, the prime impulse of a security person is to look not at what can go right, but at what can go wrong. Hierarchies are brittle, and because they are brittle, there is a natural tendency to limit the scope of a hierarchy. In general, passports and driver's licenses are not unified, for example. Government documents rarely become credit documents. And because they are brittle, different hierarchies tend to look askance at each other. The badge that gets you into your workplace cannot get you onto a plane, despite a chain of trust! The badge comes from a hierarchy at your employer that is backed by identity documents into the banking and tax systems. At least in theory, they could be tied together. They are not tied, however, because of a lack of trust between the hierarchies.

The simplest cumulative trust system is represented by the question, "May I see two forms of ID, please?" The two forms of ID are a cumulative trust system. The security assumption is that it is much harder to have two erroneous trust paths than one. That idea, that the relying party collects at least one trust path, makes it cumulative. The accumulation might also use different types of trust. For example, when you give a merchant your credit card and the merchant asks to see your driver's license as well, that is also cumulative trust. Note that the credit card is a financial credential, and the driver's license is a quasi-identity credential. The merchant, however, accumulates the trust from the two credentials and completes the transaction.

Note that cumulative trust can encompass both direct trust and hierarchical trust. It is easy to set up in a cumulative trust system both direct trust and hierarchies of trust. We can also consider a hierarchy to be a special case of a cumulative system where we accumulate to one. Direct trust is also a special case of both a hierarchy and accumulation.

In public key infrastructure, the most widely used cumulative trust system is the PGP Web of Trust. However, cross-certification and bridge CAs are closely related to cumulative trust, if not precisely an accumulation system.

DEFINITIONS

Although most of the terms in this chapter are in common use in the security field, some definitions are useful, in order to keep us on the same page. PGP terminology is intentionally colloquial; it was created to be a common-language alternative to technical terms. Let us define some of those technical terms as well as the PGP-related terms:

PKI

Public Key Infrastructure. A PKI is a set of technologies and mechanisms for creating, distributing, and maintaining public keys and certificates.

Certificate

A certificate is a data structure that contains a public key, some information, and signatures that declare that the key and the information go together. Identity certificates are the most common. They bind a name and a public key (an email address is just a type of name) together. An attribute certificate binds information about the key holder to the key. For example, a certificate that says "the holder of this certificate is over 21 years of age" is an attribute certificate.

Certification

A certification is a single binding of information and the key with a digital signature. X.509 certificates contain a single certification. OpenPGP certificates may contain a number of certifications.

A certification (and thus a certificate) is created by a certificate authority (CA) when it creates the signature that binds the key and information together.

Key

OpenPGP's term for what other PKIs call a certificate. Whitfield Diffie coined this term because it is easier to say, type, and understand than "certificate." The average person has an intuitive sense of what a key is and what it is used for. Today, the term can be confusing in some contexts. An OpenPGP key (certificate) can contain many certifications, and in fact many related public keys, each governed by its own contexts and policies.

Keyring

A collection of keys. It may be a private database maintained by one user, but can also be shared among a number of users, as on the keyservers mentioned in the following item.

Keyserver

A directory that shares large collections of keys over a network. People can upload keys to a keyserver and use it as a reliable storage facility where they can keep all their key-related information up-to-date.

Sign

OpenPGP uses the colloquialism "sign" where other PKIs would say "certify." In OpenPGP's lingo, Alice signs (rather than certifies) Bob's key.

Introducer

A key that creates a certification. Thus, an introducer is OpenPGP's term for a certificate authority. Like the term *key*, Whitfield Diffie coined the term *introducer* as a more colloquial and human term than *certificate authority*.

The Basic PGP Web of Trust

For those who are familiar with other public key infrastructures (PKIs), PGP differs from the basic, hierarchical system with one tweak that everything else derives from. In the PGP trust model, all users are also certification authorities. Of course, not all authorities are created equal. Alice can certify Bob, but that doesn't mean Fran should accept the certification. This is why PGP uses the term *introducer* instead of *authority*. We have a natural tendency to trust an authority, but we attach realistic skepticism to an introduction.

"Phil, this is Bob," says Alice, making the introduction. Based on how accurate Phil thinks Alice is, he makes a decision. Phil can fully trust Alice as an introducer and accept Bob as valid. He can also wait until Jon says, "Hey, Phil, have you ever met Bob?" before he truly accepts the other person as accurately Bob.

There is a common misconception that since the Web of Trust is relative, in that all frames of reference are equally valid, there can be no recognized authorities and no organizational use. To think this is to confuse architecture and implementation. Many implementations and deployments hand a group a set of introductions to the end users, and they use them, the same way they accept the root certificates baked into other software.

But to understand the way it works, let us examine Figure 7-1, which shows the Web of Trust and all its facets. Each node in this figure is a key in a keyring. Each arrow represents a certification signature. An arrow going from Alice to Bob means that Alice has signed or certified Bob's key.

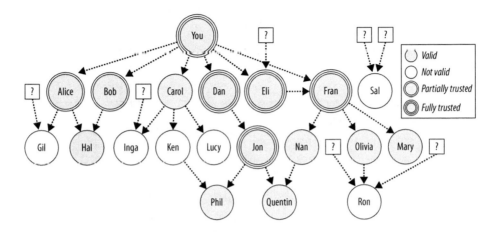

FIGURE 7-1. The PGP Web of Trust

At the top of Figure 7-1, the key labeled You is the owner's key. It is a triple circle to denote that it is fully trusted, which means that any key it signs will be valid. We also say that it is implicitly trusted, because you hold the private key as well as the public key. There are arrows that indicate that you have signed the keys belonging to Alice, Bob, Carol, Dan, Eli, and Fran.

There are also signatures that are dangling references to keys that are not in this keyring. For example, some key that you don't have has signed Eli's key.

The keys on the graph that are filled with gray are valid keys; we consider them to be accurate because the cumulative system of the Web of Trust calculates that they are valid. The accumulation works as follows: *partially trusted introducers* are denoted in the graph by a key with a double circle, and their signatures score one point; *fully trusted introducers* are denoted in the graph by a key with a triple circle, and their signatures score two points. If a key accumulates signatures from introducers that are worth two or more points, it is considered valid. Keys with zero or one point are not considered valid.

To see some examples, let's look at some specific subgraphs:

- Alice and Bob have each signed Hal. Therefore, Hal is valid, but Hal is not trusted.
- Gil is signed by Alice, but you only partially trust Alice, and so Gil's key is not valid.
- Carol has signed a number of keys that are also in this keyring, but none of them are valid. Interestingly, Ken signed Phil, which is valid, but not because Ken signed it.

- There is a tight cluster of keys with Dan, Eli, and Fran. You have signed each of them. Also, they are all fully trusted introducers. Eli's signature on Fran's key is redundant, because you directly certified it. Or perhaps your direct certification is redundant because Eli signed it.

- Nan, Olivia, and Mary are valid because Fran signed them. If we trace up from any of them, we see that there are two validity paths, one including Eli and the direct path from Fran to you.

- While you consider Jon valid because Dan signed his key, you also fully trust him. Consequently, Phil and Quentin are valid. Any other keys you discover that Jon signed are also going to be valid. This is of course true of the other fully trusted introducers, but Jon is someone you haven't directly trusted. The pair of Dan and Jon very closely resemble a hierarchical certification authority.

- Also note that while there are two upward paths from Quentin, one of them goes through Nan, who is valid but not trusted. Thus, while Nan has two upward paths of validity, Quentin only has one.

- Ron has three signatures, but none of them are from people you trust.

- Sal is signed by two dangling keys, which represent people unconnected to your Web of Trust.

We can now distinguish those two easy-to-confuse concepts of validity and trust another way: using the figure. Validity is a quality of a *node* (circle), whereas trust is a quality of the *edges* going between nodes. It is through the trust paths that we determine validity.

Rough Edges in the Original Web of Trust

The basic Web of Trust in early versions of PGP works very well as a cumulative trust system. However, there are a number of architectural and semantic rough edges in it. We fixed these rough edges in later versions of PGP, but we will review them here first.

Supervalidity

In Figure 7-1, Fran is a special key, in that she has a score of four: two from being signed by you and two from being signed by Eli. The Web of Trust makes no allowance for supervalid keys, yet intuitively there should be something special about Fran. There should also be something about a key that both Fran and Jon signed. We have yet to turn that intuition into a useful mechanism.

The social implications of signing keys

Despite this, many people are uncomfortable signing a key that belongs to someone they don't like.

Assigning trust can also be thorny from a social aspect. Still looking at Figure 7-1, suppose that you trust Carol with your very life (she might be your best friend), but you don't trust her to sign keys accurately, particularly because of her trusting nature. Similarly, Fran may be a picayune, compulsive nitpicker whom you can barely stand to be in the same room with, but you made her a fully trusted introducer for this very character flaw.

This underlines the point made when we defined trust at the beginning of this chapter: Web of Trust trust is a specialized trust limited to the sphere of validating keys, not a real-world trust.

Nonetheless, signing someone's key can be a very personal decision. Many people feel very strongly about it. Part of the strength of the Web of Trust is that this personal touch is part of PGP's zeitgeist. But it can also be a weakness that something so very simple—stating that you believe someone is who they claim to be—can become so emotionally charged. That's why the *xkcd* comic strip in Figure 7-2[†] is funny. For many people, certifying a key is an intensely personal thing.

FIGURE 7-2. *Responsible behavior*

A related emergent property of the Web of Trust is that key signatures acquire a cachet. They become like autographs, and develop social value.

Some of this social value is simply operational. If you have gone to the trouble to get several people you value to sign your key[‡] and then get a new key, you have to obtain all of those signatures again. Many people keep their key longer than they should because the keys are signed by other people who are impressive in the right social circles, or whose relationships with the key holder are simply important emotionally.

This basic problem applies even to your own keys. There is presently no way to automatically roll forward the validity of your 1998 key to your 2008 key. If the old key signs the new key

---

[†] *http://imgs.xkcd.com/comics/responsible_behavior.png*, Randall Munroe, used by permission.

[‡] Here the social value issue comes up again! Why should you get signatures from people you value rather than those who can make accurate statements?

and vice versa, this creates a manual roll-forward that is supported in the trust model, but it is not automated, and requires people to have both keys.

The social implications of the Web of Trust are its most fundamental and lasting rough edge. They create a social network out of security credentials. They make security credentials fun and personal, but by being fun and personal they acquire emotional value. We have no feelings about the SSL certificates on our website, but reviewing our PGP keys involves reviewing relationships.

PGP and Crypto History

A large number of myths unfortunately circulate through the technical community about PGP. It's important to know its true history to understand the technical choices made in the Web of Trust, so here we tell some of it.[§]

Early PGP

Phil began working on some of the early designs of PGP when he was a peace activist in the 1980s during the Nuclear Weapons Freeze campaign. The world was a different place then: Reagan was in the White House, Brezhnev was in the Kremlin, FEMA was telling cities to prepare evacuation plans, and millions of people feared the world was drifting inexorably toward Nuclear War. A million Americans marched for peace in Central Park.

It was in that political climate, in 1984, that Phil saw the need to develop what would later become PGP, both for protecting human rights overseas and for protecting grassroots political organizations at home. He started on the early design of PGP, but the more pressing matters of the peace movement postponed the bulk of the development effort until years later.

Phil wrote the first working version of PGP in 1991. He published PGP in the wake of Congressional discussion[ǁ] of requiring that all communications equipment and services have a "trap door" in them to permit government anti-criminal and counterterrorism activities.

While that discussion passed with no legislative outcome, Phil rushed to produce PGP 1.0 so that there would be freely available strong encryption in wide distribution while it was still legal to do so. One of PGP's explicit design goals was to metaphorically shoo the horses out of the barn before the door was closed.

[§] The sources for PGP can be downloaded from *http://www.pgp.com/downloads/sourcecode*. This includes not only the sources to PGP Desktop, but the PGP Command Line sources and the PGP Universal GPL-modified sources. You can also find PGP's policies on assurance and special build requirements at *http://www.pgp.com/company/pgpassurance.html*.

[ǁ] This was Senate Bill 266 of 1991. It never passed into law.

Although there were other message-encryption systems at the time, notably Privacy Enhanced Mail (PEM),# they were so tightly controlled that they were not suitable for mass deployment.*

PGP 1.0 captured the attention of many people, but it was flawed. In particular, it used the Bass-O-Matic cipher designed by Phil, in which Eli Biham found cryptographic flaws. So Phil—along with Hal Finney, Peter Gutmann, and Branko Lancaster—worked on its successor version, PGP 2.0.

PGP 2.0 replaced the Bass-O-Matic cipher with the International Data Encryption Algorithm (IDEA) cipher, designed by Xuejia Lai and James Massey. It also introduced the PGP trust model in a state that was close to its RFC 1991 form.

PGP 2 captured the imagination of many people who wanted to use strong cryptography in an ad hoc, unregulated environment. It became a grassroots phenomenon.

Patent and Export Problems

While cryptographically quite strong, PGP 2 had other issues, dealing with patents and export control. The IDEA cipher was patented, and the patent owner, Ascom-Tech AG, licensed it freely for noncommercial use but had inconsistent licensing for commercial users. The RSA public-key algorithm was patented in the United States by MIT, and was licensed to RSA Data Security Incorporated (RSADSI).

Phil met in 1986 with RSADSI's CEO, Jim Bidzos, and discussed licensing the RSA algorithm for freeware. Those meetings ended with Phil believing that he had permission to use the RSA algorithm in software so long as its cost was zero (i.e., that it was true freeware), and Bidzos believing the opposite. Years of disagreement about this agreement followed. Part of the difficulty in the legal status of PGP included the fact that the RSA algorithm was patented only in the United States, and that the actual owner of the RSA patent, MIT, was favorably disposed to PGP software.

The end result was that RSADSI created a library, RSAREF, for use in freeware and shareware, and PGP software was released in a version 2.5 that used RSAREF in the U.S. but broke compatibility with all previous versions. This meant that there were several versions of PGP:

- The pre-PGP 2.5 versions of the software, which were cut off from future development and support

---

PEM was originally defined by John Linn and Steve Kent in RFC 1113, RFC 1114, and RFC 1115. These were revised with David Balenson and Burt Kaliski in RFC 1421, RFC 1422, RFC 1423, and RFC 1424.

* Jon Callas was at Digital Equipment Corporation at the time, and had a PEM certificate. Getting a PEM certificate involved a notary public and sending his passport to a certification authority by courier. He and his colleagues switched to PGP from PEM solely because it was impossible to get certificates to people who needed them in less than a month, or to people without passports.

- An "international" version of PGP software, developed completely outside of the United States (for export-control reasons), which used the original implementation of the RSA algorithm

- An "RSAREF" version of PGP software, developed inside the United States, using the RSAREF implementation of the RSA algorithm

In all of these versions, the IDEA cipher was free for noncommercial use, but not for commercial purposes.

While the intellectual-property disagreements were going on, Public Key Partners filed a complaint in 1992 with U.S. Customs, complaining that Phil was exporting cryptography without the appropriate licenses, namely the PGP program, which by then had spread throughout the Internet. That started the notorious investigation of Phil and PGP software. The investigation lasted until January 1996, when it was dropped.

There are many misconceptions about l'affaire Zimmermann that we can correct.

Phil was the target of a criminal investigation, but was not prosecuted. No criminal charges were filed about PGP against him or anyone else. Nor were there any lawsuits filed, nor any other legal action other than an investigation, nor did anyone spend any time in prison. The investigation covered the actual distribution of the PGP software itself, and not the PGP team's development practices. The PGP team consisted of developers in the United States, New Zealand, and Europe. The practice of developing software internationally was apparently never the subject of the investigation.

The U.S. government (in particular, the National Security Agency [NSA]) did not start the investigation in response to the software's existence. The popular misconception is that somehow the government did not like mass-distributed cryptography, and therefore started the investigation. U.S. Customs conducted the investigation in response to a complaint from Jim Bidzos. While the NSA was consulted in the matter, they apparently did not start it, and there is evidence that they were instrumental in dropping the investigation.†

The Crypto Wars

Part of the political context of the 1990s was what is often called *The Crypto Wars*. The Crypto Wars were the result of the changing role of cryptography in society. Until 1997, international regulation considered cryptography a weapon of war. Free and open cryptosystems were regulated as munitions in the United States, banned in France, and of mixed status throughout the rest of the world. In 1997, the U.S. reclassified cryptography as a dual-use item. France opened up nearly all cryptography in 1999, and export controls on cryptography were radically

---

† William Crowell, then deputy director of the NSA, stated in separate personal communications with Jon and Phil that he was consulted before the investigation started, and opined that an investigation was warranted, but that he also pressed to cancel the investigation, and claimed credit for its being canceled. Others within the Justice Department also later claimed credit for that decision.

liberalized in 2000. Those liberalizations have continued since then despite international concern about terrorism.

Part of the struggle to end the U.S. export controls on crypto involved the publication of PGP source code in its entirety, in printed book form. Printed books were and are exempt from the export controls. This happened first in 1995 with the publication of *PGP Source Code and Internals* (MIT Press). It happened again later when Pretty Good Privacy, Inc., published the source code of PGP in a more sophisticated set of books with specialized software tools that were optimized for easy optical character recognition (OCR) scanning of C source code. This made it easy to export unlimited quantities of cryptographic source code, rendering the export controls moot and undermining the political will to continue imposing the export controls.

Today, there has been nearly an about-face in government attitude about cryptography. National and international laws, regulations, and expectations about privacy, data governance, and corporate governance either imply or require the widespread use of strong cryptography. In 1990, the cultural attitude about cryptography could be described as, *Why do you need that? What do you have to hide?* Twenty years later, the cultural attitude is closer to, *Why don't you have it? Don't you understand that you have to protect your data?*

The definitive history of The Crypto Wars and the cultural shift in cryptography has not yet been written. Nonetheless, a good place to start is Steven Levy's *Crypto: How the Code Rebels Beat the Government Saving Privacy in the Digital Age* (Penguin).

From PGP 3 to OpenPGP

After the status of PGP 2 became calmer, Phil, along with Derek Atkins and Colin Plumb, started work on a new version of PGP software, PGP 3. PGP 3 contained a number of improvements to the RFC 1991 protocol, including:

- Support for multiple public-key pairs in a PGP key. In particular, its design called for separate signing and encryption keys, as a way to enforce key use.
- Support for DSA public-key signatures, as well as ElGamal for public-key encryption.
- Support for CAST5 and Triple DES for symmetric encryption.
- Replacing the MD5 hash function with SHA-1, after Hans Dobbertin found pseudo-collisions in its compression function (see "References" on page 129).

In 1996, Phil formed the company Pretty Good Privacy, Inc. with private investors and the company Viacrypt, which had produced commercial versions of PGP software. Since Viacrypt had released versions of the RFC 1991 system under the product name PGP 4, the PGP 3 cryptosystem was released as PGP 5.

At the time, members of the PGP software development team started to advocate a profile of the PGP 3 protocol they informally called Unencumbered PGP, a set of parameters that eschewed algorithms encumbered with intellectual property. The team took Unencumbered PGP to the IETF as a successor to RFC 1991, and it became OpenPGP.

Enhancements to the Original Web of Trust Model

Although the model described earlier in this chapter is classic and fairly well known, few people know about the many extra features and enhanced sophistication that has been added to various later versions of PGP. As we recognized the limitations of the basic model, we added these elements to improve scaling and smooth over the rough edges.

The overarching areas of concern that came up again and again concerned revocation (or other reasons for keys becoming invalid), scaling problems, and the bloat caused as outdated signatures built up in keys. This section addresses each of those areas and a few other interesting enhancements.

Revocation

All PKIs need a way to revoke certificates. People are fallible creatures and they sometimes lose control of computers and keys. Systems can be lost or compromised, and the keys and certificates have to be declared invalid before they expire on their own.

Revocation is theoretically simple (although often still hard to propagate) in a hierarchical PKI such as X.509. Central authorities distribute revocations using the same channels they use to distribute the original authorizations to use keys.

The basic model for revocation

The original PGP Web of Trust described in the previous section offered two mechanisms for revocation:

Key revocation
> Someone who has lost control of her key must be able to revoke the whole thing; she can't depend on getting everyone who has signed it to revoke their signatures. This kind of revocation, like the previous one, is itself a kind of signature. (Signatures are the general way of transferring trusted information in PGP.) Signing a key with this key revocation signature invalidates all of its certifications.

Signature revocation
> A key can create a signature declaring that another signature is no longer valid. For instance, if Alice discovers that Bob cheated her into signing his key, she can revoke her certification of that key. If Charlie has also signed the key and doesn't revoke his signature, other people may trust Charlie and continue accepting Bob's key as valid. Note that this form of revocation is good for both data signatures and certification signatures.

Key revocation and expiration

Key revocation is a rough edge in all PKIs—perhaps the sharpest rough edge in public key cryptography. Although the PGP model is flexible and avoids some revocation pitfalls (such as the unmanageable sizes that certificate revocation lists tend to reach), it has its own issues with revocation. Here are some of them:

- There is no mechanism to distribute revocation information out-of-band, separately from the distribution of the keys themselves. If Alice revokes her key, she can place the revocation signature on a keyserver, but there is no way to broadcast this mechanism to everyone who has her key.

- There is no way for someone to revoke a lost key. It is not uncommon for a new PGP user to create a key, upload it to a keyserver, and then promptly forget the passphrase that protects it. The key has to remain there unused until it expires.

- Revocation (and expiration too, for that matter) includes no semantics for interpreting their meaning over time. For example, let us suppose that Alice creates a key in 2002 that expires in 2006. Suppose that she signs a document in 2003 and revokes her key in 2005. In 2008, what do we do with that signature? Certainly, in 2003, that signature was good, but is the signature still valid after she revokes her key?

  In practice, of course, it depends a lot on why she revoked her key. If she revoked it because she created a new one, the signature is still good. If she revoked it because identity thieves stole her laptop and wrote bad checks, then that signature should be considered a forgery, as there's no way for us to distinguish it from a forged, backdated signature.[‡]

These difficulties meant that keys were rarely revoked, except in obvious cases of key loss. At least in theory, it should be easy and desirable to revoke a key because it was superseded with a new key, or was otherwise retired. But because revocation was always looked upon with the worst-case scenario—that the key had truly been compromised—users rarely revoked keys.

A way to avoid revocation is to use expiration instead. The expiration date of a PGP key is held in a self-signature, which adds some additional flexibility because the key holder can change the expiration date simply by creating a new self-signature. Expiration, then, is not irrevocable. Unfortunately, people rarely used the expiration features.

Despite the improvements we describe next, revocation is still a conundrum.

Designated revokers

A designated revoker is a second key that has rights to generate revocation signatures for a primary key. A revocation coming from the designated revoker is as valid as one coming from the primary key itself.

[‡] This particular problem could be helped by a third-party notary signature or timestamp signature. If the document in question has another signature from a notary or timestamping service, that extra signature states that Alice's signature in 2003 was valid at the time. In practice, however, no one ever does this.

Suppose that you designate Dan to be your designated revoker. When you do this, there is a self-signed signature in your key that states that Dan is your revoker. Additionally, this signature is itself marked as an irrevocable signature. The designation of a revoker must be irrevocable, because in the case of a true key compromise, the compromiser could otherwise just revoke the revoker.§

The designated revoker need not be an active key. You might, for example, create a key specifically as your revoker and store it offline in a safe, where it will remain until it is needed. The designated revoker feature provides a great deal of resilience against lost private keys, forgotten passphrases, and compromised keys. Everyone should define a designated revoker for their keys.

Designated revokers first appeared in PGP 3, and are a part of OpenPGP.

Freshness

Freshness is an alternative way to manage expiration and revocation. Freshness-based systems use standard expiration and revocation, but de-emphasize revocation over expiration. (See Rivest in "References" on page 129.)

Consider a key holder who creates a key that will expire in two weeks but re-creates the expiration signature every week. This holder has unilaterally constructed a freshness-based system. His need for revocation is minimized, since any given copy of his key expires in two weeks or less. In many cases, freshness can permit a holder to ignore revocation completely and rely on expiration.

Key signers can also use freshness-based systems to avoid revocation on their signatures.

Note, though, that freshness requires the signers to continually update their signatures. It also requires more rigorous policies in superseding replacement signatures.

Freshness-based OpenPGP systems were first described in a 2003 article by Jon, "Improving Message Security With a Self-Assembling PKI" (see "References" on page 129).

Reasons for revocation

As we noted earlier, there are many reasons to revoke a key, but only the most dramatic reason was covered by the initial implementation of the Web of Trust. Starting with OpenPGP, a revocation signature can be annotated to state whether the revocation is for key retiring, key compromise, or because the key has been superseded by a new key. This annotation can even include a human-readable string.

---

§ Irrevocable signatures were created at the same time as designated revokers because that feature created the need for them.

Scaling Issues

In its basic form, the Web of Trust scales excellently at the low end, up to a few thousand people. Inside a single organization, it even scales to tens or hundreds of thousands of people.

But large, disconnected networks of people may find it difficult to use the basic Web of Trust because there are few paths between people who do not already know each other. As the Web of Trust includes more nodes with relatively few edges, finding trust paths becomes difficult.

The Web of Trust works at its best with groups of people who have some connections. It does not work well with a large, ubiquitous network like the Internet. However, there are two saving graces—modern social networking reconstructs the sorts of small networks that are ideal for the Web of Trust. It may not work well on the Internet as a whole, but it works well in the Internet that most of us use.

Additionally, it is also important to remember the power of direct trust. If Alice has no connections to Zeke, she can always just ask him to send her his key.

Extended introducers

Extended introducers, also called *meta-introducers*, are a way to improve the scaling mechanisms of the Web of Trust by expanding it to multilevel hierarchies. The basic Web of Trust already supports multilevel hierarchies, but each signing node in the tree must be given trust. Extended introducers can automatically introduce introducers to a specified depth.

Examine Figure 7-1 again. Assume that Dan is given a meta-introducer signature with a depth of 1. With this trust signature, Jon's certificate is automatically a fully trusted introducer with no further signature. So is any other key that Dan signs.

Note that this gives Dan great power, the same as a root certificate authority with one level of delegation. In the real world, individuals are rarely given such power, but consider an organization broken up into departments: if a top-level key for the organization is given a meta-introducer signature and that key signs department keys, the departments automatically trust each other's keys without further interaction.

Extended introducers first appeared as part of OpenPGP.

Authoritative keys

Although extended introducers permit one key to be a trust point for a whole community, they are a limited solution to scaling that works only on a local level for a few relationships. The original Web of Trust succeeded in creating a usable PKI from nothing, when there were no authorities.

A much broader scaling mechanism is one of our most recent additions to the PGP Web of Trust. The notion of *authoritative keys*, first described by Jon in "Improving Message Security With a Self-Assembling PKI," helps build a fully distributed PKI.

The notion of authoritative keys is that there may be some certificates or keys that may be presumed to be genuine, not because they descend from cryptographic trust, but because they come from an appropriate authority, such as an Internet domain. For example, if we want to encrypt to a key identified by alice@example.com, we can accept the authority of example.com even if it has no trust anchors in common with us.

From a security standpoint, this isn't unreasonable—if example.com is being forged, then we all have many problems. Also, eventually DNSSEC will use digital signatures to protect the DNS domains, and this will make authoritative keys cryptographically secured. Authoritative keys rely on a network reality: although DNS may be easy to subvert on a small scale, it is hard to subvert on a large scale. Even the recent problems found in the DNS infrastructure have had the result of making DNS a reasonable trust point.

Authoritative keys address one of the most important issues of scaling: organizations have to be able to manage their own PKIs. The alternative is to have dozens or hundreds of hierarchies (which is in fact what happens with X.509 certificates). This alternative has its own scaling problems.

The notion of authoritative keys is also an integral component of the DKIM email-authentication protocol (see Allman et al. in "References" on page 129).

Signature Bloat and Harassment

PGP software systems typically agglomerate signatures on keys, which is the easiest way to handle the signatures and usually stays faithful to their meaning. However, there are three basic cases where this is not desired:

Replacement signatures

> If a new signature supersedes an older one, the older signature should be thrown away. For example, let's suppose Alice signs Bob's key in 2007 with an expiration date of 2008. Then, in 2008, after the first signature expires, she signs Bob's key again with an expiration date in 2009. It seems that the 2008 signature should replace the 2007 one. However, it is not always clear what makes a signature a successor to a previous one. It is also not clear in the basic Web of Trust whether the signature that was superseded should be deleted or kept as a historical record.

Expired signatures

> Consider the previous case, but let us suppose that after Alice's first signature expires, she had not yet created a new one. Should we delete the signature from Bob's key? An expired signature is not included in trust calculations, so why not delete it? The basic Web of Trust does not address this, and in general, implementations have taken the lazy way out and kept all expired signatures.

Unwanted signatures

Suppose Bob doesn't want Alice's signature on his key. There can be a number of reasons. Perhaps he has no idea who she is.[||] Perhaps Bob despises Alice and wants no reminder of her. It is, after all, Bob's key.

There are two other related issues. In the Dudley/Snidely case, Dudley wants to sign Snidely's key for the public good, and Snidely understandably doesn't like this. So there's a conflict between Snidely's control of his own good and the public good at large. It is hard to come to some reconciliation of this conflict without burdening the concept of signing keys with the sort of value-based policies that we have tried so carefully to excise.

The second issue is that the basic Web of Trust provides no authentication of a signer. Let us suppose, for example, that the Dudley signature on Snidely's key comes not from Dudley but from Boris Badenov (a villain in another cartoon), who has created a false Dudley key strictly for the purpose of annoying Snidely.

We call this last case *signature harassment*. While we were developing OpenPGP, we discussed signature harassment internally, but never published any of these discussions, because harassment was so easy to carry out and so hard to guard against. The agglomerating policies of that generation of keyservers left them open to that form of signature abuse.

We instituted several new features over time to address these problems.

Exportable signatures

One of the main causes of signature bloat is the mechanics of importing keys. If Alice wants to import Phil's key and consider it valid, she is likely to need to sign it herself. If she accidentally (or intentionally) sends Phil's key back to a keyserver, it will have her signature on it.

A good way to stop this is to differentiate between signatures that someone makes as a public statement of certification and signatures they make for their own purposes, such as trust calculations. The former are *exportable*, whereas the latter are *nonexportable*.[#]

When a software implementation exports a key or sends it outside its own scope of control, it strips all nonexportable signatures. Additionally, when an implementation imports a key, it also strips nonexportable signatures.

This allows the Web of Trust to differentiate between certifications made for the world at large and certifications that exist for just the use of a single person to build a cryptographically secure set of valid keys.

Exportable signatures first appeared in PGP 3, and are a part of OpenPGP.

[||] Both authors are irked by seeing signatures appear on our key that come from people we don't know.

[#] "Public" and "private" might have been better terms; "nonexportable" is a mouthful. But all the good terms were taken.

Key-editing policies

As another way to combat signature bloat, OpenPGP introduced two key-editing policies that the key owner can announce to a keyserver:

- Direct the server to permit only edits that have been authorized by the key owner
- Direct the server to replace an old copy of the key with a new copy, rather than simply agglomerate all key signatures

These two policies give a key owner control over the signatures on each of her keys. Alone, the first policy agglomerates signatures, but only under the owner's control. The two policies together give the key owner complete control over how her key is presented.

An addition to these policies is a URI embedded into the key that states where the definitive copy of the key resides. This location can be a keyserver or even a file accessed by HTTP or FTP. This URI permits a key owner to direct the world of users to a definitive copy of the key. The definitive copy helps the owner distribute revocation information as well. If the URI points to a keyserver, it also helps with signature revocations.

All of these policies, which first appeared as part of OpenPGP, are implemented as attributes of a self-signature, so a key can have different policies for each user ID on the key.

In-Certificate Preferences

While not strictly part of the trust model, an important feature introduced in OpenPGP allows it to store a number of user preferences in the self-signature of a key. For example, there are a number of options related to symmetric ciphers, compression functions, and hash functions.

OpenPGP permits users to state their preferences in an ordered list of values for each option that is placed in the user's self-signature.

This has a number of desirable features, some related to the Web of Trust. The option list is an authenticated store of a user's options and allows two implementations of OpenPGP to resolve differences of opinion between users.

For example, let's suppose Alice likes the colors red, blue, and purple, whereas Bob likes purple, green, white, and blue. In common, they share blue and purple, but in nearly opposite orders. The OpenPGP mechanism allows each of them to use whichever they like. Alice might use purple because it's Bob's preference, or blue because it's hers. What matters is that there is a guaranteed intersection. OpenPGP has a basic set of mandatory algorithms that ensure interoperability.

These in-certificate preferences are so useful that X.509 standards are in the process of adding their own in-certificate preferences.

The PGP Global Directory

The PGP Global Directory is a revised LDAP-based keyserver that improves upon previous generations of keyservers through better authentication and key editing. It works as follows:

- The Global Directory requires authentication for a key submitted to it, via an email round-trip. The Global Directory sends an email message with an authentication URL to all supplied email addresses. Only after the Global Directory is revisited via an authentication URL does it place the key in the directory. This procedure is similar to the email confirmations sent out by weblog, mailing list, and social network servers to prevent people from being signed up without their consent.

- The Global Directory permits the holder of an email address to delete a key for that email address via an email round-trip authentication, similar to adding a key.

- The Global Directory permits only one key per email address. This is not a perfect solution to key bloat, because there are many cases where a key holder could have more than one legitimate key for a specified email address. However, in this case, there is a secondary problem in how third parties decide which key to use. The oldest? The newest? Both? Listing only one key neatly sidesteps this issue, even though it doesn't address it to everyone's satisfaction.

- The Global Directory requires that a key be reverified semiannually. It sends each key an update email, and if there is no response to the email, the corresponding key is removed from the Global Directory.

- The Global Directory implements the OpenPGP key-editing policies described earlier.

- The Global Directory signs each key it holds with its own certification key. These signatures use freshness on a two-week interval. Thus, if a user deletes or revokes his key, it remains valid for two weeks at most in the Global Directory. This permits the Global Directory to forego its own revocation mechanisms.

These operational policies improve the accuracy of the Global Directory; its users know that every key on it was authenticated via an email exchange between the Directory and the key holder sometime in the last six months.

Note that some of these policies still have the potential for abuse. For example, Boris Badenov could still update Snidely Whiplash's key periodically. These issues are addressed through appropriate software that throttles requests, as well as anti-harassment mechanisms similar to those commonly used in anti-spam software.

The Global Directory is a consolidation of a number of ideas that circulated in the OpenPGP community, including:

- The Robot CA, first proposed by Phil Zimmermann, written about by Seth Schoen, and then refined and implemented by Kyle Hasselbacher (see "References" on page 129).

- The Self-Assembling PKI described earlier, designed by Jon Callas and Will Price

- Existing OpenPGP keyservers
- Email round-trip authentication, used by email mailing list servers such as Mailman (*http://www.list.org*), the GNU mailing list manager

Variable Trust Ratings

The cryptographer Ueli Maurer (see "References" on page 129) developed an extension to the PGP Web of Trust that allows for a continuous scale of trust assignments. In his model, the usual PGP scale would be zero, one-half, and one, with validity granted when enough trust accumulates to get to one. However, he permits any fraction to be assigned to an introducer. You can have one introducer given a value of 0.9 and another a value of 0.15.

Interesting Areas for Further Research

The Web of Trust has promoted human rights and international relations by allowing thousands of people to establish connections over the Internet without having to physically meet. It has also provided a fascinating environment for studying human-relationship-building and reputation. Several issues have come up over the years for which we don't currently have solutions; these can provide a starting point for another generation of research and coding.

Supervalidity

In Figure 7-1 earlier in this chapter, Fran is a special key, in that she has a score of four—two from your signature and two from Eli's. The Web of Trust makes no allowance for supervalid keys, yet intuitively one feels there should be something special about Fran. There should also be something special about a key that both Fran and Jon signed. We have yet to turn that intuition into a useful mechanism.

Social Networks and Traffic Analysis

Many people have observed that the Web of Trust forms a social network, a generalized directed graph that shows connections between people through their keys and signatures. This graph can be analyzed for social connection information.

If a given person subscribes to the theory that her signatures should be value-neutral, or even if she makes a point of signing "hostile" keys (such as Dudley signing Snidely's key), someone cannot assume a relationship between two people based upon the existence of a key signature. Moreover, PGP "key-signing parties," where a number of people get together and collectively certify each other's keys, blur the semantic meaning of the social network.

Neal McBurnett (see "References" on page 129) analyzed the network structure of the Web of Trust digraph. He examined the digraph for path lengths, connectedness, degree of scale, and other features.

Mark Reiter and Stuart Stubblebine created PATHSERVER (see "References" below), a way to evaluate multiple signature paths between keys.

These analyses are inspired by the Web of Trust and derive from the Web of Trust, but we must note that they are orthogonal to the Web of Trust proper. It is an integral feature of the Web of Trust that it consists of viewpoints; it may be considered relativistic, in that no frame of reference in the Web of Trust is inherently more valuable or trusted than any other. The *trust* portion of the Web of Trust relies completely on the user-specific trust markings and the weights that the key holder places on keys. The mesh of keys is an interesting object that we believe is useful on its own, and helps the overall use of the Web of Trust, but it is an orthogonal construct to the Web of Trust.

The Web of Trust's directed graph says something about the people in it. What it says, though, is open to both further research and debate.

References

Allman, E., J. Callas, M. Libbey, J. Fenton, and M. Thomas. *DomainKeys Identified Mail (DKIM) Signatures*, RFC 4871, *http://www.ietf.org/rfc/rfc4871.txt*.

Atkins, D., W. Stallings, and P. R. Zimmermann. *PGP Message Exchange Formats*, RFC 1991, *http://www.ietf.org/rfc/rfc1991.txt*.

Callas, J. "Improving Message Security With a Self-Assembling PKI," in *Proceedings of the 2nd Annual PKI Research Workshop*, Gaithersburg, MD, April 2003.

Callas, J., L. Donnerhacke, H. Finney, D. Shaw, and R. Thayer. *OpenPGP Message Format*, RFC 4880, *http://www.ietf.org/rfc/rfc4880.txt*.

Callas, J., L. Donnerhacke, H. Finney, and R. Thayer. *OpenPGP Message Format*, RFC 2440, *http://www.ietf.org/rfc/rfc2440.txt*.

Dobbertin, H. "Cryptanalysis of MD5 Compress," Announcement on the Internet, 1996.

Elkins, M., D. Del Torto, R. Levien, and T. Roessler. *MIME Security with OpenPGP*, *http://www.ietf.org/rfc/rfc3156.txt*.

Ellison, C. *SPKI Requirements*, RFC 2692, September 1999, *http://www.ietf.org/rfc/rfc2692.txt*.

Ellison, C., B. Frantz, B. Lampson, and R. Rivest. *SPKI Certificate Theory*, RFC 2693, September 1999, *http://www.ietf.org/rfc/rfc2693.txt*.

Garfinkel, S. *PGP: Pretty Good Privacy (http://oreilly.com/catalog/9781565920989/index.html)*. O'Reilly, 1995.

Gordon, J. "The Alice and Bob After Dinner Speech," given at the Zurich Seminar, April 1984, *http://downlode.org/etext/alicebob.html*.

Hasselbacher, K. "ROBOT CA," *http://www.toehold.com/robotca*.

Hasselbacher, K. "Robot CA: toward zero-UI crypto," *http://www.kuro5hin.org/story/2002/11/18/135727/66*.

Levy, S. *Crypto: How the Code Rebels Beat the Government—Saving Privacy in the Digital Age*, Diane Pub Co., 2003.

Maurer, U. "Modeling a Public-Key Infrastructure," in *Proceedings of the 1996 European Symposium on Research in Computer Security* (ESORICS '96), *Lecture Notes in Computer Science*, Springer-Verlag, Sept. 1996, Vol. 1146, pp. 325–350, *http://citeseer.ist.psu.edu/maurer96modelling.html*.

McBurnett, N. "PGP Web of Trust Statistics," *http://bcn.boulder.co.us/~neal/pgpstat*.

Reiter, M. and S. Stubblebine. "Path independence for authentication in large-scale systems," in *Proceedings of the 4th ACM Conference on Computer and Communications Security*, Zurich, Switzerland, April 1997, pp. 57–66, *http://stubblebine.com/97ccs.pdf*.

Reiter, M. and S. Stubblebine. "Resilient Authentication Using Path Independence," *IEEE Transactions on Computers*, Vol. 47, No. 12, December 1998.

R. Rivest. "Can We Eliminate Certificate Revocation Lists?" in *Proceedings of Financial Cryptography '98*, Springer Lecture Notes in Computer Science, No. 1465 (Rafael Hirschfeld, ed.), February 1998, pp. 178–183.

Schneier, B. *Applied Cryptography: Protocols, Algorithms, and Source Code in C*, Second Edition. John Wiley & Sons, 1996.

Schoen, S. "Casual PKI and making e-mail encryption easy," *http://www.advogato.org/article/391.html*.

Zimmermann, P. R. *The Official PGP User's Guide*. The MIT Press, 1995.

Zimmermann, P. R. *PGP: Source Code and Internals*. The MIT Press, 1997.

CHAPTER EIGHT

Open Source Honeyclient: Proactive Detection of Client-Side Exploits

Kathy Wang

CLIENT SOFTWARE VULNERABILITIES ARE CURRENTLY BEING EXPLOITED at an increasing rate. Based on a September 2004 survey, Dell Computers estimates that 90% of Windows PCs harbor at least one spyware program. Microsoft's Internet Explorer browser has had over 50 vulnerabilities in the past six months, according to the Common Vulnerabilities and Exposures (GVE) database (*http://cve.mitre.org*). By taking advantage of client software vulnerabilities, attackers are able to infect and control systems that are protected by firewalls or otherwise inaccessible.

As is well known, client-side exploits can be used by the attacker for many other malicious activities once a victim machine is compromised. The exploit could steal valuable information, such as the user's online banking credentials. Among other things, the attacker could hijack the victim machine and add it to growing bot networks, in which each bot becomes part of a distributed denial of service (DDoS) attack or a spam delivery system.

How will attackers utilize client software vulnerabilities? As far back as 2002, a paper titled *How to 0wn the Internet In Your Spare Time*[*] came up with a disturbing possible scenario: a *contagion worm* exploit that targets both server and client vulnerabilities. First, the attack uses typical Web server security flaws, such as buffer overflows or SQL injection, to upload malicious

---

[*] S. Staniford, V. Paxson, and N. Weaver, *How to 0wn the Internet In Your Spare Time, http://www.icir .org/vern/papers/cdc-usenix-sec02* (last visited September 4, 2008).

code that is then downloaded whenever a targeted browser visits the website. Then, the downloaded code exploits vulnerabilities on the browser client.

Today, attackers target client software because many of these software applications are developed by people who are not trained to create secure software. In addition, far more people use client software than server software, and many of them are just your average Internet user who is less likely to install security updates. Compare this to your average server administrator, who is more likely to be technically trained and follow through with updating the server software.

Even if the user is savvy enough to update her operating system software and diligently runs the most recent signatures in her anti-virus product, most malware that attacks through client software will still work on the user's system, and it will not be detected by the anti-virus software. The anti-virus manufacturers just can't keep up.

THE BUSINESS OF EXPLOITS

While I was pondering the risk of client-side attacks, I looked at vulnerability databases such as CVE, as well as the SecurityFocus database (*http://www.securityfocus.com/bid*). It occurred to me that the security industry was much farther ahead in identifying and fixing server vulnerabilities than they were for client application vulnerabilities. In fact, it seems we're roughly 5 to 10 years behind with regard to just understanding client vulnerabilities and exploits. We have a lot of catching up to do!

Compounding the lack of research, all sorts of "businesses" are popping up that utilize client-side exploits as part of their business strategies. According to InformationWeek,[†] a Russian company named Iframedollars.biz developed a one-line exploit and marketed it to web server administrators. Administrators download that exploit, install it on their web servers, and get paid six cents from Iframedollars.biz for each web browser that visits the server and gets infected by the exploit code.

I have to admit that I was interested in seeing this one-line exploit. So I went to Iframedollars.biz to see where I could download it. It turns out that in order to get the exploit, I would need to send Iframedollars.biz a bunch of information, including my name, address, and credit card number. That's fairly comical—would you trust these people with your personal information? It's not clear to me how any web administrator could possibly agree to send all that sensitive data to Iframedollars.biz. Of course, I didn't end up getting the exploit.

---

† InformationWeek article on Iframedollars.biz: *http://www.informationweek.com/news/security/ vulnerabilities/showArticle.jhtml?articleID=163701736.*

Enter Honeyclients

In network security management, the quality of a security analyst's response to compromises often depends on his knowledge of existing vulnerabilities and exploits. This knowledge can be used to create intrusion detection system (IDS) signatures, or to proactively patch vulnerable systems. One popular tool for acquiring advanced knowledge is the *honeypot*, a specialized system that is intended as a target for new attacks and is instrumented to provide detailed information about an exploit when an attack is successful.

However, honeypots are passive devices, and all publicly known honeypot systems to date are limited to discovering server software attacks. A large and growing proportion of vulnerabilities these days are discovered in client software, such as web browsers or mail clients. Since existing honeypot systems cannot detect exploits for these vulnerabilities, we need a new technology, one that instruments client software and drives it in such a way as to detect new exploits. This concept is the *honeyclient*.

Honeyclients are systems that drive a piece of potentially vulnerable client software, such as a web browser, to potentially malicious websites, and then monitor system behavior for indicators of compromise. A honeyclient emulates the client side of a connection, and in normal mode acts as a spider or a bot, constantly surfing random sites. The client probably runs inside of a sandbox that monitors client behavior to see whether it falls outside of normal operational bounds. For example, the requests from the honeyclient could be monitored to see whether the honeyclient's requests start deviating from a known good request (e.g., the honeyclient system isn't writing an executable file). If the honeyclient begins to behave abnormally, we know that it has already been infected. This monitoring process would have the added benefit of detecting malicious or compromised web servers.

Traditional honeypots are passive, unable to detect malicious behavior until the attacker happens upon them. Honeyclients therefore possess the advantage of being able to seek out suspicious remote systems. Still, each is suited to its own domain: honeypots for server-side exploits and honeyclients for client-side exploits.

Introducing the World's First Open Source Honeyclient

In 2004, I started designing a honeyclient prototype. One of the first decisions I made was to open-source the prototype code. My hope was that this would inspire others in the security community to start thinking about honeyclients as a technology area, and that a few might contribute to the project.

To detect exploits, I used a comprehensive check for changes on the client, just as Tripwire (*http://sourceforge.net/projects/tripwire*) does on a server. I took a baseline of the honeyclient by recording MD5 hashes of files and enumerating Windows registry keys. After visiting each suspected website, I then looked for changes between the initial baseline and the new snapshot.

I had already decided to start with a Windows honeyclient host, because that's what the average user has installed on his computer.

I also chose Microsoft Internet Explorer (IE) as the browser to use when visiting suspected websites. There may be exploits designed specifically for another operating system or another browser, and my honeyclient might not detect them. But I had to choose one operating system and browser, so it made sense to choose those with the largest population of users. These are the ones most likely to be chosen by the developers of malware, and the ones where exposing the exploits can help the most people.

The truly critical decision was to let a real web browser visit each site instead of simulating browser behavior by downloading files through a tool such as *wget*. A simulation would never reveal the hidden effects of malware that I wanted to uncover. The honeyclient software actually had to be compromised when it encountered a malicious website so that I could collect the malware and analyze it to better understand the latest attack vectors. Using that information, I could then warn the user community about bad websites and potential consequences of infections. If the honeyclient were to emulate a web browser, it would not necessarily get compromised, since there's no underlying system to attack.

The honeyclient operational steps look something like this:

1. Create a baseline consisting of MD5 hashes and registry key values.

2. The honeyclient host invokes Internet Explorer (IE) by calling the *iexplore.exe* process.

3. A previously created URL list file is opened, and URLs are taken from the file one by one.

4. IE is driven to visit the specified URL.

5. As soon as the URL is visited, a snapshot of MD5 hashes and registry key values on the system is created.

6. If the snapshot in step 5 differs from the baseline created in step 1, the honeyclient considers a suspicious event to have occurred, and it sets a flag to warn the user.

7. If the snapshots match, the website is spidered (each link is visited recursively) until there are no more internal links left to visit on that website.

8. Once a website is completely spidered, the honeyclient pulls the next external link from the URL list, and the process begins again.

The original honeyclient prototype was also developed with a driver-proxy architecture (see Figure 8-1). The driver code was responsible for creating an initial baseline as well as invoking the Internet Explorer browser, while the proxy created sockets to pass HTTP requests from the IE browser. The driver also performed the checks on the state of the system.

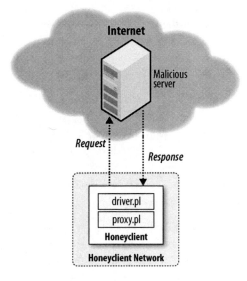

FIGURE 8-1. First-generation open source honeyclient prototype

In June 2005, the initial honeyclient prototype was presented and released to the public at the RECon Conference in Montreal.[‡] The audience showed a lot of interest and posed many questions to me after the talk. In addition to introducing the honeyclient prototype, I raised many related questions.

The technology is great, but what will the resulting arms race be like? Would attackers set up detectors of honeyclients via web bugs, color-on-color URLs, or *robot.txt* files? How about Flash sites that honeyclients will not be able to automatically "click" on? One enhancement I knew I should develop further was letting the honeyclient follow links embedded in JavaScript applications.

We will see shortly how honeyclient operations have been affected by these types of countermeasures to detection.

Second-Generation Honeyclients

Later on in the summer of 2005, the Honeyclient Project was funded at the MITRE Corporation, and our new project team[§] began to work on more advanced honeyclients. We wanted to keep parts of the original prototype, notably the baseline integrity check system, but we also wanted to add completely new features, such as running the honeyclients in virtual machines. It was

[‡] Honeyclient presentation at RECon: *http://2005.recon.cx/recon2005/papers/Kathy_Wang/Wang -Honeyclients-RECON.pdf.*

[§] The Honeyclient project team and contributors are listed at *http://www.honeyclient.org/trac/wiki/about.*

tiring to run the original honeyclient up until it got compromised, and then reimage that operating system in preparation for the next attack. Also, if we wanted to quickly retain compromised operating systems for later attack forensics analysis, we needed to move toward honeyclient virtualization. Our team wanted speed, ease of use, and scalability. These factors were always on our minds as we worked to create our next honeyclient prototype.

One of the first decisions we made was to modularize the new honeyclient architecture. This allows us to develop optional plug-ins that can easily be enabled or disabled, depending on the user's goal. Modularization makes it easier for contributors outside of our project team to develop a plug-in that will work with the rest of the existing honeyclient code. We also decided to license this second-generation honeyclient under the GNU Public License v2. I've always been a big supporter of open source code, and it is a great way to give back to the community, as well as encourage other people to create their own open source honeyclient prototypes.

Another important decision was to go with a client-server model, where the *client* or *agent* side of the honeyclient is located in the honeyclient virtual host and the *server* or *manager* side sits on the physical server that hosts the honeyclient virtual host. The server controls higher-level operations for the honeyclient, which include cloning and suspending virtual machines, detecting changes to the honeyclient system, communicating with an external honeyclient database, and logging full packet captures of the traffic between the honeyclient and the remote server. This new architecture is almost a complete rewrite of the old version. We changed our terminology as well, nixing "driver-proxy" in favor of "client-server." Part of the reason for the semantic change is that client-server better reflects one of the main things we were able to accomplish with this generation: distributed honeyclients. Our team's lead developer, Darien Kindlund, was responsible for implementing the virtual-machine-based honeyclient model.

From an architecture standpoint, the new honeyclient prototype is a virtual machine (VM) designed to drive a locally running target application to one or more remote resources (see Figure 8-2). In this architecture, the honeyclients are structured as follows:

- Hosted on VMware[||] virtual machines
- Running a variant of the Microsoft Windows[#] operating system
- Configured to automatically log in as the system administrator upon boot
- Upon login, automatically executes the Perl module, called `HoneyClient::Agent`, that runs as a daemon inside a Cygwin[*] environment and starts the web visits

We chose VMware Server for virtualization because it is free to all users, and we didn't want to burden the open source community users with having to purchase software to run our

---

[||] VMware's corporate website is *http://www.vmware.com.*

[#] Windows XP is found at *http://www.microsoft.com/windowsxp.*

[*] The Cygwin utility can be obtained at *http://www.cygwin.com.*

honeyclient prototype. Although VMware is not open source, we found it more suited to our needs than open source virtualization projects. It also runs on many operating systems; a later section explains why we chose Linux as the host.

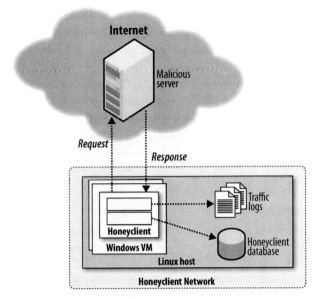

FIGURE 8-2. Honeyclient architecture

The honeyclient system is implemented as a series of Perl modules that execute on a Windows XP platform. The Perl modules drive a Microsoft Internet Explorer browser, and automatically spider given websites. After the driver script gives the honeyclient a URL (such as *http://news .google.com*) as a starting point, the simulated Internet Explorer browser grabs each URL on the site and recursively hits every link, with the driver script extracting links for future spidering.

The honeyclient Perl server checks file and registry key integrity. Even before the first connection to a remote server is made by the honeyclient, the integrity check module starts monitoring files, registry key values, and process-related information on the honeyclient host. After the honeyclient visits each site, the integrity-checking module compares the file checksums and registry key values against the known good list to see whether any changes have been made to sensitive system files or keys. If a change occurs, the server flags this URL as potentially malicious, saves all the network traffic generated during the spidering of this URL, and alerts the analyst that the site deserves further examination.

The honeyclient prototype is installed in a virtual machine environment (currently VMware) in order to ease the restoration of the system to a known good state. To further minimize risk, our physical host operating system is a Linux distribution. Because the honeyclient virtual host is Windows, for reasons explained earlier, deploying a different operating system as a physical host helps to limit the risks of breakout from the virtual host to the physical host. As we collect and analyze the payload data, we will better understand our honeyclient prototype's limitations and modify it continually to improve its performance.

An exploit often enlists the client system in attacks such as spamming and denial of service, so we wanted to prevent our honeyclient from being used by the attacker as a springboard to launch other attacks. Therefore, another piece of our design is a firewall-enabled router running on a virtual host alongside the honeyclients' virtual hosts. The firewall router filters honeyclient traffic as it passes between the internal network and the DMZ network. As a honeyclient is driven to a remote resource, the firewall is configured to permit that honeyclient to access the minimum set of resources required to process all fetched content from the remote resource. Honeywall (*https://projects.honeynet.org/honeywall*), another open source effort by the Honeynet Project, filled our requirements very well, so team member JD Durick integrated it into our architecture for this purpose.

If the host system were to drive a honeyclient to the *http://www.cnn.com* page, the firewall would allow the honeyclient to contact all web servers that mapped to the *http://www.cnn .com* domain (including any additional servers that may host external inline content, such as externally linked advertisements from *http://www.doubleclick.net*) over TCP port 80. Once the firewall grants the honeyclient access, the honeyclient is then signaled to drive to *http:// www.cnn.com*. The firewall allows us to protect the honeyclient from being utilized as a launching pad for other attacks once it becomes compromised. If the attacker tried to launch email or DDoS attacks from the honeyclient host, that action would be blocked by the firewall.

Although we initially utilized Honeywall, we quickly realized that restricting outbound traffic through this firewall prevented the honeyclient host from becoming compromised some of the time. For example, if a web page made use of third-party ad banners, where the exploit was hosted at a different server, the honeyclient would miss that exploit because the firewall would block access to the latter server's domain. This scenario was a trade-off we needed to explore. Is it more important for us to get compromised so that we catch more exploits? Or is it more important to limit the chance of becoming part of a botnet? This is strictly a decision that each honeyclient user needs to make.

Besides utilizing Honeywall from the Honeynet Project, we also incorporated an integrity-checking algorithm from the Capture-HPC[†] honeyclient. Originally, our server simply checked for baseline changes in files and registry keys on our honeyclient system. A bit later, we decided to change the architecture to real-time checks for changes in files, registry keys, and system processes. Capture's integrity check code met our criteria, and a member of our team, Xeno Kovah, worked with Christian Seifert to integrate the integrity check functionality for our honeyclients.

[†] The Capture-HPC honeyclient is at *https://projects.honeynet.org/capture-hpc*, and the project is described at *https://projects.honeynet.org/capture-hpc/wiki/AboutCapture*.

Honeyclient Operational Results

Our second-generation prototype went fully operational in 2006. While developing the honeyclient framework was a necessary step, going live with the second-generation prototype was a learning experience in itself. The first hurdle we had to resolve was the false positives generated with this new prototype.

Transparent Activity from Windows XP

For example, if we visited a foreign language website, IE would pop up a window asking if we wanted to install the language pack for the particular language the website was written in. During that process, we noticed that the same six Windows XP registry keys would be modified as follows:

```
HKEY_CURRENT_USER\Software\Microsoft\Internet Explorer\IntelliForms (added)
HKEY_CURRENT_USER\Software\Microsoft\Internet Explorer\International (changed)
HKEY_CURRENT_USER\Software\Microsoft\Internet Explorer\International\CpMRU (added)
HKEY_USERS\S.+\Software\Microsoft\Internet Explorer\IntelliForms (added)
HKEY_USERS\S.+\Software\Microsoft\Internet Explorer\International (changed)
HKEY_USERS\S.+\Software\Microsoft\Internet Explorer\International\CpMRU (added)
```

Since we were able to replicate the same results while visiting a bunch of known benign foreign language websites, we knew this action alone was not an indication of malicious behavior. At that point, we decided to add these known benign actions to our whitelist. Another interesting case results consistently when we visit SSL-based URLs. The following files are repeatedly modified within the Windows XP environment:

```
Cab1.tmp, Cab2.tmp, ... Cabx.tmp
Tar1.tmp, Tar2.tmp, ... Tarx.tmp
```

Building this whitelist has been—and continues to be—an interesting experience. Until we started testing known good websites, we had little insight as to how many modifications occur in the course of normal operations within the Windows XP environment. Even if we can see all of the modifications in files and registry keys, it doesn't necessarily mean we know for sure whether a file or registry key change is malicious. For example, we encountered the following change in a file upon visiting a shady website:

C:\WINDOWS\fla1.tmp

Is this file benign or malicious? When we did a Google search on this filename, it seemed that even among anti-virus researchers there are questions about the "goodness" of this file. As the name suggests, it may be associated with Flash Player, but it also seems be associated with things you wouldn't want on your system. In general, not only is there a lot of activity during normal (benign) operations, but many of the operations are also quite complex. Our current whitelist can be viewed on our project website.

The substantial time we had to invest in generating whitelists led us to realize that there's very little sharing by the anti-virus research community with the public. So when we look into identifying false positives, we share our results with the public so that everyone can understand what "normal" behavior is for a particular operating system, such as Windows XP.

It's ridiculous that even seasoned security researchers can have a hard time identifying whether a state change on the system is a malicious event. If experienced security researchers have trouble sorting out good from bad, how can we expect the rest of the users on the Internet to know better? This is one reason why client-side exploits are so pervasive today.

Storing and Correlating Honeyclient Data

Early during the development of my first-generation prototype, I realized that one of the real values behind honeyclient technology was the database of vulnerabilities and compromised websites it would produce. This database would store information associated with each honeyclient compromise, including filesystem changes, registry key modifications, and process executions that the remote web server caused when visited by a honeyclient. The database records the URLs visited when these system changes occurred, along with a timestamp marking when the incident happened. Team member Matt Briggs took on the role of implementing the exploit database.

In the process of developing the exploit database, we realized that we might want to store additional information that's not necessarily related to an exploit itself, such as VMware identification numbers for the compromised images.

We also wanted the ability to store information in this database about what application the honeyclient was driving. For example, we will likely get different results by visiting a web page with IE 6 versus IE 7. (Our prototype can also support Mozilla Firefox browsers now.) We will also most likely get different results using Windows XP-based honeyclients versus Windows Vista-based honeyclients. I won't even go into other future possibilities, such as driving non-HTTP-based applications. The database allows us to store all of this information about different environments and results, and allows us to correlate the data between results from driving different applications in various OS environments.

In short, our database grew to become much more than just an exploit database; it should really be called a honeyclient database.

This brings me to another reason why our modularized honeyclient architecture turned out to be a good idea. Because we develop in modules, we can now allow the user to decide which application she wants to send out onto the Internet.

Analysis of Exploits

Now let's talk about some interesting malware that we discovered while operating honeyclients, along with some of the difficulties in detecting it.

Most malware appears to be financially motivated. Thus, we saw a lot of new malware variants that were gaming trojans, where the user's game account information is sent to the attacker's machine. Another type of malware that we saw often was banking trojans, which allow the attacker to obtain access to the victim's online banking account credentials. But we have even seen politically motivated malware, where the attackers attempt to evangelize their political message by installing and/or printing HTML files on the user's desktop.

Perhaps the most interesting example of malware we've seen is one that is able to detect that we're using VMware and proceeds to shut down the guest operating system within seconds. Plenty of malware have the ability to detect virtual platforms such as VMware. Are there other honeyclient implementations that utilize different virtualization platforms? This leads us to the next section.

As I've explored the client-side exploit landscape over the past several years, it has become clear to me that attackers are extremely opportunistic. The bulk of client-side exploits today target Microsoft's IE 6 browser, but this can change as market shares shift. Many people ask me whether it's a good idea to use Mozilla Firefox instead. My answer is always something like, "Sure, but keep in mind that if everyone in the world used Firefox, there would be a lot of exploits that target the Firefox browser." In other words, don't rely on using Firefox alone to protect you from these attacks. The user still needs to be somewhat savvy and not get duped into clicking on every link that comes his way.

What about anti-virus software? It was not until we started capturing a lot of malware with our honeyclients that we were truly able to appreciate what a difficult job the anti-virus industry has. First of all, most anti-virus products are signature-based, which means that the company has isolated each attack and found an embedded set of byte-strings that uniquely identify the attack. Because products are signature-based, the manufacturers need to understand at some level how an attack works in order to detect that attack. Developing a signature can be as simple as running the strings utility against malware binaries and extracting a particular unique string that appears in all of them. Developing a signature can also involve more complex research, but as signature development is not the focus of this chapter, I recommend checking out other books if this topic interests you.[‡]

It's difficult to keep up with developing signatures for every new attack—I'm talking about new malware variants here, not just new exploits—and keep up with all the attacks. There are literally thousands of new malware variants released each day, and anti-virus companies have a finite amount of resources. So a lot of the malware that we capture with our honeyclients

---

[‡] One that I particularly like is *The Art of Computer Virus Research and Defense* by Peter Szor (Symantec Press).

are very poorly detected by major anti-virus companies. The backlog of signatures to develop is so large that it sometimes takes these anti-virus companies weeks after new malware is found to actually develop the signature. Their users are not protected from the malware in the meantime. And some malware never yields a usable signature.

One of the things our project lacks is a dedicated malware analysis team; we currently just don't have the resources. When we capture malware with the honeyclients, we have useful information in the form of filesystem modifications, registry key changes, and processes executed. We even have a module that will do full packet captures of network traffic between the honeyclient and the remote web server at the time of compromise. However, our prototype is not an automated malware analysis tool. This means we do not automatically reverse-engineer captured malware binaries to determine further information about the malicious binary. What we end up doing when we capture new malware is scan the malware binaries with tools such as VirusTotal.com (*http://www.virustotal.com*). VirusTotal gives us a quick glance at how well known the malware is that was captured with our honeyclients. VirusTotal manages a backend of anti-virus scanning tools, all updated with the most recent detection signatures. Figure 8-3 shows a typical scan that we run on a malicious binary via the VirusTotal interface.

Complete scanning result of "mssrv32.exe", received in VirusTotal at 06.19.2007, 23:07:30 (CET).   STATUS: FINISHED

Antivirus	Version	Update	Result
AhnLab-V3	2007.6.16.0	06.19.2007	no virus found
AntiVir	7.4.0.34	06.19.2007	TR/Pakes.A.1604
Authentium	4.93.8	06.19.2007	no virus found
Avast	4.7.997.0	06.19.2007	no virus found
AVG	7.5.0.467	06.19.2007	Generic5.SI
BitDefender	7.2	06.19.2007	no virus found
CAT-QuickHeal	9.00	06.19.2007	(Suspicious) - DNAScan
ClamAV	devel-20070416	06.19.2007	no virus found
DrWeb	4.33	06.19.2007	no virus found
eSafe	7.0.15.0	06.19.2007	Suspicious Trojan/Worm
eTrust-Vet	30.7.3727	06.19.2007	no virus found
Ewido	4.0	06.19.2007	no virus found
FileAdvisor	1	06.19.2007	no virus found
Fortinet	2.91.0.0	06.19.2007	no virus found
F-Prot	4.3.2.48	06.19.2007	no virus found
F-Secure	6.70.13030.0	06.19.2007	Trojan.Win32.Pakes
Ikarus	T3.1.1.8	06.19.2007	Trojan.Win32.Pakes
Kaspersky	4.0.2.24	06.19.2007	Trojan.Win32.Pakes
McAfee	5056	06.19.2007	no virus found
Microsoft	1.2607	06.19.2007	no virus found
NOD32v2	2339	06.19.2007	no virus found
Norman	5.80.02	06.19.2007	no virus found
Panda	9.0.0.4	06.19.2007	Suspicious file
Sophos	4.18.0	06.12.2007	no virus found
Sunbelt	2.2.907.0	06.16.2007	no virus found
Symantec	10	06.19.2007	no virus found
TheHacker	6.1.6.134	06.18.2007	no virus found
VBA32	3.12.0.2	06.19.2007	no virus found
VirusBuster	4.3.23:9	06.19.2007	no virus found
Webwasher-Gateway	6.0.1	06.19.2007	Trojan.Pakes.A.1604

FIGURE 8-3. Output of a VirusTotal scan on malware

As you can see, very few anti-virus products even thought this file was suspicious to begin with. Apparently, this malware binary was obfuscated. Obfuscation is a popular technique used by malware authors to bypass detection by anti-virus scanners, as well as thwart further analysis of the malware binary itself by security researchers. This is why some of the vendors shown in the figure tagged this binary with a "Pakes" name. It means the binary was obfuscated, and the anti-virus scanner could not deobfuscate or unpack that binary.

Limitations of the Current Honeyclient Implementation

That is not to say that honeyclient detection is perfect. In information security, no solution is going to prevent attacks 100% of the time, and if you encounter someone who suggests otherwise, you should be very wary. While operating our honeyclient prototype, we came across several limitations. If a malicious website inserts a delay before launching an attack against the web browser client, honeyclients will not detect the attack. This is because honeyclients operate in such a manner that after the website contents are rendered and no suspicious changes are detected, the honeyclient moves on to the next URL.

Many websites host advertisement banners, and attackers have been known to buy ad banner space and embed malicious code in active ads. An active ad is based on JavaScript or Flash technology, and does not require the user to click on the ad for the content to animate. Therefore, users' computers can be compromised via a web browser vulnerability through one of these active ads. Any site can host these ads, including popular sites that users know and trust. Our honeyclient prototype has the ability to detect these malicious ads, and we have detected these ads while operating. However, if we visit a website that another user also visits, we may not get served the same ads as the other user. Therefore, honeyclients have difficulties detecting malware when that malware is embedded in an ad that rotates. We are currently working on the ability to more accurately detect a particular component of a web page that causes a compromise. Being able to pinpoint this might allow us to identify certain advertising companies that are more prone to leasing ads to malicious parties.

While we were testing our second-generation honeyclient prototype, we encountered a lot of malware that required user interaction and acknowledgment in order to execute and compromise the machine. This type of malware can be in executable (*.exe*) format, and clicking on that *.exe* link will result in the Windows IE browser asking the user if she would like to allow install or download that *.exe* file. It was difficult (at least at the time) for us to develop an automatic "OK" or "Download" clicking mechanism for this prompt. So we made the decision that our honeyclients would be primarily focused on detecting drive-by malware downloads, not malware that requires user permission to execute. Drive-by malware downloads are not the majority of all client-side attacks, but they are more subtle (nearly impossible for the average user to stop, in fact) and their prevalence will only increase in the next couple of years.

Related Work

Although honeyclient technology is relatively new compared to honeypots, anti-virus, and intrusion detection system (IDS) technologies, currently there are at least several separate honeyclient efforts occurring. Various honeyclients were developed for different purposes, but most of them focused on detecting malicious websites.

Back when I started working on the first-generation open source honeyclient, Microsoft was developing honeyclients (which they call *honeymonkeys*). Microsoft and I were developing honeyclients in parallel, and it wasn't until I had already written the first prototype that I found out about Microsoft honeyclients, and vice versa. Unfortunately, I was never able to get information from Microsoft about their honeymonkey internals, and there's not a lot of information on the implementation details of honeymonkeys.§

As a researcher, I cannot emphasize enough the importance of communicating with other researchers about a technology that you're working on. Some people I've talked to feel conflicted about this. On the one hand, if they share their ideas, they may be able to find others who have also thought about the idea, and in return, their original idea can get more refined. On the other hand, they are worried that people will steal their idea if they mention it. I would argue that very few people have such striking ideas that absolutely no one else in the world has ever thought of them. So in the end, the people who want to just hold onto their idea often find that other people came up with the same idea, and had even developed it further than they had! And even if someone was the first to think up something, he may end up losing the chance to claim some credit because he was too obsessed with perfecting the idea to tell anyone about it.

Many anti-virus companies operate software similar to honeyclients, mainly to collect malware for subsequent signature development. Mostly, these anti-virus companies prefer to talk about malware characteristics rather than honeyclient technology. I've talked to Dan Hubbard of Websense about the honeyclients they operate there. Robert Danford is another researcher who implemented the Pezzonavante honeyclient.‖ From prior conversations with Robert, I know his implementation is mainly focused on collecting malware and visiting as many URLs in as short of a time as possible. This is a valid approach, but it sacrifices accuracy in determining the specific URL that caused the compromise.

In late 2005, Aidan Lynch and Daragh Murray from Dublin City University developed a new extension to my original open source honeyclient. Lynch and Murray's extension allowed the user to use Outlook to grab email URLs and send them back to the honeyclient. This allows the honeyclient user to use email as another source of URLs. They also added a feature to allow

---

§ The Microsoft HoneyMonkey Project is discussed at *http://research.microsoft.com/HoneyMonkey*.

‖ A presentation on Pezzonavante can be found at *http://handlers.dshield.org/rdanford/pub/Honeyclients _Danford_SANSfire06.pdf*.

integrity checks for newly spawned processes. Their source code is currently hosted on one of our servers.[#]

Thorsten Holz had been involved with honeyclient technology through the efforts of the German Honeynet Project. The Honeynet Project calls honeyclient technology "client-side honeypots," mainly because they were one of the pioneers of honeypot technology. Since traditional honeypots are server-side, it follows that they would choose the term "client-side" for their other honeypots. However, I have noticed in talking to many people over the years that often honeyclients are confused with honeypots, even though the two technologies address different areas. So, it probably does not help to have the word "honeypot" in the phrase when describing a honeyclient.

Through Thorsten Holz, our honeyclient project team started discussions with Christian Seifert and his Capture client-side honeypot team in 2006. Capture was designed to be a high-interaction honeyclient, like ours. What our honeyclient team really liked about Capture was the real-time integrity check capability. Essentially, it is installed as a benign rootkit on the honeyclient system and begins to monitor for changes in files, registry keys, and processes, right when the honeyclient starts up. There are many benefits to this, but one of the most important is that by integrating Capture's integrity check, we were able to reduce the time we expended checking for system changes, from three or four minutes to less than five seconds.

Since our Honeyclient Project and the Capture Project shared a common GPLv2 license, we were able to utilize each other's code without legal complications, and we were able to develop a wrapper script to call Capture as a module. The Capture code also added the process-checking feature I mentioned earlier.

Since then, there have been other honeyclient implementations,[*] especially in the low-interaction side of things. The implementations mentioned earlier have all been high-interaction honeyclients, where the web browser is actually driven as a process. Low-interaction honeyclients emulate web browsers rather than allow a real one to be infected. Examples of low-interaction honeyclients include SpyBye (*http://spybye.org*), developed by Niels Provos. Google has operational honeyclients that seek out bad websites and create blacklists based on those URLs. This blacklist is part of the Google Safe Browsing API (*http://code.google.com/apis/safebrowsing*), which is currently integrated with the Mozilla Firefox browser. Recently, Jose Nazario released PhoneyC (*http://svn.mwcollect.org/log/phoneyc*), which focuses on the automatic browser script deobfuscation and analysis.

[#] The source code is at *http://www.synacklabs.net/honeyclient/email-honeyclient.zip*.

[*] See the Wikipedia entry on honeyclients: *http://en.wikipedia.org/wiki/Honeyclient*.

The Future of Honeyclients

There are over 240 million websites on the Internet today (and of course the number keeps growing by leaps and bounds), and there's not one group that can cover all of those websites with honeyclient technology. To better fight these attackers that damage our machines and steal our data, we need to band together and learn from each other.

We should envision a future where honeyclients take a SETI@home ("Search for Extraterrestrial Intelligence at home") approach, in which each honeyclient is able to process its own data and send it back to a central database repository that can more effectively correlate the data. This can help us identify targeted domains: for example, if company A's employees are being targeted by company B in order to compromise someone's computer and steal corporate documents.

For now, we're supporting mainly web browsers, but I'm interested in seeing a peer-to-peer (P2P) honeyclient. There's a lot of malware stored in P2P networks, and driving a P2P application could be a very interesting way to find new malware. We may make the decision to actually develop a P2P honeyclient in the future. Currently, our time is taken up just finding new and interesting web-based malware.

The average user should not have to live in fear when all she really wants to do is open her web browser and seek information on the Internet. We have already seen that many users think they are completely safe from being attacked because they installed a signature-based anti-virus scanner. We should help protect those users, many of whom are compromised, not from visiting "shady" websites, but because a supposedly safe site they visit happens to be hosting a malicious advertisement.

The field's understanding of client-side exploits is about five years behind its understanding of server-side exploits. As an industry, we've only recently started to better understand how client-side exploits are developed. Clearly, there's still a lot of work to be done, and I believe honeyclient technology will be an instrumental part of this process. Sharing both code and results is a critical step forward.

CHAPTER NINE

Tomorrow's Security Cogs and Levers

Mark Curphey

Without changing our patterns of thought, we will not be able to solve the problems that we created with our current patterns of thought.

—Albert Einstein

INFORMATION SECURITY IS NOT JUST ABOUT TECHNOLOGY. It is about people, processes, and technology, in that order—or more accurately, about connecting people, processes, and technology together so that humans and entire systems can make informed decisions. It may at first seem rather odd to start a chapter in a book about the future of security management technology with a statement that puts the role of technology firmly in third place, but I felt it was important to put that stake in the ground to provide context for the rest of this chapter.

This doesn't mean that I belittle the role of technology in security. I firmly believe that we are at the very beginnings of an information technology revolution that will affect our lives in ways few of us can imagine, let alone predict. It's easy to dismiss futuristic ideas; many of us still laugh at historical predictions from the 1970s and 1980s portraying a future where self-guided hovercars will whisk us to the office in the mornings and where clunky humanoid robots will mix us cocktails when we get home from work, yet fundamental technological breakthroughs are emerging before our eyes that will spark tomorrow's technological advances.

One such spark, which feeds my conviction that we are on the cusp of an exponential technology curve, is the development of programming languages and artificial intelligence technology that will improve itself at rates humans can't match. Think about that for a moment: programming languages that can themselves create better languages, which in turn can create better languages, and so on. Software that can reprogram itself to be better based on what it learns about itself, designing and solving solutions to problems that we didn't even imagine were solvable (assuming we even knew about them in the first place). Many people debate ethical medical research and cry foul about how human cloning could change the planet, but they may well be focused on the wrong problem.

Information security and its relationship with technology, of course, dates back through history. The Egyptians carved obfuscated hieroglyphs into monuments; the Spartans used sticks and wound messages called *scytales* to exchange military plans; and the Romans' Caesar ciphers are well documented in school textbooks. Many historians attribute the victory in the Second World War directly to the code breakers at Bletchley Park who deciphered the famous Enigma machine, yet even this monumental technological event, which ended the World War and changed history forever, may pale into insignificance next to changes to come.

The packet switching network invented by Donald Davies in 1970 also changed the world forever when the sudden ability of computers to talk to other computers with which they previously had no relationship opened up new possibilities for previously isolated computing power. Although the early telegraph networks almost a century before may have aroused the dream of an electronically connected planet, it was only in the 1970s, 1980s, and 1990s that we started to wire the world together definitively with copper cables and later with fiber-optic technology. Today that evolution is entering a new phase. Instead of wiring physical locations together with twisted copper cables, we are wiring together software applications and data with service-oriented architectures (SOAs) and, equally importantly, wiring people into complex social networks with new types of human relationships.

While I would be foolish to think I could predict the future, I often find myself thinking about future trends in information security and about the potential effect of information security on the future—two very distinct but interrelated things. Simply put, I believe that information security in the future will be very different from the relatively crude ways in which we operate today.

The security tools and technology available to the masses today can only be described as primitive in comparison to electronic gaming, financial investment, or medical research software. Modern massive multiplayer games are built on complex physics engines that mimic real-world movement, leverage sophisticated artificial intelligence engines that provide human-like interactions, and connect hundreds of thousands of players at a time in massively complex virtual worlds. The financial management software underpinning investment banks performs "supercrunching" calculations on data sets pulled from public and private sources and builds sophisticated prediction models from petabytes of data.* Medical research systems

---

* One could, of course, argue that the 2008 credit crunch should have been predicted. The lapse may be the fault of prejudices fed to the programmers, rather than the sophistication of the programs.

analyze DNA for complex patterns of hereditary diseases, predicting entire populations' hereditary probability to inherit genetic traits.

In stark contrast, the information security management programs that are supposed to protect trillions of dollars of assets, keep trade secrets safe from corporate espionage, and hide military plans from the mucky paws of global terrorists are often powered by little more than Rube Goldberg machines (Heath Robinson machines if you are British) fabricated from Excel spreadsheets, Word documents, homegrown scripts, Post-It notes, email systems, notes on the backs of Starbucks cups, and hallway conversations. Is it any wonder we continue to see unprecedented security risk management failures and that most security officers feel they are operating in the dark? If information security is to keep pace (and it will), people, processes, and (the focus of this chapter) information security technology will need to evolve. The Hollywood security that security professionals snigger at today needs to become a reality tomorrow.

I am passionate about playing a part in shaping the security technology of the future, which to me involves defining and creating what I call the "security cogs of tomorrow." This chapter discusses technology trends that I believe will have a significant influence over the security industry and explores how they can be embraced to build information security risk management systems that will help us to do things faster, better, and more cheaply than we can today. We can slice and dice technology a million ways, but advances usually boil down to those three things: faster, better, and cheaper.

I have arranged this chapter into a few core topics:

- "Cloud Computing and Web Services: The Single Machine Is Here" on page 150
- "Connecting People, Process, and Technology: The Potential for Business Process Management" on page 154
- "Social Networking: When People Start Communicating, Big Things Change" on page 158
- "Information Security Economics: Supercrunching and the New Rules of the Grid" on page 162
- "Platforms of the Long-Tail Variety: Why the Future Will Be Different for Us All" on page 165

Before I get into my narrative, let me share a few quick words said by Upton Sinclair and quoted effectively by Al Gore in his awareness campaign for climate change, *An Inconvenient Truth*, and which I put on a slide to start my public speaking events:

> It's difficult to get a man to understand something when his salary depends on him not understanding it.

Challenging listeners to question the reason why they are being presented ideas serves as a timely reminder of common, subtle bias for thoughts and ideas presented as fact. For transparency, at this time of writing I work for Microsoft. My team, the Connected Information

Security Group, has a long-term focus of advancing many of the themes discussed here. This chapter represents just my perspective—maybe my bias—but my team's performance depends on how closely the future measures up to the thoughts in this chapter!

Cloud Computing and Web Services: The Single Machine Is Here

Civilization advances by extending the number of important operations which we can perform without thinking of them.

—Alfred North Whitehead
An Introduction to Mathematics (1911)

Today, much is being made of "cloud computing" in the press. For at least the past five years, the computer industry has also expressed a lot of excitement about web services, which can range from Software as a Service (SaaS) to various web-based APIs and service-oriented architecture (SOA, pronounced "so-ah").

Cloud computing is really nothing more than the abstraction of computing infrastructure (be it storage, processing power, or application hosting) from the hardware system or users. Just as you don't know where your photo is stored physically after you upload it to Flickr, you can run an entire business on a service that is free to run it on any system it chooses. Thus, part or all of the software runs somewhere "in the cloud." The system components and the system users don't need to know and frankly don't care where the actual machines are located or where the data physically resides. They care about the functionality of the system instead of the infrastructure that makes it possible, in the same way that average telephone users don't care which exchanges they are routed through or what type of cable the signal travels over in order to talk to their nanas.

But even though cloud computing is a natural extension of other kinds of online services and hosting services, it's an extremely important development in the history of the global network. Cloud computing democratizes the availability of computing power to software creators from virtually all backgrounds, giving them supercomputers on-demand that can power ideas into reality. Some may say this is a return to the old days when all users could schedule time on the mainframe and that cloud computing is nothing new, but that's hardly the point. The point is that this very day, supercomputers are available to anyone who has access to the Internet.

Web services are standards-based architectures that expose resources (typically discrete pieces of application functionality) independently of the infrastructure that powers them. Web services allow many sites to integrate their applications and data economically by exposing functionality in standards-based formats and public APIs. SOAs are sets of web services woven together to provide sets of functionality and are the catalyst that is allowing us to connect (in the old days we may have said "wire together") powerful computing infrastructure with software functionality, data, and users.

I'm not among the skeptics who minimize the impact of cloud computing or web services. I believe they will serve up a paradigm shift that will fundamentally change the way we all think about and use the Internet as we know it today. In no area will that have effects more profound than in security—and it is producing a contentious split in the security community.

Builders Versus Breakers

Security people fall into two main categories:

- Builders usually represent the glass as half full. While recognizing the seriousness of vulnerabilities and dangers in current practice, they are generally optimistic people who believe that by advancing the state they can change the world for the better.

- Breakers usually represent the glass as half empty, and are often so pessimistic that you wonder, when listening to some of them, why the Internet hasn't totally collapsed already and why any of us have money left unpilfered in our bank accounts. Their pessimism leads them to apply the current state of the art to exposing weaknesses and failures in current approaches.

Every few years the next big thing comes along and polarizes security people into these two philosophical camps. I think I hardly need to state that I consider myself a builder.

Virtual digital clouds of massive computing power, along with virtual pipes to suck it down and spit it back out (web services), trigger suspicions that breakers have built up through decades of experience. Hover around the water coolers of the security "old school," and you will likely see smug grins and knowing winks as they utter pat phrases such as, "You can't secure what you don't control," "You can't patch a data center you don't own," and the ultimate in cynicism, "Why would you trust something as important as security to someone else?"

I've heard it all, and of course it's all hard to argue against. These are many valid arguments against hosting and processing data in the cloud, but by applying standard arguments for older technologies, breakers forget a critical human trait that has been present throughout history: when benefits outweigh drawbacks, things almost always succeed. With the economic advantages of scalable resources on demand, the technological advantages of access to almost unlimited computing resources, and the well-documented trend of service industries, from restaurants to banking, that provide commodity goods, the benefits of cloud computing simply far outweigh the drawbacks.

One reason I deeply understand the breaker mentality springs from a section of my own career. In 2002, I joined a vulnerability management firm named Foundstone (now owned by McAfee) that sold a network vulnerability scanner. It ran as a client in the traditional model, storing all data locally on the customer's system. Our main competitor, a company called Qualys, offered a network scanner as a service on their own systems with data stored centrally at their facilities. We won customers to our product by positioning hosted security data as an outrageous risk. Frankly, we promoted FUD (Fear, Uncertainty, and Doubt). Most customers at the time agreed, and it became a key differentiator that drove revenue and helped us sell the company to McAfee. My time at Foundstone was among the most rewarding I have had, but I also feel, looking back, that our timing was incredibly fortunate. Those inside the dust storm watched the cultural sands shift in a few short years, and we found more and more customers not only accepting an online model but demanding it.

The same is true of general consumers, of course. Over five million WordPress blog users have already voted with their virtual feet, hosting their blogs online. And an estimated 10% of the world's end-user Internet traffic comes from hosted, web-based email, such as Yahoo! Mail, Gmail, and Live Mail. Google is renowned for building megalithic data centers across the world; Microsoft is investing heavily in a cloud operating system called Azure, along with gigantic data center infrastructures to host software and services; and Amazon has started renting out parts of the infrastructure that they built as part of their own bid to dominate the online retailing space.

Clouds and Web Services to the Rescue

The question security professionals should be asking is not "Can cloud computing and web services be made secure?" but "How can we apply security to this new approach?" Even more cleverly, we should think: "How can we embrace this paradigm to our advantage?"

The good news is that applying security to web services and cloud computing is not as hard as people may think. What at first seems like a daunting task just requires a change of paradigm. The assumption that the company providing you with a service also has to guarantee your security is just not valid.

To show you how readily you can see the new services as a boon to security instead of a threat, let me focus on a real-world scenario. Over Christmas I installed a nice new Windows Home Server in our house. Suddenly, we are immersed in the digital world: our thousands of photos and videos of the kids can be watched on the TV in the living room via the Xbox, the six computers scattered around the house all get backed up to a central server, and the family at home once again feels connected. Backing up to a central server is all well and good, but what happens if we get robbed and someone steals the PCs and the server?

Enter the new world of web services and cloud computing. To mitigate the risk of catastrophic system loss, I wrote a simple plug-in (see the later section "Platforms of the Long-Tail Variety: Why the Future Will Be Different for Us All" on page 165) to the home server that makes use of the Amazon Web Services platform. At set intervals, the system copies the directories I chose onto the server and connects via web services to Amazon's S3 (Simple Storage System) cloud infrastructure. The server sends a backup copy of the data I choose to the cloud. I make use of the WS-Security specification (and a few others) for web services, ensuring the data is encrypted and not tampered with in transport, and I make use of an X.509 digital certificate to ensure I am communicating with Amazon. To further protect the data, I encrypt it locally before it is sent to Amazon, ensuring that if Amazon is hacked, my data will not be exposed or altered. The whole solution took 30 minutes to knock up, thanks to some reusable open source code on the Internet.

So, storing your personal data on someone else's server seems scary at first, but when you think it through and apply well-known practices to new patterns, you realize that the change is not as radical as you first thought. The water cooler conversations about not being able to control security on physical servers located outside your control may be correct, but the solution is to apply security at a different point in the system.

It is also worth pointing out that the notion of using services from other computers is hardly new. We all use DNS services from someone else's servers every day. When we get over the initial shock of disruptive technologies (and leave the breaker's pessimism behind), we can move on to the important discussions about cloud computing and web services, and embrace what we can now do with these technologies.

A New Dawn

In a later section of this chapter, I discuss *supercrunching*, a term used to describe massive analysis of large sets of data to derive meaning. I think supercrunching has a significant part to play in tomorrow's systems. Today we are bound by the accepted limitations of local storage and local processing, often more than we think; if we can learn to attack our problems on the fantastically larger scale allowed by Internet-connected services, we can achieve new successes.

This principle can reap benefits in security monitoring, taking us beyond the question of how to preserve the security we had outside the cloud and turning the cloud into a source of innovation for security.

Event logs can provide an incredible amount of forensic information, allowing us to reconstruct an event. The question may be as simple as which user reset a specific account password or as complex as which system process read a user's token. Today there are, of course, log analysis tools and even a whole category of security tools called Security Event Managers (SEMs), but these don't even begin to approach the capabilities of supercrunching. Current tools run on standard servers with pretty much standard hardware performing relatively crude analysis.

A few short years ago I remember being proud of a system I helped build while working for a big financial services company in San Francisco; the system had a terabyte of data storage and some beefy Sun hardware. We thought we were cutting-edge, and at the time we were! But the power and storage that is now available to us all if we embrace the new connected computing model will let us store vast amounts of security monitoring data for analysis and use the vast amounts of processing power to perform complex analysis.

We will then be able to look for patterns and derive meaning from large data sets to *predict* security events rather than *react* to them. You read that correctly: we will be able to predict from a certain event the probability of a tertiary event taking place. This will allow us to provide context-sensitive security or make informed decisions about measures to head off trouble.

In a later section of this chapter ("Social Networking: When People Start Communicating, Big Things Change" on page 158), I discuss social networking. Social networking will have a profound impact on security when people start to cooperate efficiently. Sharing the logfiles I mentioned earlier with peers will enable larger data sets to be analyzed and more accurate predictions to be made.

It's also worth noting that a cloud service is independent from any of the participating parties, and therefore can be a neutral and disinterested facilitator. For a long time, companies have been able to partition their network to allow limited access to trusted third parties, or provide a proxy facility accessible to both parties. This practice was not lost on the plethora of folks trying to compete for the lucrative and crucial identity management area. Identity management services such as OpenID and Windows Live ID operate in the cloud, allowing them to bind users together across domains.

Connecting People, Process, and Technology: The Potential for Business Process Management

> **Virtually every company will be going out and empowering their workers with a certain set of tools, and the big difference in how much value is received from that will be how much the company steps back and really thinks through their business processes, thinking through how their business can change, how their project management, their customer feedback, their planning cycles can be quite different than they ever were before.**
>
> —*Bill Gates*

New York Times columnist Thomas Friedman wrote an excellent book in 2005 called *The World Is Flat* (Farrar, Straus and Giroux) in which he explored the outsourcing revolution, from call centers in India and tax form processing in China to radiography analysis in Australia. I live Friedman's flat world today; in fact, I am sitting on a plane to Hyderabad to visit part of my development team as I write this text. My current team is based in the United States (Redmond), Europe (London and Munich), India (Hyderabad), and China (Beijing). There's a lot of media attention today on the rise of skilled labor in China and India providing goods and services to the Western world, but when you look back at history, the phenomenon is really nothing new. Friedman's book reveals that there has been a shift in world economic power about every 500 years throughout history, and that shift has always been catalyzed by an increase in trading.

And furthermore, what has stimulated that increase in trading? It's simple: connectivity and communication. From the Silk Road across China to the dark fiber heading out of Silicon Valley, the fundamental principle of connecting supply and demand and exchanging goods and services continues to flourish. What's interesting (Friedman goes on to say) is that in today's world workflow software has been a key "flattener," meaning that the ability to route electronic data across the Internet has enabled and accelerated these particular global market shifts (in this case, in services). Workflow software—or more accurately, Business Process Management (BPM) software, a combination of workflow design, orchestration, business rules engines, and business activity monitoring tools—will dramatically change both the ways we need to view the security of modern business software and how we approach information security management itself.

Diffuse Security in a Diffuse World

In a flat world, workforces are decentralized. Instead of being physically connected in offices or factories as in the industrial revolution, teams are combined onto projects, and in many cases individuals combined into teams, over the Internet.

Many security principles are based on the notion of a physical office or a physical or logical network. Some technologies (such as popular file-sharing protocols such as Common Internet File System [CIFS] and LAN-based synchronization protocols such as Address Resolution Protocol [ARP]) take this local environment for granted. But those foundations become irrelevant as tasks, messages, and data travel a mesh of loosely coupled nodes.

The effect is similar to the effects of global commerce, which takes away the advantage of renting storefront property on your town's busy Main Street or opening a bank office near a busy seaport or railway station. Tasks are routed by sophisticated business rules engines that determine whether a call center message should be routed to India or China, or whether the cheapest supplier for a particular good has the inventory in stock.

BPM software changes the very composition of supply chains, providing the ability to dynamically reconfigure a supply chain based on dynamic business conditions. Business transactions take place across many companies under conditions ranging from microseconds to many years. Business processes are commonly dehydrated and rehydrated as technologies evolve to automatically discover new services. The complexity and impact of this way of working will only increase.

For information security, of course, this brings significant new challenges. Over thousands of years, humans have associated security with physical location. They have climbed hills, built castles with big walls, and surrounded themselves with moats. They have worked in office buildings where there are physical controls on doors and filing cabinets, put their money in bank vaults (that seems so quaint nowadays), and locked their dossiers (including the ones on computers) in their offices or data centers. Internet security carried over this notion with firewalls and packet filters inspecting traffic as it crossed a common gateway.

Today, groups such as the Jericho Forum are championing of the idea of "deperimeterization" as companies struggle to deal with evolving business models. A company today is rarely made up of full-time employees that sit in the same physical location and are bound by the same rules. Companies today are collaborations of employees, business partners, outsourcing companies, temporary contractors (sometimes called "perma-vendors"), and any number of other unique arrangements you can think of. They're in Beijing, Bangalore, Manhattan, and the Philippines. They are bound by different laws, cultures, politics, and, of course, real and perceived security exigencies. The corporate firewall no longer necessarily protects the PC that's logged into the corporate network and also, incidentally, playing *World of Warcraft* 24/7. Indeed, the notion of a corporate network itself is being eroded by applications that are forging their own application networks connected via web services and messaging systems through service-oriented architectures.

When a company's intellectual property and business data flow across such diverse boundaries and through systems that are beyond their own security control, it opens up a whole new world of problems and complexity. We can no longer have any degree of confidence that the security controls we afford our own security program are effective for the agent in a remote Indian village. Paper contracts requiring vendors to install the latest anti-malware software is of little comfort after the botnet was activated from Bulgaria, bringing the key logger alive and altering the integrity of the system's processing. Never has the phrase "security is as only good as the weakest link" been more apt, and systems architects are being forced to operate on the premise that the weakest link can be very weak indeed.

BPM As a Guide to Multisite Security

Despite these obvious concerns, I believe the same technologies and business techniques encompassed by the term BPM will play a critical role in managing information security in the future.

For example, if we examine today's common information security process of vulnerability management, we can easily imagine a world where a scalable system defines the business process and parcels various parts of it off to the person or company that can do it faster, better, or more cheaply. If we break a typical vulnerability management process down, we can imagine it as a sequence of steps (viewed simplistically here for illustrative purposes, of course), such as the analysis of vulnerability research, the analysis of a company's own data and systems to determine risk, and eventual management actions, such as remediation.

Already today, many companies outsource the vulnerability research to the likes of iDefense (now a VeriSign company) or Secunia, who provide a data feed via XML that can be used by corporate analysts. When security BPM software (and a global network to support it) emerges, companies will be able to outsource this step not just to a single company, in the hope that it has the necessary skills to provide the appropriate analysis, but to a global network of analysts. The BPM software will be able to route a task to an analyst who has a track record in a specific obscure technology (the best guy in the world at hacking system X or understanding language Y) or a company that can return an analysis within a specific time period. The analysts may be in a shack on a beach in the Maldives or in an office in London; it's largely irrelevant, unless working hours and time zones are decision criteria.

Business rules engines may analyze asset management systems and decide to take an analysis query that comes in from San Francisco and route it to China so it can be processed overnight and produce an answer for the corporate analysts first thing in the morning.

This same fundamental change to the business process of security research will likely be extended to the intelligence feeds powering security technology, such as anti-virus engines, intrusion detection systems, and code review scanners. BPM software will be able to facilitate new business models, microchunking business processes to deliver the end solution faster, better, or more cheaply. This is potentially a major paradigm shift in many of the security technologies we have come to accept, decoupling the content from the delivery mechanism. In the future, thanks to BPM software security, analysts will be able to select the best anti-virus engine and the best analysis feed to fuel it—but they will probably not come from the same vendor.

When Nicholas Carr wrote *Does IT Matter?*,[†] he argued that technology needs to be realigned to support business instead of driving it. BPM is not rocket science (although it may include rocket science in its future), but it's doing just that: realigning technology to support the business. In addition to offering radical improvements to information security by opening new markets, BPM can deliver even more powerful changes through its effects on the evolution of the science behind security. The Business Process Management Initiative (BPMI) (*http://www .bpmi.org*) has defined five tenets of effective BPM programs. These tenets are unrelated to information security, but read as a powerful catalyst. I'll list each tenet along with what I see as its most important potential effects on security:

1. Understand and Document the Process

    Security effect: Implement a structured and effective information security program

2. Understand Metrics and Objectives

    Security effect: Understand success criteria and track their effectiveness

3. Model and Automate Process

    Security effect: Improve efficiency and reduce cost

4. Understand Operations and Implement Controls

    Security effect: Improve efficiency and reduce cost

    Security effect: Fast and accurate compliance and audit data (visibility)

5. Optimize and Improve

[†] *Does IT Matter?*, Nicholas Carr, Harvard Business School Press, 2004.

Security effect: Do more with less

Security effect: Reduce cost

Put another way: if you understand and document your process, metrics, and objectives; model and automate your process; understand and implement your process; and optimize and improve the process, you will implement a structured and effective information security program, understand the success criteria and track effectiveness, improve efficiency and reduce cost, produce fast and accurate compliance, audit data, and ultimately do more with less and reduce the cost of security. This is significant!

While the topic of BPM for information security could of course fill a whole book—when you consider business process modeling, orchestration, business rules design, and business activity modeling—it would be remiss to leave the subject without touching upon the potential BPM technologies have for simulation. When you understand a process, including its activities, process flows, and business rules, you have a powerful blueprint describing how something should work. When you capture business activity data from real-world orchestrations of this process, you have powerful data about how it actually works.

Simulation offers us the ability to alter constraints and simulate results before we spend huge resources and time. Take for example a security incident response process in which simulation software predicts the results of a certain number or type of incidents. We could predict failure or success based on facts about processes, and then change the constraints of the actual business to obtain better results. Simulation can take place in real time, helping avoid situations that a human would be unlikely to be able to predict. I believe that business process simulation will emerge as a powerful technique to allow companies to do things better, faster, and more cheaply. Now think about the possibilities of BPM when connected to social networks, and read on!

Social Networking: When People Start Communicating, Big Things Change

Human beings who are almost unique (among animals) in having the ability to learn from the experience of others, yet are also remarkable in their apparent disinclination to do so.

—Douglas Adams

One night at sea, Horatio Hornblower, the fictional character from C. S. Forester's series of novels, is woken up by his first officer, who is alarmed to see a ship's light in his sea lane about 20 miles away, refusing to move. Horatio quickly joins the deck and commands the ship via radio communications to move starboard 20 degrees at once. The operator refuses and indignantly tells 1st Baron Horatio that it is he who should be moving his ship starboard 20 degrees at once. Incensed and enraged, Horatio Hornblower pulls rank and size on the other ship, stating that he's a captain and that he's on a large battleship. Quietly and calmly, the operator replies, informing Captain Hornblower that his is in fact the biggest vessel, being a lighthouse on a cliff above treacherous rocks.

Each time I tell this story, it reminds me just how badly humans communicate. We are all guilty, yet communication is crucial to everything we do. When people communicate, they find common interests and form relationships.

Social networking is considered to be at the heart of Web 2.0 (a nebulous term that describes the next generation of Internet applications), yet it is really nothing new. Throughout history people have lived in tribes, clans, and communities that share a bond of race, religion, and social or economic values, and at every point, when social groups have been able to connect more easily, big things have happened. Trading increases, ideas spread, and new social, political, and economic models form.

I started a social network accidentally in 2001 called the Open Web Application Security Project (OWASP) (*http://www.owasp.org*). We initially used an email distribution list and a static website to communicate and collaborate. In the early days, the project grew at a steady rate. But it was only late in 2003, when a wiki was introduced and everyone could easily collaborate, that things really took off. Today the work of OWASP is recommended by the Federal Trade Commission, the National Institute for Standards, and the hotly debated Payment Card Industry Data Security Standard, or PCI-DSS. I learned many valuable life lessons starting OWASP, but none bigger than the importance of the type of social networking technology you use.‡

The State of the Art and the Potential in Social Networking

Today Facebook and MySpace are often held up as the leading edge of social networking software that brings together people who share a personal bond. People across the world can supposedly keep in touch better than they could before it was created. The sites are certainly prospering, with megalevels of subscribers (250 million+ users each) and their media darling status. But in my observations, the vast majority of their users spend their time digitally "poking" their friends or sending them fish for their digital aquariums. To the older kids like me, this is a bit like rock 'n' roll to our parents' parents—we just don't get it—but I am ready to accept I am just getting old.

Equally intriguing are social networks forming in virtual worlds such as Second Life. With their own virtual economy, including inflation-capped monetary systems, the ability to exchange real-world money for virtual money, and a thriving virtual real estate market, Second Life has attracted a lot of interest from big companies like IBM. Recently, researchers were able to teleport an avatar from one virtual world to another, and initiatives such as the OpenSocial

---

‡ I can't take credit for starting the wiki (Jeff Williams can); on the contrary, I actually opposed it because I thought it was unstructured and would lead to a deterioration in content quality. I learned a good lesson.

API indicate that interoperability of social networks is evolving. Networks of networks are soon to emerge!

Social networking platforms like these really offer little for corporations today, let alone for security professionals, but this will change. And when it changes, the implications for information security could be significant.

If social networking today is about people-to-people networking, social networking tomorrow may well be about business-to-business. For several years, investment banks in New York, government departments in the U.S., and other industry groups have shared statistical data about security among themselves in small private social networks. The intelligence community and various police forces make sensitive data available to those who "need to know," and ad hoc networks have formed all over the world to serve more specific purposes. But in the grand scheme of things, business-to-business social networking is very limited. Information security is rarely a competitive advantage (in fact, studies of stock price trends after companies have suffered serious data breaches indicate a surprisingly low correlation, so one could argue that it's not a disadvantage at all), and most businesses recognize that the advantages in collaborating far outweigh the perceived or real disadvantages.

This still begs the question, "Why isn't social networking more prevalent?" I would argue that it's largely because the right software is lacking. We know that humans don't communicate well online without help, and we can cite cases such as the catalytic point when OWASP moved to a wiki and theorize that when the right type of social networking technology is developed and introduced, behavior similar to what we have seen throughout history will happen.

Social Networking for the Security Industry

What this may look like for the security industry is hard to predict, but if we extrapolate today's successful social networking phenomenon to the security industry, some useful scenarios emerge.

Start with the principle of reliability behind eBay, for instance, a highly successful auction site connecting individual sellers to individual buyers across the globe. Its success is based partially on a reputation economy, where community feedback about sellers largely dictates the level of trust a buyer has in connecting.

Now imagine a business-to-business eBay-type site that deals in information security. It could list "security services wanted" ads, allowing companies to offer up service contracts and the criteria for a match, and allow service providers to bid for work based on public ratings and credentials earned from performing similar work for similar clients.

eBay-type systems not only act as conduits to connect buyers and sellers directly, but potentially can provide a central data of market information on which others can trade. Take, for example, security software. How much should you pay for a license for the next big security source code scanning technology to check your 12 million lines of code? In the future, you may be able to consult the global database and discover that other companies like you paid an average of *X*.

In order for these types of social networks to succeed, they will likely have to operate on a "pay to play" model. It will be a challenge to seed them with enough data to make them enticing enough to play at the beginning, but I have no doubt the networks will emerge. Virus writers in Eastern Europe and China have long traded techniques via old-school bulletin boards, and we are starting to see the first stages of exploit exchanges and even an exploit auction site. Why shouldn't the white hats take advantage of the same powerful networks?

Actually, large social networks of security geeks already exist. They typically use email distribution lists, a surprisingly old-school, yet effective, means of communication.

Before the 2008 Black Hat Conference, a U.S.-based "researcher" named Dan Kaminsky announced he was going to discuss details of a serious vulnerability in DNS. Within days, mailing lists such as "Daily Dave" were collaborating to speculate about what the exploit was and even share code. Imagine the effectiveness of a more professional social network where security engineers could share empirical data and results from tests and experiments.

Security in Numbers

Social networking isn't just about connecting people into groups to trade. It's a medium for crowdsourcing, which exploits the wisdom of crowds to predict information. This could also play an interesting role in the future security market.

To give you a simple example of crowdsourcing, one Friday at work someone on my team sent out a simple spreadsheet containing a quiz. It was late morning on the East Coast, and therefore late on Friday afternoon in Europe and late evening in our Hyderabad office. Most people on the team were in Redmond and so were sitting in traffic; most Brits were getting ready to drink beer and eat curry on Friday evening; and most Indians were out celebrating life. Here are the stats of what happened in the next 50 minutes:

- Request started at 11:07 AM EST
- Crowd size of 70+ across multiple time zones
- Active listening crowd of probably less than 30 due to time zone differences
- Participation from 8
- Total puzzles = 30
- Initial unsolved puzzles = 21
- Total responses = 35
- Total time taken to complete all puzzles = 50 minutes

The brain is still the most powerful computer created (as of today), and when we build distributed networks of such powerful computers, we can expect great results. Networks can support evolving peer groups who wish to share noncompetitive information in a sheltered network. For social networking to be truly useful to the security industry, it will likely need to develop a few killer applications. My money is on the mass collection, sharing, and analysis of information and benchmarking. Participants can run benchmarks of service quality in relation to software cost, corporate vulnerabilities, and threat profiles. The potential scope is enormous, as shown through the MeMe map in Figure 9-1, taken from a security industry source.

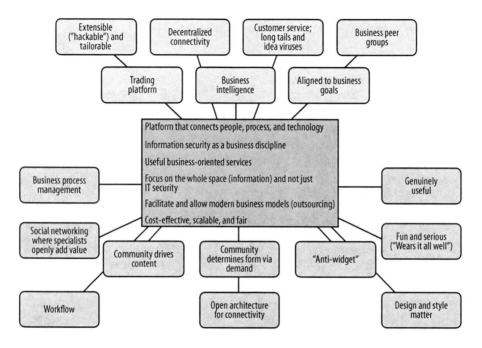

FIGURE 9-1. Possibilities of social networking for security professionals

Information Security Economics: Supercrunching and the New Rules of the Grid

> Curphey turned to his friend Jeff Cave in an investment bank server room in London in the late '90s and said, "What's the time?" Cave replied, "Quite simply the measurement of distance in space, dear chap."

Scene 1: Imagine you are picnicking by a river and you notice someone in distress in the water. You jump in and pull the person out. The mayor is nearby and pins a medal on you. You return to your picnic. A few minutes later, you spy a second person in the water. You perform a second rescue and receive a second medal. A few minutes later, a third person, a third rescue, and a third medal, and so on through the day. By sunset, you are weighed down with medals and honors. You are a local hero! Of course, somewhere in the back of your mind there is a sneaking suspicion that you should have walked upriver to find out why people were falling in all day—but then again, that wouldn't have earned you as many awards.

Scene 2: Imagine you are a software tester. You find a bug. Your manager is nearby and pins a "bug-finder" award on you. A few minutes later, you find a second bug, and so on. By the end of the day, you are weighed down with "bug-finder" awards and all your colleagues are congratulating you. You are a hero! Of course, the thought enters your mind that maybe you should help prevent those bugs from getting into the system—but you squash it. After all, bug prevention doesn't win nearly as many awards as bug hunting.

Simply put: *what you measure is what you get*. B. F. Skinner told us 50 years ago that rats and people tend to perform those actions for which they are rewarded. It's still true today. As soon as developers find out that a metric is being used to evaluate them, they strive mightily to improve their performance relative to that metric—even if their actions don't actually help the project. If your testers find out that you value finding bugs, you will end up with a team of bug-finders. If prevention is not valued, prevention will not be practiced. The same is of course true of many other security disciplines, such as tracking incidents, vulnerabilities, and intrusions.

Metrics and measurement for information security has become a trendy topic in recent years, although hardly a new one. Peter Drucker's famous dictum, "If you can't measure it, you can't manage it," just sounds like common sense and has been touted by good security managers as long as I can remember.

Determining the Return on Investment (ROI) for security practices has become something of a Holy Grail, sought by security experts in an attempt to appeal to the managers of firms (all of whom have read Drucker or absorbed similar ideas through exposure to their peers). The problem with ROI is that security is in one respect like gold mining. You find an enormous variance in the success rates of different miners (one could finish a season as a millionaire while another is still living in a shack 20 years later), but their successes cannot be attributed to their tools. Metrics about shovels and shifters will only confuse you. In short, ROI measures have trouble computing return on these kinds of high-risk investments. In my opinion, security ROI today is touted by shovel salesmen.

I have high hopes for metrics, but I think the current mania fails to appreciate the subtleties we need to understand. I prefer the term Economics to Metrics or Measurement, and I think that Information Security Economics will emerge as a discipline that could have a profound impact on how we manage risk.

Information Security Economics is about understanding the factors and relationships that affect security at a micro and macro level, a topic that has tremendous depth and could have a tremendous impact. If we compare the best efforts happening in the security industry today against the complex supercrunching in financial or insurance markets, we may be somewhat disillusioned, yet the same advanced techniques and technology can probably be applied to the new security discipline with equally effective results.

I recently read a wonderful story in the book *Super Crunchers: Why Thinking-by-Numbers Is the New Way to Be Smart* by Ian Ayres (Bantam Press) about a wine economist called Orley Ashenfelter. Ashenfelter is a statistician at Princeton who loves wine but is perplexed by the pomp and circumstance around valuing and rating wine in much the same way I am perplexed by the pomp and circumstance surrounding risk management today. In the 1980s, wine critics dominated the market with predictions based on their own reputations, palate, and frankly very little more. Ashenfelter, in contrast, studied the Bordeaux region of France and developed a statistic model about the quality of wine.

His model was based on the average rainfall in the winter before the growing season (the rain that makes the grapes plump) and the average sunshine during the growing season (the rays that make the grapes ripe), resulting in simple formula:

```
quality = 12.145 + (0.00117 * winter rainfall)
        + (0.0614 * average growing season temperature)
          (0.00386 * harvest rainfall)
```

Of course he was chastised and lampooned by the stuffy wine critics who dominated the industry, but after several years of producing valuable results, his methods are now widely accepted as providing important valuation criteria for wine. In fact, as it turned out, the same techniques were used by the French in the late 19th century during a wine census.

It's clear that from understanding the factors that affect an outcome, we can build economic models. And the same principles—applying sound economic models based on science—can be applied to many information security areas.

For the field of security, the most salient aspect of Orley Ashenfelter's work is the timing of his information. Most wine has to age for at least 18 months before you can taste it to ascertain its quality. This is of course a problem for both vineyards and investors. But with Ashenfelter's formula, you can predict the wine's quality on the day the grapes are harvested. This approach could be applied in security to answer simple questions such as, "If I train the software developers by X amount, how will that affect the security of the resulting system?" or "If we deploy this system in the country Hackistanovia with the following factors, what will be the resulting system characteristics?"

Of course, we can use this sort of security economics only if we have a suitably large set of prior data to crunch in the first place, as Ashenfelter did. The current phase, where the field is adopting metrics and measurement may be generating the data, and the upcoming supercrunching phase will be able to analyze it, but social networking will probably be the catalyst to prompt practitioners to share resources and create vast data warehouses from which we can analyze information and build models. Security economics may well provide a platform on which companies can demonstrate the cost-benefit ratios of various kinds of security and derive a competitive advantage implementing them.

Platforms of the Long-Tail Variety: Why the Future Will Be Different for Us All

> A "platform" is a system that can be programmed and therefore
> customized by outside developers—users—and in that way,
> adapted to countless needs and niches that the platform's
> original developers could not have possibly contemplated,
> much less had time to accommodate.
>
> —*Marc Andreessen, founder of Netscape*

In October 2004, Chris Anderson, the editor in chief of the popular *Wired Magazine*, wrote an article about technology economics.§ The article spawned a book called *The Long Tail* (Hyperion) that attempts to explain economic phenomena in the digital age and provide insight into opportunities for future product and service strategies.

The theory suggests that the distribution curve for products and services is altering to a skewed shape that concentrates a large portion of the demand in a "long tail": many different products or service offerings that each enjoy a small consumer base. In many industries, there is a greater total demand for products and services the industries consider to be "niches" than for the products and services considered to be mainstays. Companies that exploit niche products and services previously thought to be uneconomical include iTunes, WordPress, YouTube, Facebook, and many other Internet economy trends.

I fundamentally believe that information security is a long-tail market, and I offer three criteria to support this statement:

- Every business has multiple processes.
- Processes that are similar in name between businesses are actually highly customized (i.e., no two businesses are the same).
- Many processes are unique to small clusters of users.

To understand the possible implications of the long-tail theory for the information security industry, we can look to other long-tail markets and three key forces that drive change.

Democratization of Tools for Production

A long time ago, I stopped reading articles in the popular technology press (especially the security press). I sense that these journals generally write articles with the goal of selling more advertising, while bloggers generally write articles so people will read them. That is a subtle but important difference. If I read an article in the press, chances are that it includes commentary from a so-called "industry insider." Usually, these are people who tell the reporter

---

§ See *http://www.wired.com/wired/archive/12.10/tail.html*.

what they want to hear to get their names in print, and they're rarely the people I trust and want to hear from. I read blogs because I listen to individuals with honest opinions. This trend is, of course, prevalent throughout the new economy and will become more and more important to information security. A practitioner at the heart of the industry is better at reporting (more knowledgeable and more in tune) than an observer.

Much as blogging tools have democratized publishing and GarageBand has democratized music production, tools will democratize information security. In fact, blogging has already had a significant effect, allowing thousands of security professionals to offer opinions and data.

The most far-reaching change will be the evolution of tools into *platforms*. In software terms, a platform is a system that can be reprogrammed and therefore customized by outside developers and users for countless needs and niches that the platform's original developers could not have possibly contemplated, much less had time to accommodate. (This is the point behind the Andreessen quote that started this section.) When Google offered an API to access its search and mapping capabilities, it drove the service to a new level of use; the same occurred when Facebook offered a plug-in facility for applications.

As I'll describe in the following section, a security platform will allow people to build the tools they want to solve the problems they are facing.

When we talk about platforms, we of course need to be careful. Any term that has the potential to sell more technology is hijacked by the media and its essence often becomes diluted. Quite a few tools are already advertised as security platforms, but few really are.

Democratization of Channels for Distribution

There's no shortage of security information. Mailing lists, BBSs (yes, I am old), blogs, and community sites abound, along with professionally authored content. There's also no shortage of technology, both open source and commercial. But in today's economy, making information relevant is paramount, and is one of the key reasons for the success of Google, iTunes, and Amazon.com. Their rise has been attributed largely to their ability to aggregate massive amounts of data and filter it to make it relevant to the user. Filtering and ordering become especially critical in a world that blurs the distinction between what was traditionally called "professionally authored" and "amateur created." This, in essence, is a better information distribution model.

Another characteristic that has democratized distribution in other long-tail markets is *microchunking*, a marketing strategy for delivering to each user exactly the product she wants—and no more. Microchunking also facilitates the use of new channels to reach customers.

The Long Tail uses the example of music, which for a couple decades was delivered in CD form only. These days, delivery options also include online downloads, cell phone ringtones, and materials for remix.

The security field, like much of the rest of the software industry, already offers one type of flexibility: you can install monitoring tools on your own systems or outsource them. In tomorrow's world, security users will also want to remix offerings. They may want the best scanning engine from vendor A combined with the best set of signatures from Vendor B. In Boolean terminology, customers are looking for "And," not "Or."

The underlying consideration for security tools is that one size doesn't fit all. Almost all corporate security people I talk to repeat this theme, sharing their own version for the 80/20 rule: 80% of the tool's behavior meets your requirements, and you live with the 20% that doesn't—but that 20% causes you 80% of your pain!

Let's take threat-modeling tools for software. The key to mass appeal in the future will be to support all types of threat-modeling methodologies, including the users' own twists and tweaks. Overlaying geodata on your own data concerning vulnerabilities and processing the mix with someone else's visualization tools might help you see hotspots in a complex virtual world and distinguish the wood from the trees. These types of overlays may help us make better risk decisions based on business performance data. In an industry with a notoriously high noise-to-signal ratio, we will likely see tools emerge that produce higher signal quality faster, cheaper, and more efficiently than ever before.

Connection of Supply and Demand

Perhaps the biggest changes will take place in how the next generation connects people, process, and technology. Search, ontology (information architecture), and communities will all play important roles.

The advice from *The Long Tail* is this: people will tell you what they like and don't like, so don't try to predict—just measure and respond. Recommendations, reviews, and rankings are key components of what is called the *reputation economy*. These filters help people find things and present them in a contextually useful way.

Few information security tools today attempt to provide contextually useful information. What we will likely see are tools that merge their particular contributions with reputation mechanisms. A code review tool that finds a potential vulnerability may match it to crowdsourced advice, which is itself ranked by the crowd and then provides contextual information like "50% of people who found this vulnerability also had vulnerability X." Ratings and ranking will help connect the mass supply of information with the demand.

To summarize the three trends in the democratization of security tools, I believe that real platforms will emerge in the security field that connect people, processes, and technology. They will be driven by the democratization of tools for production, the democratization of tools for distribution, and the connection of supply and demand. No two businesses are the same, and a true security platform will adapt to solving problems the original designers could have never anticipated.

Conclusion

I was fortunate enough to have been educated by the Information Security Group (*http://isg
.rhul.ac.uk*) of Royal Holloway, University of London. They are the best in the business, period.
Readers of *The Da Vinci Code* will recognize the name as the school where Sophie Neveu, the
French cryptographer in the book, was educated.

Several years before I worked for Microsoft, Professor Fred Piper at the Information Security
Group approached me for an opinion on the day that he was to speak at the British Computer
Society. He posed to me a straightforward question: "Would Microsoft have been so successful
if security was prominent in Windows from day one?" At this point, I should refer you back
to my Upton Sinclair quote earlier in this chapter; but it does leave an interesting thought about
the role security will have in the overall landscape of information technology evolution.

I was once accused of trivializing the importance of security when I put up a slide at a
conference with the text "Security is less important than performance, which is less important
than functionality," followed by a slide with the text "Operational security is a business support
function; get over your ego and accept it." As a security expert, of course, I would never
diminish the importance of security; rather, I create better systems by understanding the
pressures that other user requirements place on experts and how we have to fit our solutions
into place.

I started the chapter by saying that anyone would be foolish to predict the future, but I hope
you will agree with me that the next several years in security are an interesting time to think
about, and an even more interesting time to influence and shape. I hope that when I look back
on this text and my blog in years to come, I'll cringe at their resemblance to the cocktail-mixing
house robots from movies of the 1970s. I believe the right elements are really coming together
where technology can create better technology.

Advances in technology have been used to both arm and disarm the planet, to empower and
oppress populations, and to attack and defend the global community and all it will have
become. The areas I've pulled together in this chapter—from business process management,
number crunching and statistical modeling, visualization, and long-tail technology—provide
fertile ground for security management systems in the future that archive today's best efforts
in the annals of history. At least I hope so, for I hate mediocrity with a passion and I think
security management systems today are mediocre at best!

Acknowledgments

This chapter is dedicated to my mother, Margaret Curphey, who passed away after an epileptic fit in 2004 at her house in the south of France. When I was growing up (a lot of time frankly off the rails), she always encouraged me to think big and helped me understand that there is nothing in life you can't achieve if you put your mind to it. She made many personal sacrifices that led me to eventually find my calling (albeit later in life that she would have hoped) in the field of information security. She always used to say that it's all good and well thinking big, but you have to do something about it as well. I am on the case, dear. I also, of course, owe a debt of gratitude for the continued support and patience of my wife, Cara, and the young hackers, Jack, Hana, and Gabe.

CHAPTER TEN

Security by Design

John McManus

> **"Beauty is truth, truth beauty,"—that is all**
> **Ye know on earth, and all ye need to know.**
>
> *—John Keats, "Ode on a Grecian Urn"*

BEAUTY IS NOT SKIN DEEP. TRUE BEAUTY IS A REFLECTION OF ALL ASPECTS OF A PERSON, object, or system. In security, beauty appears in simplicity and graceful design, a product of treating security as a critical goal early in the system design lifecycle. In properly designed systems, security is an integral attribute of the system, designed, built, and tested; it is lightweight and adaptive, allowing the overall system to remain agile in the face of evolving requirements. When security is treated as an afterthought, or developed independently from the overall system design requirements, it is most often ugly and inflexible.

Several experiences during my career have had a profound impact on my views on information security and my overall system development philosophy. The first was at NASA's Langley Research Center. The second was a four-year period where I worked on software quality, reliability, usability, and security, first at Reliable Software Technologies (now known as Cigital) and then as the vice president of the Software Technology Center at Bell Labs. The lessons I learned and the fantastic teams I had the opportunity to work with demonstrated to me that security and all of the other important "ilities" (e.g., quality, reliability, availability, maintainability, and usability) are highly interrelated, and are achievable in a cost-effective way. The early experience at NASA helped me understand what would not work and why it wouldn't. The experiences at Cigital, Bell Labs, and a second stint at NASA helped me develop and refine a strategy for delivering high-quality, secure systems on schedule and on budget.

Both NASA and Lucent had the mistaken perception that the systems they were developing and deploying were "closed," or on a highly controlled, dedicated network infrastructure. The reality was significantly different. The rapid growth of computer networking and the global Internet fundamentally changed the way systems were accessed and interconnected. Many of the networks the system administrators thought were "closed" were actually interconnected with research and academic networks that had significantly different security postures and access control mechanisms. The network interconnects provided new access points for attackers to exploit and increased the overall attack surface of the systems.

This misconception created a large blind spot in the overall security posture and fed the view that perimeter security was sufficient to protect the systems. Unfortunately, if you don't have a clearly known, clearly defined perimeter, you can't have an effective perimeter-based security posture. Since the perception of having a known, well-monitored perimeter was inaccurate, the systems were exposed to security risks they were not designed to protect against. The perimeter defense model was often referred to as the "M&M" model, or the "hard outer shell, soft center" model. Once the perimeter defenses were bypassed or overcome, the internal infrastructure elements and software of the systems were not properly secured and could not defend themselves.

Metrics with No Meaning

I was working at NASA in the early 1990s when a new administrator took the helm. He came from private industry and set out to improve the agency's overall project performance. His goals were simple: reduce project cost, decrease project delivery time, and increase the overall quality of the resulting systems. While I greatly appreciated these goals, it soon became clear that the plan was not well thought out.

The new initiative focused on delivering "Better, Faster, Cheaper" programs. When someone pointed out that safety was key to human spaceflight and the aeronautics program, the initiative became "Better, Faster, Cheaper, and Safer." The working-level folks at NASA added: "Pick any two."

Why the humor? It was simple: the initiative assumed that all the key system characteristics—quality, schedule, cost, and safety—were independent and that the current processes in place were so poor that all aspects could be simultaneously improved. More importantly, other key system "ilities," such as security, operability, and maintainability, were pushed to the side. The sharp focus of the initiative pulled resources and attention away from security just as new threats were emerging and swift action was necessary.

I admit that the existing system development lifecycle at NASA had room for improvement. This is not a criticism of the existing processes: all processes can benefit from continuous improvement programs. The "better, faster, cheaper, safer" initiative, however, was based on unvalidated assumptions about the root causes of the problems. The core business process analysis required to develop an effective program was missing. The metrics program and associated push for Total Quality Management were positive, but misdirected. There were no clear baselines for better, faster, cheaper, or safer, and in many cases the metrics developed were in direct conflict. Human flight (both spaceflight and aeronautics) is a difficult endeavor. Improving safety is not always aligned with faster delivery or cheaper overall program cost.

The metrics that were established to support the initiative were very stove piped. For example, there were detailed metrics to measure cost versus planned budget, but the fundamental concepts of Earned Value Management (EVM) were not applied, so the metrics were a one-dimensional assessment. The metrics related to cost, schedule, and scope were not integrated or correlated. The cost metrics were based on the amount of the budget expended, not the value gained. For example, if a project manager accelerated the purchase of some critical items to provide for additional test and integration time, the metrics showed the project as over-budget. This false positive happened even though the costs *were* planned, just planned to occur later in the schedule. More importantly, the "flat" metrics were easily manipulated and could mask serious problems in a project. If a project deferred spending for a major item and spent a lesser amount on unforeseen items, the delayed purchase masked the budget risk. The metrics would show green until the planned expense occurred, suddenly tilting the metric from green to red.

The quality and security metrics suffered from similar shortcomings. They didn't account for security's role in quality, speed, cost reduction, or safety. The minimal security metrics that were included in the program addressed the security of final components and system perimeter defense. Quality and security were not tested at the component level. Key issues were masked by a lack of unit testing and system integration testing, only to be uncovered in final system test, or, even worse, when systems failed in flight.

There was no concept of good enough, fast enough, cost-effective enough, or safe enough. The metrics were binary, and often were not collected at the unit and component level. Overall program and project success criteria were not clearly defined. There was a lot of energy expended; a lot of flat, one-dimensional metrics defined and collected; and few tangible results. I watched in horror as we spiraled deeper into trouble, addressing the symptoms of problems without identifying the root causes. The "metrics for the sake of metrics" approach left a very bad impression on me.

Around the turn of the century I had the opportunity to spend an extended period focusing on security, quality, reliability, and supportability, first at Reliable Software Technologies (RST) and then at Lucent's Bell Labs. At the height of the "Internet boom," many companies focused on time to market or features that would differentiate their products. The single focus was on capturing market share, in many cases to drive the company to a large initial public offering (IPO). Unfortunately, most companies did not consider the core "ilities" (e.g., quality, reliability, availability, maintainability, security, and usability) to be market differentiators. The focus was on beating the competitors to market. Robust system architecture, security, design, development, testing, and deployment were often seen as detrimental to getting products to market quickly. A host of academic and industry research, as well as common sense, demonstrated the flaws in this approach, but the push for a quick market share dominated. Key strategic decisions were driven by perceived market opportunities and not by solid engineering best practices.

After the tech bubble burst, the impact to the broader IT community was clear: a host of poorly designed, poorly constructed products on the market. The companies that survived were in no position to clean up their products. They did not have the staff or financial resources to redesign their systems and applications. Recovery from the shortsighted "time to market" focus has been going on for six years now and is still not complete. Some companies have made the investment in re-architecting their products, with marked improvements as a result. Others have continued to deliver products based on failed design and development practices. Such systems have deep architectural and programming flaws that undermine their security.

Time to Market or Time to Quality?

Bell Labs has a proud history of excellence in computer science research, but the best practices developed in the labs were not being applied consistently across Lucent's product development teams. The same design, development, and test practices that resulted in security vulnerabilities also contributed to poor system performance, low reliability, and overall poor quality. The lessons were not being transferred; they were being painstakingly documented and placed on shelves to gather dust. We had "lessons noted," not "lessons learned."

Poor project management and a weak system development lifecycle were allowing feature bloat and requirements creep to divert critical architecture, engineering, development, and test resources away from the core product elements. Instead of focusing on achieving quality and security at the product core and then expanding the feature set product, teams tried to deliver bloated products that could be all things for all people. As is often the case with the "be all things" approach, the products missed the core market requirements. In the drive for additional features, some products intended to solve simple problems became research projects that chased premature technologies, delivering complex, difficult to maintain solutions. Instead of investing in developing a simple solution to a common problem and reusing it across multiple products teams, we allowed, and in some cases actively encouraged, teams to develop custom solutions. The ever-growing code base made system design, development, testing, maintenance, and security more complex and more costly.

Soon after I arrived at Bell Labs, I had the opportunity to co-lead a team that was focused on addressing quality and security issues with the current family of products. The problem statement for the project was clear and concise: "To compete in the marketplace, Lucent needs to improve software quality, productivity, and predictability."

Lucent had just completed an internal survey that evaluated perceived organization goals across several product development groups. Five goals were rated as "High," "Medium," or "Low" priority (Figure 10-1). Security did not appear at all. This is a critical point, that security was not even on the radar as an important organizational goal.

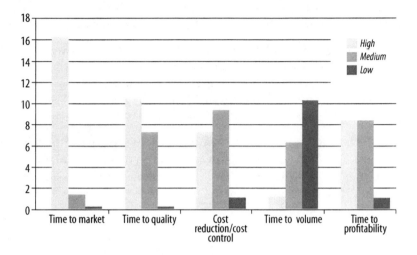

FIGURE 10-1. Organizational goals at Lucent

Nearly all survey respondents had a high focus on time to market (TTM). There was low focus on time to volume, which directly drives time to profitability. The dominant focus on TTM echoed weaknesses in reliability and performance engineering documented in the survey. The complex interrelationships between quality, security, reliability, availability, time to volume, and time to profitability were not recognized or managed effectively. Highly interrelated attributes were either treated as independent attributes or ignored.

In reality, you should not transition a product to volume production before achieving appropriate levels of quality and security. If you do, you directly impact overall product development and support costs and delay the time to profitability. In several cases at Lucent, products had been prematurely transitioned to volume production to meet TTM goals. The resulting products had high warranty and service costs that reduced overall product profitability, and the quality, reliability, and security issues harmed Lucent's reputation for delivering quality products.

For all project or product development programs, it is important to determine the attributes that need to be measured, their interdependencies, and the acceptable levels for each attribute. The project team must have a consistent view of success. Success criteria must be realistic and driven by the overall goals of the project. It is important to know what is acceptable for each metric and to make the proper trades between metrics.

The survey also measured the respondents' views of the gaps between Lucent's current performance in critical practices areas and the performance required to ensure successful projects. Again, much to my surprise, the survey did not explicitly ask about security. The data collected showed gaps in all areas, with the largest gaps covering reliability, metrics, system performance, training, early requirements development, and management and system testing. It was clear that a set of system issues needed to be addressed by a comprehensive program; we could not just improve one of the "ilities" without addressing the related root-cause issues.

In addition, Software Engineering Institute (SEI) assessments showed that the majority (over 60%) of Lucent's software development teams were performing at the lowest level of process maturity and effectiveness. Internal analysis and reviews documented a need to focus on deploying standard metrics and processes and improving the "ilities" of products prior to initial release.

In response to the findings, a cross-organizational team developed an end-to-end program focused on improving software by deploying a consistent set of software design and development best practices. Figure 10-2 shows the program's three key best practice clusters: engineering for the "ilities," engineering for test and configuration management (CM), and the deployment of standard foundational elements.

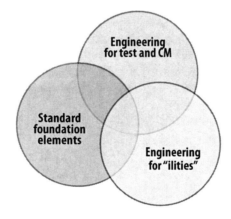

FIGURE 10-2. The best practices clusters

Engineering for the "ilities" focused on performance and capacity, reliability and availability, serviceability, and usability and security. Engineering for test and configuration management focused on test planning and architecture, test automation, and one-day build and test. The standard foundation elements were project management, standard operational metrics, and training.

The team recommended a pilot model with four pilot projects phased by fiscal quarters: one project would be started in the first quarter, the second in the second quarter, dependent upon a successful review by the project sponsors. In the two succeeding quarters, additional pilots would begin—again, dependent upon a successful review by the project sponsors.

At the start of the engagement, a pilot jump-start team conducted a lightweight self-assessment with the project team. The jump-start team worked directly with the project team, providing technical expertise to support the focused project improvement plan and transferring the detailed knowledge to the project team. The joint team developed and implemented the detailed project plan with the project team maintaining "ownership" of the identified issues and their resolution. The partnership worked well. It kept the project team fully engaged, and they maintained accountability for overall project success.

The team developed a high-level lifecycle to help understand the dependencies between best practices and the proper project lifecycle phase to deploy them. The three phases of the lifecycle were explore, execute, and volume deploy. Figure 10-3 shows the dependencies documented for the Performance and Capacity focus area of the Engineering for the "ilities" practice area, and Figure 10-4 shows the dependencies documented for the Reliability and Availability focus area.

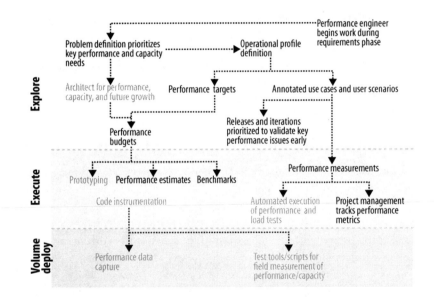

FIGURE 10-3. Best practices dependencies: Performance and Capacity

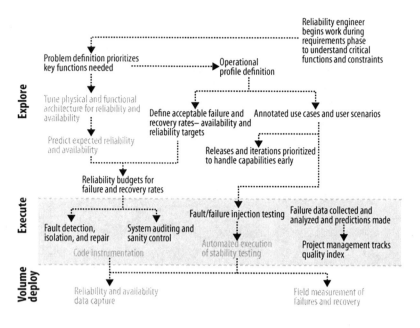

FIGURE 10-4. Best practices dependencies: Reliability and Availability

The program was very successful in focusing attention back onto the key behaviors and best practices required to improve Lucent's products and properly position them in terms of security, cost and profitability, customer satisfaction, and timeliness.

How a Disciplined System Development Lifecycle Can Help

When I returned to NASA in January of 2003, I had the pleasure of working on a project to redesign the NASA nonmission (i.e., general purpose) wide area network. The project had strong support from two critical senior leaders who understood the value of applying a strong system development lifecycle approach, to ensure that the new design was secure, robust, and scalable. I co-led the project with Betsy Edwards, the owner of the current network. We assembled a cross-functional team that included Jim McCabe, an excellent network architect; John McDougle, a strong Project Manager; and a team of security specialists, end users, network architects, network operations engineers, and network test engineers.

John McDougle kept the team on a disciplined design process (shown in Figure 10-5), where we developed options and evaluated them against the full suite of metrics. The final design was a major departure from the existing network architecture, but all of the design decisions were clearly documented and founded on the prioritized system requirements. The final system was deployed on budget and on schedule; it provided 10 times the bandwidth of the network it replaced at a lower monthly operational cost. John did an excellent job keeping all of the disciplines supporting the project—including security and the operations and management staff—engaged throughout the lifecycle.

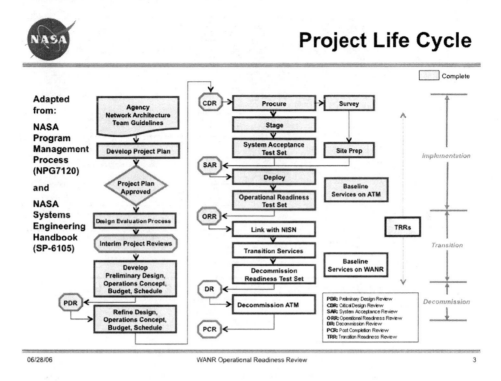

FIGURE 10-5. The NASA program management process

Jim McCabe led the team through a detailed requirements capture, prioritization, and management process. The resulting requirements documents captured not just the functional requirements (e.g., bandwidth, latency, etc.), but also all of the nonfunctional and operational requirements (e.g., security, maintainability, scalability) for the final system. At each phase in the development lifecycle, the requirements were updated and revalidated. The team used detailed modeling to evaluate preliminary design alternatives and assessed the nonfunctional requirements at each review. We also assessed security at each review, and our strategy and final implementation matured as a part of the overall system design.

One of the critical lessons I learned during the project was the effective use of risk management tools. John used a 5×5 matrix (shown in Figure 10-6) to track project risks. The matrix has the likelihood of occurrence (rated low to high) on one axis and the consequence (low to high) on the other. During each project meeting, we added risks John identified to the project risk log and analyzed them. All risks were actively tracked until they were retired. The matrix created a powerful visual image that made communicating risk to project sponsors and review members easy, regardless of the type of risk.

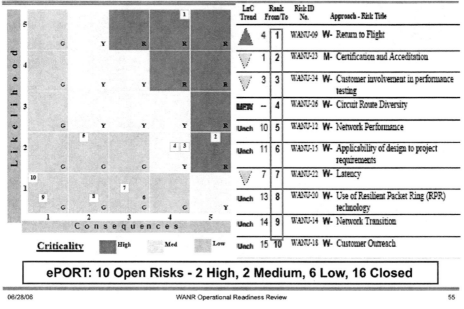

FIGURE 10-6. The 5×5 risk management matrix

This project was one of the most successful projects I have worked on in my career. A portion of its success was directly attributable to the strength of the team members (this was an all-star team) and the excellent leadership that John and Jim provided. The discipline the team applied was also a direct contributor to the project success. The team developed a clear set of requirements, including security, reliability, availability, bandwidth, latency, usability, and maintainability at the start of the projects. All of the "ilities," including security, were addressed in the system design phase and alternatives analysis, and all of the requirements were prioritized. The resulting system is simple, yet beautiful. There are no extra layers or bolt-ons that detract from the design or prevent the system from adapting to evolving requirements and security threats.

I applied the same 5×5 risk model at the Department of Commerce to evaluate information security risks and the risks associated with the loss of Personally Identifiable Information (PII). We evaluated each PII loss against two axes: the controls that were in place to protect the information (High to Low) against the risk of identity theft if the information was compromised (Low to High). This approach allowed us to make consistent, risk-based decisions on how to respond to PII losses. We also applied the model as a part of the security assessments of systems under design and during our security audits. This model allows us to clearly identify specific risks and decide to either mitigate a risk or accept it. There are very few perfect systems: in most cases, you end up deciding (I hope it is a conscious decision) to accept some level of residual risk. As more teams move to risk-based security strategies, a clear risk identification and management strategy is critical to success.

Conclusion: Beautiful Security Is an Attribute of Beautiful Systems

I am gravely concerned by the "quick and dirty" approach that I still see being applied to security. It seems like we did not learn the lessons of the late 1990s and the dotcom bust. We documented the lessons and placed them in binders on a shelf to gather dust. As I said earlier, we have lessons noted, not lessons learned. It is not good enough to gather the lessons; we must apply them in order to improve. We are not developing risk-based security programs that address security at all phases of the system development lifecycle. Until we make that transition, we will have limited success.

I've been asked why "ugly" security is not good enough. The question disappoints me. We should have matured as a discipline beyond the point of asking that question. It drives home that we, as a community, have a long path of improvement in front of us. My answer to the question is simple: ugly solutions are piecemeal—not integrated into an overall system design. The security elements of the system are layered or bolted onto the system late in the development lifecycle. The resulting systems are fragile, difficult to operate, and difficult to maintain. Instead of designing security into the system, we try to test it in. Since the security layers and/or bolt-on elements were not a part of the system design, there are challenges at the integration points between the system and the security elements. The "quick and dirty" approach has a 25-year history of failing to deliver quality, reliability, or usability—why should we expect it to work for security?

A simple analogy is to look at the design of a Ferrari 430 Scuderia compared to the current wave of customized sport tuner cars. It is clear that the overall design of the Ferrari 430 integrates all aspects of vehicle (i.e., system) performance. The vehicle is beautiful, with clean lines and a balanced, lightweight chassis. Contrast that against the "customized" sport tuner vehicles, where items are independently designed, purchased separately, and then bolted onto the basic vehicle by the end user. In many cases the parts do not work well together and actually have a negative impact on the system's performance. In the case of the Ferrari, it is clear that the vehicle was designed to work as a system—balancing speed, handling, weight, and strength.

I'm sure you are thinking that the cost of the Ferrari is much greater that the cost of the customized sport turner, and that if you spent as much money on the sport tuner, you would get the same results. I disagree with that assessment; in my experience, good design is independent of the target price point. Given the corporate (e.g., intellectual property) and personal assets (e.g., personally identifiable information) we are protecting, we are negligent in our responsibilities to our clients and customers if we do not invest properly in security. We have a responsibility to deliver the best products and services possible, and it is time we took the security element seriously and clearly faced up to the risks of not doing information security properly.

I strongly believe that a well-designed and consistently implemented system development lifecycle applied to all projects will provide significant benefits in improved security. The system development lifecycle approach is proven to improve a team's ability to deliver projects and services. The lifecycle provides a lightweight framework that focuses on clear decision-making, communication, and risk management. It engages key stakeholders early in the lifecycle and provides a clear set of criteria for proceeding to the next phase in the lifecycle. The approach allows all attributes of the final system to be addressed throughout its design and development. It allows us to weave security into the fabric of the overall solution.

I have seen beautiful systems that are very cost effective and ugly systems that are very expensive. Good design discipline is not inherently expensive and, in many cases, reduces the total cost of designing, developing, and operating a system.

My experiences at NASA, Reliable Software Technologies (RST), and Bell Labs were positive and helped me develop a full lifecycle view of delivering the "ilities" and a strategy for managing project and security risks. I have a great respect for the people I've worked with and appreciate all of the time they spent helping me learn. The research and consulting teams at these organizations were talented and worked hard at improving all aspects of system performance.

In the end, beautiful security is not a standalone attribute. How do you define beautiful security for a system that has "ugly" reliability, availability, or usability? The key to beautiful security is to design, develop, and deliver overall systems that are beautiful.

CHAPTER ELEVEN

Forcing Firms to Focus: Is Secure Software in Your Future?

Jim Routh

BEAUTIFUL SECURITY IN SOFTWARE REQUIRES A FUNDAMENTALLY DIFFERENT BUSINESS model from that which exists today. In fact, the current state of security in commercial software is rather distasteful, marked by embarrassing public reports of vulnerabilities and actual attacks, scrambling among developers to fix and release patches, and continual exhortations to customers to perform rudimentary checks and maintenance.

The solution is to embrace customer requirements for security controls in commercial software development. The business model for commercial software development firms has evolved to meet *explicit* customer requirements, but not *implicit* requirements, such as security. History has clearly shown that software providers are very good at delivering core functionality to meet customers' time-to-market needs. But removing security vulnerabilities has never before been an explicit requirement. Is it possible to add it to the requirements model in a way that benefits both customers and software providers?

This chapter is a story of one firm's pursuit to change the conventional model for acquiring and developing software. The ending of the story is not yet written, but the journey to this point may benefit other organizations interested in improving their resistance to software security exploits.

Implicit Requirements Can Still Be Powerful

Acquiring software is very different from other types of consumer purchases. However, to better understand the need for a different approach for acquiring software, it is useful to consider the following scenarios for customer requirements in other consumer-oriented businesses. I encourage you to ask yourself what you would do in the following scenarios if you were the consumer:

1. You walk into a McDonald's, order a Big Mac, pay for it, and then notice when you sit down to eat the burger that it is room temperature instead of piping hot. What would you do?

2. You order a best-selling book on Amazon.com by a noted author, select overnight delivery because you can't wait to get your hands on it to begin reading, open the package upon delivery, and notice that a 16-page folio is missing and the corners of most of the pages are crumpled, along with the book cover corners. What is your next step?

3. You purchase a professional desktop printing software package that enables slick photo editing and printing for $125.00 from Best Buy and install it on one of your home computers to both edit and manage your personal photos from your many interesting travel adventures. After completing the installation and doing some preliminary testing, you are satisfied that the software is functioning properly. You post many edited pictures of you and your significant other on your Facebook homepage and Flickr site to share with your friends. A few months later, you learn from a blog posting that the version of software you paid $125.00 for contains a security vulnerability that enables anyone that you shared the files with to see previous draft versions of your photos without the editing, which you did not mean for people to see. How do you respond?

Now, I'm willing to bet that in Scenario 1, you would bring the cold Big Mac back to the counter and demand one that was piping hot. And I suspect that 9 times out of 10 you will get exactly what you request. The probability of anyone receiving a Big Mac served at or below room temperature out of the 550 million Big Macs served each year is relatively low, given McDonald's focus on quality and customer satisfaction. I wonder how many of those orders for Big Macs include an explicit request from the customer to deliver it to the counter hot. It is an implied requirement, but one that managers are anxious to fulfill. There is no need to specify your desire for a hot Big Mac upon ordering to ensure that the temperature is well above room temperature.

In Scenario 2, both you and the representatives at Amazon.com would likely agree immediately that 16 missing pages is a significant defect. I suspect that, given Amazon.com's reputation for excellent customer service, you would receive a new book with all of the pages within a day or so without paying for additional shipping, after bringing this defect to their attention. In this scenario, you never specified that the book you ordered needed to have all of the pages. But no service representative from Amazon.com would point out that you did not specify that the book needed all of the pages. Once again, the requirement that the book contain all of the pages is implied. The inability of a bookseller to sustain a profitable operation while offering only partial pages in its books reinforces the industry's common practices of offering all of the pages for every book.

Scenario 3 is much less likely to result in a satisfying outcome. The reason for this is that, although security may be an implicit part of your requirements when you purchase software, it is certainly not explicit. Furthermore, security rarely figures in the requirements when the software is developed, unfortunately. The majority of commercial software providers do very little to identify security vulnerabilities and address them during the development process.

As I said at the beginning of this chapter, the gap between adherence to explicit and implicit requirements is substantial. Commercial software providers focus on delivering functionality to meet the time-to-market demands of customers, and they do it well. New features and capabilities make it easier for them to differentiate their products from other commercial software developers and encourage their customers to purchase new software or upgrade old packages.

Clearly, the omission of security from explicit requirements is no reason to believe that customers don't care about it, or don't understand its importance. But customers don't explicitly specify security requirements for two reasons:

1. There is no standard way of assessing software security.
2. Software vulnerabilities evolve and change with the threat landscape.

Determining whether a Big Mac is hot enough is a relatively trivial exercise for a customer. Determining whether a software product has security vulnerabilities requires an entirely different level of effort and expressiveness. There is no standard measure to determine the presence of software vulnerabilities or a secure approach to software development, which would resemble using a thermometer to determine the temperature of a Big Mac.

How One Firm Came to Demand Secure Software

I have worked for several highly regulated financial service firms with core business operations that rely heavily on the resiliency of their software. One of these companies, which I'll give the fictitious name of Acme, launched an effort costing substantial money over several years and requiring intense involvement at the CIO level to reduce its security risks. The rest of this chapter explains how we started, championed, and extended these efforts.

At the time Acme committed itself to the long-term project described here, it had never made any previous attempts to improve software security. However, it had an impressive quality record, having made investments in the use of a consistent methodology for systems development and achieved a level 3 status in the Carnegie Mellon Capability Maturity Model Integration (CMMI) process. To address security, at first, Acme considered bringing in a few security vulnerability detection tools to use on selected projects in a "proof of concept" mode. This is a common approach that companies take when starting a secure software program.

But Acme's chief information security officer (yours truly) read a book (*Software Security: Building Security In*, published by Addison-Wesley) on software security written by a recognized authority, Gary McGraw. Gary clearly points out that software security is more than identifying and removing defects in software code. In fact, over 50% of software vulnerabilities are based on defects in the architecture, not the code itself. I also recognized from previous experience in software development that identifying and addressing software defects early in the lifecycle is far more cost effective than fixing defects once the code is in production. I believed that emphasizing the identification and remediation of software defects early in the lifecycle was the best approach for creating an economic incentive for more secure software that the CIO was more likely to appreciate.

I knew from my previous experience in software development that encouraging software developers to think of security vulnerabilities as defects would be a significant challenge, requiring both a comprehensive education program and organizational development techniques for managing behavior change. I decided to put our focus on teaching developers to create secure code as opposed to spending a lot of money on pen testing services once the code was developed, tested, and implemented.

How I Put a Security Plan in Place

Carrying out this ambitious plan required a series of conversions in the attitudes of Acme chief officers, developers, and ultimately outside companies providing software. The steps in launching the plan are described in this section.

Choosing a focus and winning over management

Reformers can't fix everything at once. I had to pick one area of software and strive for measurable improvements in security there. Fortunately, the concentration of vulnerabilities in modern software makes the choice easy, as it is also consistent with the highest risk exposure.

Modern software exploits, unlike such early annoyances as the Internet worm and the Melissa virus, involve money-making operations. Like any commercial enterprise, modern hackers consistently seek the method that yields the greatest financial result with the least amount of effort. That leads them to web-based exploits. On the one hand, web applications and the software platforms on which they are based tend to sprout bugs that intruders can exploit to gain entry to web servers and ultimately end-user machines. Correspondingly, the widespread use of web applications by millions of untrained computer users offers enormous paybacks for intruders interested in data theft.

Unsurprisingly, recent trends in security threat data clearly show the migration of hacker exploits away from network perimeters (routers, switches, firewalls, etc.) to the web application layer. Web applications are targeted because this area is the most economical approach to data compromise.

For more information on favorite hacking techniques for web applications, go to *http://www .owasp.org*, which shows the top 10 web-based exploits. Number one is cross-site scripting:

> Cross Site Scripting flaws occur whenever an application takes user supplied data and sends it to a web browser without first validating or encoding that content. Cross Site Scripting allows attackers to execute script in the victim's browser that can hijack user sessions, deface web sites, possibly introduce worms, etc.

At Acme, I justified the initial security focus by providing the President and COO with industry trend data clearly showing the rise in exploitation of web application vulnerabilities from the OWASP Top 10 list and from the Gartner Group (75% of hacks occur at the application level). McAfee recently released survey results that show that about two-thirds of mothers of teenagers in the U.S. are just as or more concerned about their teenagers' online safety as they are about drunk driving or experimenting with drugs.

Showing the preponderance of web vulnerabilities in security exploits is quite helpful in persuading financial service executives to invest in security programs. Most organizations have increased their reliance on web applications in order to serve customers better and deliver greater efficiency. A nudge from an industry regulator also contributes to a compelling story about addressing application security. The President of Acme clearly understood the value of detecting software vulnerabilities, and of doing so early in the software development lifecycle, in order to reduce the significant cost of remediation or fixing the defects later.

Setting up formal quality processes for security

Given the go-ahead to integrate security into Acme's development cycle, our initial work involved various forms of formalization and standardization, which would provide metrics and educational material for further efforts.

We created a list of key deliverables from CLASP (Comprehensive, Lightweight Application Security Process), a methodology for developing secure software developed by John Viega and adopted by OWASP. We integrated this into our software development lifecycle (SDLC) and enforced it through appropriate controls. For instance, one of the required deliverables near the start of each project was a document that identified the trust boundaries for an application: what data it manipulated and who was expected to have legitimate access to that data. This document helped define the application's security requirements based on the classification of the data it handled.

Another area of formalization was to subject each new software architecture to an intensive review by the security organization, which had to approve the architecture before development could proceed to the next phase. Projects leveraging standard security architectures are encouraged to proceed with little required review.

Coders also got support and were required to meet security standards. To do this, Acme chose a static code analysis tool and required all Java and C++ code to pass through this tool with a certain threshold of quality before the code could go to the quality assurance team. A key criterion when we selected the tool was its high-quality contextual help, allowing relatively untrained developers to easily identify and understand security vulnerabilities.

Developer training

After persuading the chief officers of the company to launch this security initiative, I faced my second major challenge: encouraging the software developers to adopt and use the static analysis tool in the development process. As an entry point into the teams, I selected the most competent and highly respected developers and convinced their team leaders to nominate them for a special educational program to teach them about security. Developers who passed the test at the end of the course would be recognized as part of a newly established community of top developers and be handed an explicit and accepted responsibility to teach their peers about security.

The first class included 18 top developers nominated by their respective team leaders. The educational content was custom designed for Acme's environment, based on an existing software development methodology called CLASP. Acme delivered the education in classrooms in a lecture format followed by workshops, using an outside consulting firm that specialized in software security. Several firms, such as Cigital and Aspect Security, specialize in assisting firms that are committed to implementing software security programs.

When the security process really took hold

An interesting event occurred on the third day of the security class. One of the most influential web developers, who developed a web application architecture used by multiple Acme web applications that were already in production, abruptly got up out of his chair and bolted for the door. He mumbled something about a burning need to test something. The instructor, coordinator, and I were concerned that one of the best developers had walked out on the class and began plans for damage control.

The next day, the developer returned to class and quietly sat down. The instructor felt compelled to ask the developer if everything was OK. The developer then stood up to address the instructor and the entire class: "I realized yesterday that the web application architecture I developed for several production applications had a significant security vulnerability that could be easily compromised by an external hacker using cross-site scripting. I ran the code through the static code analyzer and my worst fears were confirmed by the results, so I stayed last night and fixed the code. I used the static code analyzer and remediated the code, removing the critical vulnerabilities before turning it over for testing. It will be implemented tonight, and I'll be able to breathe easier."

From that point forward, few Acme developers were willing to challenge the need for a static code analysis tool. The attempt to win over the developers gained momentum.

Fixing the Problems

The next hurdle I faced turned out to be a debate with team leaders over the importance of handling the defects found during static vulnerability analysis. Several projects missed the threshold of acceptability and were sent back to the development team. Team leaders thus faced the need to spend more time, and therefore more money, fixing security flaws, which in turn could lead to missing delivery schedules and bringing projects in over budget.

I had anticipated extra costs and had tried to mitigate such concerns from team leaders. I had previously negotiated with the Acme CIO to add a 10–15% productivity factor into the annual budget for training, tool integration, and remediation requirements. The CIO and I had subsequently met with the business stakeholders and obtained their commitment to the additional time and budget for security.

But some team leaders were not playing along. They were unwilling to relax schedules or use the productivity factor to offset the increased time needed to fix identified vulnerabilities. They preferred to allocate time and budget to creating functionality rather than improving the vulnerability risk score of their team's code. In effect, the team leaders conveniently assumed that security vulnerabilities were not defects and could be deferred for future enhancements or projects. Acme dealt with this problem by making two significant adjustments.

The CIO made the first key decision by reversing his earlier agreement and removing the 15% productivity factor, purely as a way of reducing the budget for software development and removing a level of contingency for all phases of the lifecycle. I initially dreaded this decision since it limited the leverage I had to encourage project leaders to identify and remediate security vulnerabilities. The results proved that this decision actually increased compliance with the security plan. With the requirement to pass the static analysis test still hanging over teams, they felt the need to remove defects earlier in the lifecycle so that they would avoid last-minute rejections.

The second decision was the implementation of a detailed reporting framework in which key performance metrics (for instance, percentage of high-risk vulnerabilities per lines of code) were shared with team leaders, their managers, and the CIO on a monthly basis. The vulnerability information from the static code analyzer was summarized at the project, portfolio, and organization level and shared with all three sets of stakeholders. Over time, development leaders focused on the issues that were raising their risk score and essentially competed with each other to achieve better results. This was not lost on the CIO, who would have no hesitation about calling a development leader up to his office to answer questions about an SQL injection vulnerability based on the monthly report.

Further resistance to the controls diminished. Although there remained Acme developers and team leaders who believed that the security controls were burdensome and constraining, they accepted them over time as core requirements.

Acme later added dynamic testing and manual penetration testing, run by outside services, to its core controls. The company spent a great deal of time to integrate the reporting of the vulnerability information into a model linked to Acme's accountability model. This reinforced the desired behavior at all levels of the organization. The initial core team of 18 developers trained in security grew to over 70 within a three-year time frame. We also created a formal process for providing performance feedback on selected developers to their team leaders, which helped the developers trained in security to achieve promotions and rotations, bolstering their career development.

Extending Our Security Initiative to Outsourcing

The steps described so far took place at Acme's main development site, where close monitoring and personal contact could reinforce the lessons and adherence to rules. But some development took place by outside service providers, who could not be reached by the intensive controls available in-house. Therefore, Acme designed some specific controls for off-site development. They were based on a few core controls:

- Off-site developers had to integrate their code with code developed by Acme following the same core controls, such as the analysis tools.
- Acme imposed standards on remote access architecture, including specific controls.
- Access to development environments was monitored and strictly controlled by Acme, limiting access to essential development servers and tools.

Over the first years of the software security initiative, Acme increased the amount of off-shore development due to the attractive economics of using contractors in lower-cost foreign countries. This led to the emergence of new security issues. For instance, offshore vendor staff could potentially have access across applications to source code beyond what they needed for their respective project. Acme added a few selected controls to both monitor and restrict this access to files and development servers.

Enforcing Security in Off-the-Shelf Software

With a relatively mature application security program in place, Acme decided to tackle commercial off-the-shelf software, or COTS. Like most firms, Acme's reliance on purchased software for business and workstation software was growing, and we had no security review prior to implementation of the software.

Within Acme there was a great deal of skepticism about the possibility of adopting any security controls for commercial software. The IT leaders were reluctant to support anything that added hurdles and time to the process of evaluating and selecting software packages. Acme business leaders were uncertain how software companies were going to react to customers requiring information on security controls in the development process.

But I was anxious to push for the adoption of security controls for at least a subset of commercial software applications. I recognized that software was playing an increasing role in commercial infrastructure, and that economics was driving companies such as Acme to depend increasingly on purchases from commercial software vendors. My rationale also took into account that over time, regulatory requirements were likely to include application security and that Acme needed to be ahead of the curve by adopting controls to avoid paying more for a "knee-jerk" reaction to a new regulation. For example, in April 2008 the Office of the Comptroller of the Currency (OCC) published comprehensive guidance on software security requirements for the financial service firms they regulate. It's the first comprehensive regulatory requirement in the U.S. that is explicitly for software security. Attempting to adopt and implement a program to fully comply with the OCC requirements is a significant undertaking for firms without an established and mature program in place for software security. The cost alone for immediate compliance would be significant, in addition to the time and resource effort required. In addition, any control that we could implement would represent a significant improvement over the current situation, where we had no way to identify the security risks of using purchased software and no leverage over the providers. From my perspective, commercial software was simply one more important dimension of the IT supply chain that required appropriate controls.

When I presented the concept of commercial software controls to the Security Committee, there was significant debate. They ultimately agreed to try out this new process in a "proof-of-concept" project. I defined the evaluation criteria for the project, and I promised to provide the results to the committee.

I recognized that software companies were likely to resist the new requirements and that added delays in software procurement would be poorly received by business stakeholders. So I developed an approach where I would intervene in the negotiations with a software vendor prior to making a buying decision and simply request whatever artifacts the software vendor could provide to demonstrate effective controls in their software development process.

This request mirrored the information Acme was prepared to share with other customers who requested similar information from Acme. Acme had artifacts from the requirements, design, development, and testing phases of our software development lifecycle that demonstrated our security controls. The artifacts requested by Acme are identified in Figure 11-1. Each of the four boxes represents a core phase of a conventional waterfall methodology, identified by the label at the top of the box. The bottom of each box lists the categories of vulnerability detection tools and services we use.

In short, Acme laid out a conventional software development process and the types of tools and services we used for quality control and security checking, and asked vendors for similar information.

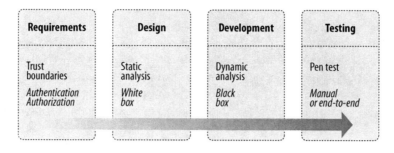

Requirements	Design	Development	Testing
Trust boundaries	Static analysis	Dynamic analysis	Pen test
Authentication Authorization	White box	Black box	Manual or end-to-end

FIGURE 11-1. Acme's security controls, as shown to customers

In addition, I decided to test out a new service from a young start-up firm that developed an innovative way to scan code binaries; for this article I'll call it Verify. This new method did not require access to source code, a significant obstacle for commercial software vendors who go to great lengths to protect their proprietary intellectual capital. Acme offered the use of Verify to its suppliers as an alternative to providing Acme with the information previously mentioned about the four stages of development. If vendors opted to use Verify, Acme would use it to scan the binaries from their latest release of software. The software vendors receive the detailed scan results so they could identify and remediate the vulnerabilities based on risk and their priorities. I could then influence their priorities based on Acme's needs. The Verify service provides a risk score using a consistent framework, and Acme is able to establish the required risk score for each software product or type of software product. So the level of vulnerabilities detected are comparable with other software products, applications developed by third parties, and systems that Acme has internally developed.

My proof-of-concept project included three mid-sized software firms. Two out of the three software vendors resisted the initial request for artifacts and reluctantly agreed to the Verify service. The third firm had coincidentally been asked to use the Verify service by another financial services firm as part of its own vendor evaluation process. This software vendor actually scored lower than its competitor in vulnerabilities discovered by Verify, but was selected by the financial services firm anyway because it showed a commitment to address the vulnerabilities and improve the software. This software firm hired Verify too and incorporated the service into its controls on a consistent basis, ultimately improving its risk score and the resiliency of its software. Several other firms, including Acme, asked for and received the vulnerability summary information from the software firm.

The results for the three software vendors that we asked for security controls were generally positive. Two of the three firms responded well to the vulnerability information and used the results to prioritize their remediation work effort. One of these vendors actually received a relatively lower risk score than its competitor in a separate evaluation by a financial services firm that was using the risk rating as an evaluation criteria, but the vendor's response to the vulnerability risk information was so proactive and effective that it won the business anyway and later improved its risk score for Acme.

Acme does not expect perfect risk scores; it is more encouraged by vendors that demonstrate a willingness to learn how to improve their security controls over time.

The third vendor received a relatively low vulnerability score and then challenged the accuracy of the binary scanning technology. This firm had invested in the Common Criteria for Software from BITS, a financial services industry organization. This is a rigorous documentation exercise for controls and vulnerabilities that is labor intensive and whose value is tied directly to the specific version of software reviewed. Acme agreed to accept this as an artifact from this vendor but encouraged the vendor to engage with Verify. The ensuing dialogue with the vendor provided an effective assessment of security controls within the vendor's environment and a significantly better understanding of the security risks that would go with the adoption of the vendor's product into Acme's environment.

The proof of concept demonstrated enough success for Acme to move forward and enforce security requirements for all future business application software purchases. I analyzed the existing inventory of desktop applications currently offered by Acme and selected products where we should require a security assessment prior to the annual license renewal. The Vendor Management Office contacted each vendor, explained the new security requirements, and gave them our choices of options for compliance.

Once again, Acme decided to take a gradual approach to improving software security by applying new security requirements only to a subset of the software purchased, business application software, which is typically web-based and offers the highest risk of exploit. Our plan was to evolve security assessment until we felt it was mature, and then apply similar requirements to all software procured by Acme.

Analysis: How to Make the World's Software More Secure

Software, whether commercially produced or internally developed by IT organizations, has penetrated to the core infrastructure of the global economy. Very few commercial products or services can be provided effectively today without the contribution of software. The planes we fly for air travel were designed, manufactured, operated, and maintained by processes dependent on software functionality. The food we eat, the cars we buy, and the goods we acquire are enabled by software. Yet with all of this demand for functionality from software, companies and consumers still have a limited understanding of processes for creating resilient software with control of security vulnerabilities.

The Best Software Developers Create Code with Vulnerabilities

Designing software that is functional and works consistently is a challenge in the best of circumstances, and most software developers understand that there is really no way to guarantee quality in software design and development, regardless of their level of talent.

In regard to security, Acme understands how difficult it is to design and develop software with limited vulnerabilities and low risk. After all, we've developed software ourselves for years. But a cursory overview of the software development process clearly reinforces the need to perform code reviews that enable software developers to identify and correct software flaws during the development lifecycle. Acme believes that software code must be tested for security vulnerabilities during development as well as within the quality assurance testing cycles, leveraging multiple controls. This requirement applies equally to commercial software developers, off-shore application outsourcing service providers, and internal IT organizations.

The best software developers create great functionality that can be hacked due to vulnerabilities in the code. Software developers are typically very good at creating functional code, but the skill necessary for a malicious hacker to break an application is unique and very difficult to teach to a software developer.

Luckily, there are improvements in the tools and services available to detect vulnerabilities early in the software development lifecycle and correct them before the cost of remediation escalates. The analysis tool chosen by Acme provided context-sensitive help that actually promoted developer education as well as identifying immediate flaws that needed fixing.

A large body of evidence suggests that using a consistent, repeatable process followed by established practices does improve the probability of success in any engineering or manufacturing effort. The same is true for designing and building software that has limited security vulnerabilities. Consumers or business users can and should require the adoption of good practices to eliminate software defects related to security within the software development lifecycle.

Acme understands the need for security controls in the software development process for two fundamental reasons:

- Security flaws are likely to be discovered in design, in the security and authorization architecture, in the actual software code, and in the configuration settings of the devices supporting the application. Therefore, multiple controls at different phases are essential.

- Identification and remediation of vulnerabilities earlier in the software lifecycle lowers operating costs.

Acme has applied these principles to the design of our own program, along with the requirements we use with software vendors. That is why Acme believes that requesting a description of the security controls within a software development methodology is an effective way to engage software vendors in a joint assessment of the effectiveness of controls, in order to understand the inherent risk of commercial software.

Microsoft Leading the Way

One of the most common complaints Acme receives, when we give our security requirements to software vendors, is that one of the largest commercial software providers (which happens to be based in Redmond, Washington) is not expected to comply with Acme's requirements, given the vendor's market size.

But ironically, Microsoft is one of the few commercial software providers that addresses security in the software development process. They have made significant investments in updating their software development lifecycle with security controls, and currently have one of the most mature sets of security controls within their development process today, which has been emulated by other companies. Consumer perception of Microsoft products may be influenced by the relatively large number of patches released monthly, but the reality is that Microsoft *has* listened to customer needs for security and has made progress addressing these needs.

They got started by introducing security controls into their SDLC many years ago. One of their leading advocates for improving software security is Michael Howard, who has authored several books on software security. Microsoft recently released their Software Development Lifecycle (SDL version 3.2) to the public to promote better industry practices for security in software. It is clear that their ability to improve the software vulnerabilities in their products has been significantly enhanced in recent years.

In contrast, Acme has found that several other large software firms are offering a posture of resistance when confronted with a request to demonstrate security controls in their development process.

Software Vendors Give Us What We Want but Not What We Need

Unfortunately, companies and consumers have never really specified a preference software that is free from security vulnerabilities, nor have consumer buying habits indicated that this is crucial to success. The large majority of software Requests For Proposals (RFPs) released by organizations do not specify the identification of controls in the software development process that identify and remediate security flaws. In fact, researchers—rather than actual consumers—identify most security vulnerabilities.

Software vendors have responded by consistently releasing software patches that address known vulnerabilities as quickly as they can. Acme realizes that to blame software vendors for the growing level of security vulnerabilities in commercial software products today is not all that effective at yielding better results and is somewhat off the mark. Software vendors have largely given commercial customers what they have asked for: ever-increasing functionality delivered rapidly on open-standards-based platforms. Their business models reflect the churn for new functionality delivered rapidly to the market, and those that have mastered this process meet both consumer and Wall Street expectations.

Acme is attempting to alter that churning and inject security requirements into the software evaluation criteria for commercial software purchases. Will other firms follow suit? That remains to be seen. Will consumers adjust their behaviors? Perhaps they already have. We see a growing demand for software products that deliver a higher level of security for consumers.

Acme realizes that changing consumer behavior is well beyond the scope of reducing security risks at our own site. We focus on enforcing security requirements during our own software procurement. The success of this aspect of Acme's security program will take years to evaluate.

Luckily, Acme's commitment to improving the world of software development is mirrored in an entirely different and larger scale. There is a large organization that procures billions of dollars of software annually and has in recent years adjusted its procurement process for software and hardware to include requirements for security settings that it specifies. This is, of course, the U.S. federal government, which in early 2006 successfully negotiated a set of specific security settings that applies to all purchases of Win/Tel workstations configured with Microsoft Windows and other Microsoft software.

In 2005, the Air Force CIO successfully implemented security configuration standards after obtaining an agreement from Microsoft to configure workstations and Windows with the desired settings and then to test software patches on similarly configured workstations prior to releasing them. This program was so successful that the U.S. government implemented the same configuration requirements for all of its agencies. As an example, the Department of Agriculture specified security requirements in the End User Workstation Standards published on December 12, 2007. This is a department-wide standard established for the consistent application of security controls, and drives the procurement of all workstations. The standard includes such security requirements as:

- Patch management
- Anti-virus and anti-spyware software
- Operating system security patches
- Vulnerability scanning
- Disk encryption
- Multifactor authentication

There is light at the end of the tunnel for those firms that embrace a comprehensive software security program. Acme has gone over five consecutive months without any high-risk vulnerabilities in all of the projects supported by its 600+ developers. Acme has also completed analysis indicating that it realizes an 11% savings in productivity by eliminating security vulnerabilities earlier in the lifecycle, saving costly remediation work after the code is in production. Acme's software security program reduces risk and improves productivity, enabling developers to focus on higher value activities. Every organization, both large and small, that procures software has an opportunity to apply the same type of logic to the procurement process and ask vendors to demonstrate compliance with security requirements through the three common types of vulnerability detection controls (static, dynamic, and manual). If we all make the demonstration of compliance to these types of controls a requirement in the procurement process, the software vendors, integrators, and outsourcers will respond over time by investing in these controls and sharing results with prospective customers, in order to demonstrate a competitive advantage over other firms that are less proactive. It's a beautiful thing!

CHAPTER TWELVE

Oh No, Here Come the Infosecurity Lawyers!

Randy V. Sabett

PLUS ÇA CHANGE, PLUS C'EST LA MÊME CHOSE (THE MORE THINGS CHANGE, THE MORE they stay the same).* In the area of information security, technology changes rapidly. As soon as the "good folks" catch up, the "bad folks" forge ahead with new attacks. In the area of information security, however, the saying holds true that the more things change, the more they stay the same.

Security professionals deal perennially with well-known and systemic problems, including poor user practices, buggy software, and a deliberate lack of leadership at the national level (at least in the United States, which has taken a market-driven approach up to this point). The pervasiveness of the problems, the regularity with which incidents containing common elements occur, and the depth of cultural influences that determine their continued existence suggest that legal intervention can make a difference. Indeed, information technology and law have already collided and will continue to collide at an increasing pace. In this chapter, I'll offer

---

* Alphonse Karr, *Les Guêpes* (1849). The phrase could be translated more literally as, "The more that changes, the more it is the same thing," but it is more often translated as I have here, and is sung that way by the rock band Rush in the song "Circumstances" from their *Hemispheres* album. To some extent, certain aspects of information security resemble the world that Rush describes generally in Circumstances: "Now I've gained some understanding / Of the only world that we see / Things that I once dreamed of / Have become reality."

some anecdotes and principles that will hopefully help you understand the positive potential of the interaction between law and information security.

Though you may be tempted to skip over this chapter because it is written by an attorney, consider the following: First, I was a crypto engineer in a previous life and therefore appreciate how technology and the law interrelate. Second, the intersection of information security and the law follows naturally from the notion that one person has a duty to another. Duties (and breaches of those duties) have historically been addressed via tort law, particularly as related to negligence. Although technology changes things (more and more!), the same basic argument exists for people who feel they are wronged in the area of information security. The entity with a duty to protect that person breached that duty, and the wronged party suffered damages caused by the breach. That is simply the legal principle of negligence in the context of information security. We'll spend more time on negligence later.

This book provides numerous examples of principles that the various authors consider core to the idea of beautiful security. From my perspective, four basic concepts influence any issue in this area: *culture, balance, communication*, and the notion of *doing the right thing*. Even though a tremendous amount of attention has been paid to data security breaches and numerous laws have been passed related to information security, information losses and data security breaches continue to occur. Many wonder how these can be allowed to happen, and the situation seems particularly perplexing to those who believe in the power of law to further "beautiful security." If we accept the premise that better security requires a fundamental change to the status quo, what can be done to change that status quo from a legal perspective?

Enter *pragmatic security*, a movement in the security field that reflects on the basic rationale for having a secure system and then changes the responsible people's mindset from "security is an afterthought" to "security is integrated into our daily operations."

In this chapter, I will walk through these notions of culture, balance, communication, and doing the right thing from the perspective of the law and exposure to liability. To explain these concepts, I will call on my experiences with and discussions amongst the group that I affectionately call the "crazy little band of infosec lawyers I run with."

Culture

I have not met a person in the information security field who doubts that the culture of an organization can make or break its success with information security. Thus, the stance taken by an organization's leadership toward security directly affects the culture and ultimately its security practices.

Expanding this concept further, a regional and national culture related to security will depend on the leadership shown in this area. So I'll start with one specific example of recommendations for national leadership in this area: the Commission on Cyber Security for the 44th Presidency.

The Center for Strategic and International Studies (CSIS) established the Commission on Cyber Security for the 44th Presidency in late 2007. Chaired by Jim Langevin and Mike McCaul (two members of the Subcommittee on Emerging Threats, Cyber Security and Science and Technology within the House Committee on Homeland Security), Scott Charney (Corporate Vice President for Trustworthy Computing, Microsoft Corporation), and Lt. General Harry Raduege, USAF (Ret.) (Chairman, Center for Network Innovation, Deloitte & Touche LLP), the Commission's goal was to develop nonpartisan recommendations for a comprehensive strategy to improve cyber security in federal systems and in critical infrastructure.

During my participation as a Commissioner, I experienced the very surprising revelation that the United States did not have a coordinated cyber doctrine to cover cyberspace activities. Given that this section addresses culture, one might wonder why I begin with a discussion of doctrine. It naturally follows, however, that without a broad federal doctrine and associated strategy on cyber security, development of a culture of security can be tremendously difficult. Consistent with this view, Commission members appeared before the House Homeland Cybersecurity Subcommittee in a September 2008 hearing. The members testified that the U.S. lacks a coherent and actionable national strategy for addressing the daunting challenges of securing cyberspace.

The U.S. has had various doctrines at different times in history. In the early 1800s, the Monroe Doctrine articulated a policy on political development in the rest of the Americas and the role of Europe in the Western Hemisphere. The three main concepts of (1) separate spheres of influence for the Americas and Europe, (2) noncolonization, and (3) nonintervention were meant to show a clear break between the diplomatic approach of the new United States and the autocratic realm of Europe.

Following World War II, the Truman Doctrine established a policy that drove diplomatic endeavors of the United States for several decades. The Truman Doctrine stated that "[i]t must be the policy of the United States to support free peoples who are resisting attempted subjugation by armed minorities or by outside pressures." This decisively ended the long tradition of isolationism in the United States, set the foundation for dealing with the aftermath of World War II, and heralded the ensuing six decades of intervention in world politics. In more recent times, we have seen the Carter Doctrine, which established the policy of the United States to use military force if necessary to defend its national interests in the Persian Gulf region. Some of the consequences of that doctrine are obvious in 2009.

Considering the broad scope of these doctrines and the pervasive reach of the Internet into all aspects of life (government, corporate, and individual), it seems that a cyber doctrine and associated strategy would be incredibly helpful in establishing a culture of security. Appropriately, one of the Commission's recommendations urged the U.S. government to take a strong leadership role in this area by (a) establishing a National Office for Cyberspace (NOC) within the White House and (b) developing a comprehensive doctrine and strategy for securing cyberspace.

Pointing out that cyberspace security had become a top national priority (cited in both of the 2008 presidential campaigns), the Commission provided a number of other recommendations, some of which included:

- Developing a comprehensive national security strategy for cyberspace that uses all instruments of U.S. power and builds on the Comprehensive National Cybersecurity Initiative (CNCI)
- Regulating cyberspace through a balanced approach that avoids both prescriptive mandates and overreliance on market forces
- Requiring more robust authentication of identity for access to critical infrastructure components
- Creating public-private advisory groups to support the NOC
- Partnering with the private sector to focus on key infrastructures and coordinated activities for the prevention of incidents and response to incidents

Although the long-term effect of the Commission's efforts remains to be seen, at least one critical difference between this Commission and earlier efforts was its focus on actionable recommendations. The goal of each recommendation was to provide something on which the President and the members of the Executive Office of the President could take action.

Balance

Areas of law involving responsibility and negligence, including legal analysis, risk assessment, and liability exposure, necessarily involve balance. As is often the case, the balance in information security tends to focus on competing factors that contribute to an overall security calculus. Unlike other areas of risk assessment (such as life insurance or medical insurance, where actuarial data allows strong corollaries to be calculated), information security cannot draw on a significant amount of historical information. This is especially true when considering the legal aspects of security.

Nevertheless, we can still take a holistic and (in some cases) proactive approach. In this section I'll provide two examples where balancing acts were achieved among competing interests—the Digital Signature Guidelines put out by the American Bar Association and the California Data Privacy Act (a.k.a SB 1386)—and finish on a more general note with the return on investment (ROI) that can be achieved by an information security program.

The Digital Signature Guidelines

One of my first encounters with the notion of balance as related to the legal aspects of information security occurred in the early 1990s, as I transitioned from a career as a crypto engineer to a career as a lawyer. When I entered law school, I got involved in the Information

Security Committee (ISC) within the American Bar Association (ABA).† Surprisingly, the group was not the stereotypical bunch of stuffy attorneys, but instead a dynamic and energetic collection of attorneys, technical folks, and business people (along with several international representatives and governmental representatives over the years). One interesting challenge we took on was striking an appropriate liability balance as Public Key Infrastructure (PKI) came into vogue. Few areas in computing depend on trust and long-term guarantees as PKI does. A certificate is only as good as the identity vetting done by the certificate authority (CA) who signs it. Many people downstream, with little or no sophistication in technology and law, rely on decisions made by a few trusted entities many steps away in the process. Knowing the potential governmental regulation in the area of digital signatures, the ISC decided to draft the Digital Signature Guidelines (DSG),‡ whose subtitle summarized its scope: a "Legal Infrastructure for Certification Authorities and Secure Electronic Commerce." Considering that PKI comprised then-uncharted territory from a legal perspective, we had quite a lot of ground to cover. Not only did the DSG seek to clearly articulate legal principles where none had yet existed, it needed to do so for a nascent technology.

The DSG resulted from a collaborative effort of over 70 committee members. During a multi-year effort, the group parsed through the responsibilities and liabilities of each of the stakeholders in the standard PKI model: the CA, the subscriber, and the relying party. In doing so, the ISC established definitions for numerous terms and crafted a set of general principles, including variation by agreement, reliance on certificates being foreseeable, and the fiduciary relationships that exist amongst the stakeholders.

Once the basic principles and definitions were laid out, each stakeholder (CA, subscriber, and relying party) was carefully deconstructed and examined. Various subgroups within the committee drafted principles for each entity and provided commentary for each principle. Once a draft was completed by a subgroup, it was vetted by the entire committee.

While sometimes cumbersome, this process ultimately produced a concise document with principles that were thoroughly thought through. Such a result was possible only due to a very determined leadership team and a cross-disciplinary group of very smart people working together collaboratively.

The California Data Privacy Law

Although not as proactive in its development as the DSG, the California data privacy law also provides a good example of balance between competing interests. The California data privacy law (also known as SB 1386, passed as Sections 1798.29, 1798.82, and 1798.84 of the Civil Code) places requirements on any "business that conducts business in California" that "owns

---

† See *http://www.abanet.org/scitech/ec/isc*.

‡ See American Bar Association, Information Security Committee, Section of Science and Technology Law, *Digital Signature Guidelines*, available at *http://www.abanet.org/scitech/ec/isc/digital_signature.html* (Aug. 1, 1996) (hereinafter the Digital Signature Guidelines).

or licenses computerized data that includes personal information." However, the law defines personal information rather narrowly as the person's first name or first initial and last name in combination with his or her account information. A 2008 amendment expanded this definition to include medical information.

The less well-known backstory on SB 1386, however, is that the bulk of the text that became the enacted version of the law came out of a single drafting session that I imagine must have been very interesting and intense. Once I describe the time frame, you will understand why and how that text was drafted. But first, a quick word about legislative history (or alternatively, everything you probably didn't really want or need to know about the drafting of legislation).

Once a draft bill gets introduced, it typically goes through a process of being "marked up" by a committee and then debated on the floor of the legislature. Often a bill undergoes several different revisions prior to becoming law, including compromises between the two legislative houses. In many cases, the final law will bear a close resemblance to the originally introduced bill.

What is interesting in the case of the California law, however, is that the language that passed into law bears no resemblance to the original bill. The law, in fact, underwent a complete rewrite. The original draft of the law[§] focused mainly on access to public records held by state agencies and restrictions on the disclosure of personal information by these agencies in conformance with an earlier California law that required a state-wide privacy policy.

Following a set of amendments in March 2002, the Assembly Committee on the Judiciary, in a June 2002 amendment, completely rewrote the text of the bill to focus on notification of data breaches by both state agencies and businesses within the state.[‖] In a report analyzing the pending bill, the Assembly Committee mentioned two specific events that occurred between March and June that prompted them to completely revamp the bill.

First, the report discussed an "incident at the Stephen P. Teale Data Center which saw the personal financial information of hundreds of thousands of state workers fall into the hands of computer hackers." Second, it mentioned a private sector incident in which "an unauthorized individual using an access code normally employed by Ford Motor Credit had accessed 13,000 full credit histories of consumers from Experian, including names, addresses, Social Security numbers, mortgage information and credit-card account details."[#]

Based on these incidents, the Committee went on to note that:

[§] See Bill Number: SB 1386, Introduced, Bill Text, available at *http://www.leginfo.ca.gov/pub/01-02/bill/ sen/sb_1351-1400/sb_1386_bill_20020212_introduced.html* (February 12, 2002).

[‖] See Bill Number: SB 1386, Amended, Bill Text, available at *http://www.leginfo.ca.gov/pub/01-02/bill/ sen/sb_1351-1400/sb_1386_bill_20020606_amended_asm.html* (June 6, 2002).

[#] See *http://www.leginfo.ca.gov/pub/01-02/bill/sen/sb_1351-1400/sb_1386_cfa_20020617_141710_asm _comm.html*.

All too often events of this sort go completely unreported. How can this be? The embarrassment of disclosure that a company or agency was "hacked," or the fear of lost business based upon shoddy information security practices being disclosed overrides the need to inform the affected persons. In other instances, credit card issuers, telephone companies and internet service providers, along with state and local officials "handle" the access of consumer's personal and financial information by unauthorized persons internally, often absorbing the losses caused by fraud as a matter of "customer service" without ever informing the customer of the unauthorized use of his/her account.

Customers need to know when unauthorized activity occurs on their accounts, or when unauthorized persons have access to sensitive information, in order to take appropriate steps to protect their financial health.[*]

In trying to balance the competing interests of consumers and businesses, the Committee eventually included several compromises. The resulting law, which instituted the first data breach notification requirement in the United States, ultimately balanced consumers' need to know when their personal information had been disclosed against the negative effects that would be felt by the agencies and companies making such notifications. For example, early drafts of the bill required that notification be provided "immediately." In light of the realities of investigations involving data breaches, the "immediately" requirement was removed. Similarly, because of concerns over the cost of notifying large numbers of people, a substitute notice provision was added during the drafting process.

Security's Return on Investment

Each company inevitably has to balance its obligations in the area of security against numerous other competing interests. Choices along the lines of, "Should we buy a $10,000 box to protect us against threats that may or may not materialize, or should we spend that same $10,000 on a new server that will increase our transaction processing efficiency by 20%?" are probably all too common. When viewed purely from an ROI perspective, an argument for the security investment rarely succeeds.

Therefore, the three words *return on investment* can strike terror in the hearts of even the most seasoned security professionals. Every CIO and CISO, asked to justify a security budget or particular security expenditure, knows that information security suffers from the inescapable problem of generating little or no direct revenue (an issue also addressed in detail by Peiter "Mudge" Zatko in Chapter 1, *Psychological Security Traps*). Many pundits have likened information security to an insurance policy: if everything goes well, you don't even realize you have it.

[*] *Ibid.*

Information security now vies for the top spot in the priority list (and, therefore, for the budget dollars) of many IT departments. Consider information security management's rating as the number-one technology initiative in a 2008 survey of Certified Information Technology Professionals.[†] In justifying expenditures for information security, however, this may be one of those rare situations where "lawyers are your friends." To understand what I mean, we need to first talk about a barge, a tugboat, the New York Harbor, and a rope.

Let's go back to a fateful day in January 1944 when the barge *Anna Carroll*, moored in New York Harbor, broke away from its rope and caused damage while the bargee (caretaker) was absent. In determining the liability of the barge's owners, Judge Learned Hand came up with the formulation $B < P \times L$ and stated "[i]f the probability be called P; the injury, L; and the burden, B; liability depends upon whether B is less than L multiplied by P: i.e., whether B is less than PL."[‡] In the context of information security, this could translate to the following analysis: if the burden on an organization to prevent an information security breach or lapse is less than the probability of that breach multiplied by the damages that could result, that organization should seriously consider taking on that burden (or a reasonable alternative approach).

Mapping this to pragmatic and proactive information security, the simple shorthand of $B < P \times L$ can set the stage for a powerful argument for information security budgets. A company can get a very rough estimate of its security budget by taking a look at all of the threats in its threat and risk assessment (TRA) and ascertaining two things about each threat: the probability that an attack based on that threat will actually affect the business and the cost of the resulting attack. Those numbers offer a starting point for the budget and, consequently, a calculation for Return on Security Investment (ROSI). If we view the $B < P \times L$ calculation as the risk exposure and then determine how much the risk is mitigated by a particular solution, we can then derive the ROSI. The following formula provides at least one means:[§]

```
ROSI = ( (Risk Exposure x Percent of Risk Mitigated)
          - Solution Cost) / Solution Cost
```

One other point to consider: a company's investment in security could (at least indirectly) actually come up when determining liability. In at least one data breach case that came before a court, the judge specifically noted that the company had taken steps to put in place reasonable security. Specifically, he said, "The Court concludes that Guin has not presented sufficient evidence from which a fact finder could determine that Brazos failed to comply with the GLB

[†] See the AICPA 2008 Top Technology Initiatives, available at *http://infotech.aicpa.org/Resources/Top +Technology+Initiatives/2008+Top+10+Technology+Initiatives/2008+Top+Technologies+and +Honorable+Mentions.htm*.

[‡] *United States v. Carroll Towing Co.*, 159 F.2d 169 (2d. Cir. 1947).

[§] Wes Sonnenreich, Jason Albanese, and Bruce Stout, "Return On Security Investment (ROSI) – A Practical Quantitative Model," *Journal of Research and Practice in Information Technology*, Vol. 38, No. 1, at p. 55 (February 2006). Available at *http://www.securemark.us/downloads/ROSI-Practical_Model -20050406.pdf*.

Act.... Brazos had written security policies, current risk assessment reports, and proper safeguards for its customers' personal information as required by the GLB Act."‖

Hopefully, you will never be in the docket after a data breach and have to face questions about whether you had adequate security controls. If you are, however, presenting a ROSI analysis that was prepared prior to the breach, this could be a useful tool. But even in less extreme circumstances, it's a great response to anyone quoting those pesky pundits who mischaracterize information security as an insurance policy. ROSI shows there is an ROI in security.

Communication

Communication related to information security can be stated very simply: geeks need lawyers and lawyers need geeks. This has been confirmed in policy (usually through negative examples of poor computer products and poor legal decisions), but it's just as true in a commercial setting.

How Geeks Need Lawyers

Among the things geeks can learn from lawyers is that the laws in the area of information security can provide the balance described in an earlier section of this chapter, and can also evolve in sophistication. In the early days, anti-hacking laws were passed at both the state and national level. Federal laws in this area included the Computer Fraud and Abuse Act (CFAA),# the Electronic Communications Privacy Act (ECPA),* and other criminal laws. Similarly, all states have passed their own anti-hacking laws.

While these reactive laws played (and continue to play) an important role related to information security, they have certain drawbacks when looking at security from a holistic perspective. First, they focus on only one party in the overall security calculus: the wrongdoer. Second, they focus on the after-the-fact portion of the security time line. Specifically, any laws focused on hacking are triggered only after something bad has happened. Thus, they're useful mainly as a deterrent in preventing future cyber attacks.

As mentioned earlier, in a significant development related to security on the legal landscape, California became the first state in the nation to pass a data breach notification law, which, because of the cross-border reach of commerce and information, became in effect a national law. With the passage of SB 1386, California raised information security to the consciousness level of the so-called "C-Suite" (the CEO, CFO, CIO, COO, etc.).

Recognizing that a whole other side of the equation exists (i.e., on the proactive side), a fairly recent trend in the law, also starting in California, focuses on activities prior to bad events. AB

‖ *Guin v. Brazos Higher Ed. Service Corp.*, U.S. Dist. Court, Minnesota, Civ. No. 05-668 (February 7, 2006).

18 U.S.C. § 1030 *et seq.*

* 18 U.S.C. § 2510 *et seq.*

1950† requires businesses that own or license unencrypted personal information about a California resident to implement and maintain reasonable security procedures and practices to protect that personal information from unauthorized access, destruction, use, modification, or disclosure.

At the federal level, regulatory compliance has become one of the strongest driving forces for implementing security. Depending on whom you ask, the passage of infosecurity laws and regulations can be viewed as one of the most important trends affecting information security or, conversely, the cause of the dangerous misperception that compliance equals security. This double-edged sword can wind up perpetuating unwarranted complacency. Although regulatory compliance certainly is a driver that must be taken into account in the implementation of your information security plan, it should be a result, not a goal.

Imagine back to the days before SOX, HIPAA, GLBA, and data breach disclosure laws. Numerous nonregulatory sources of guidance and several information security standards provided the direction needed for most information security professionals. Various events, however, led to the passage of the aforementioned laws.

From a glass-half-full perspective, the laws have provided a decent framework within which a reasonable security program can be built. In regulated industry silos (e.g., health care and financial services), regulation has arguably improved security over the previous status quo. For companies outside those silos, state laws requiring data breach notification and reasonable security measures brought information security to the forefront. Thus, regulation can be viewed as the catalyst needed to get many organizations focused on security. Hence, more regulation is purportedly needed.

Critics of this view point out, however, that if companies have been cavalier about their security up to now they will probably not be scared by more regulation into becoming more secure. Further, regulation sets a bar that will be the minimum level sought by many enterprises, with no reason or initiative to surpass that minimum.

Further, from a glass-half-empty perspective, some view the laws as being unsuccessful. Due in part to vague provisions and lax enforcement, they have not provided the tighter information security that many advocates would have liked. Had the laws been successful, the argument goes, we wouldn't have had numerous data breaches, along with increasing instances of identity theft and corporate data theft that have occurred over the past several years. Hence, at the very least, we should not expand regulation and, in a perfect world, should instead get rid of those regulations that are not working.

Given the real impact that security breaches have on personal, commercial, and national security—an impact the law cannot afford to ignore—there is really no point in debating whether regulation should be a part of the information security landscape. Instead, we should focus on how to implement regulation in such a way that regulatory compliance (to the extent

† See *http://info.sen.ca.gov/pub/03-04/bill/asm/ab_1901-1950/ab_1950_bill_20040929_chaptered.pdf.*

faced by any particular organization) becomes a trivial by-product instead of a horrendous burden.

I'll return then to my earlier posture: how can regulatory compliance be a result, instead of a goal? If an organization seeks to protect itself properly, pragmatic security should come into play.

Pragmatic security approaches recognize the value proposition in maintaining a secure network, understand the consequences of not having adequate security, and embrace the implementation of information security from the top of the organization down. In effect, pragmatic security creates a culture of security.

A similar pragmatic recognition of compliance and ethics exists, of all places, within the Federal Sentencing Guidelines. "To have an effective compliance and ethics program" requires an organization to implement a program that is "reasonably designed, implemented, and enforced so that [it] is generally effective in preventing and detecting criminal conduct. The failure to prevent or detect the instant offense does not necessarily mean that the program is not generally effective in preventing and detecting criminal conduct."[‡] Pragmatic security, taken seriously, really works: most successful information security programs have a C-level executive supporting them from the top down. When upper management provides the necessary leadership and incentives for establishing an information security program, it becomes much easier for the people implementing that program to create a culture of security.

So let's get out there and get management to support our information security initiatives, including the legal team. Let's proactively write our information security policies that address administrative, technical, and physical safeguards—and make sure they have been approved by the lawyers. Having gained the support of management, let's implement appropriate internal controls and reasonable security measures. Let's be ready for (but hopefully never need to provide) data breach notification. But let's hopefully be doing all this because our management and our legal team believe in it and have empowered us to do so…not because some regulation is simply telling us to do it.

A good friend of mine who spent 42 years at the same law firm used to say, "Lawyers are often wrong, but never in doubt." Despite what the lawyers may think, however, they do need the geeks. While the law moves ahead at a relatively glacial pace, technology advances very quickly. In addition, the complexity of technology continues to grow. As a result, a good technology lawyer has the monumental job of keeping up with the changes in technology while determining how to apply the law to those ever-changing complexities. The only way to do this is via good contacts with the technical community.

A lawyer can run into technology issues in numerous ways. For example, a client may need to create a license for some new technology or may have a unique business model that requires

---

[‡] 2007 Federal Sentencing Guideline Manual, Chapter 8, Sentencing of Organizations, § 8B2.1 "Effective Compliance and Ethics Program," available at *http://www.ussc.gov/2007guid/tabconchapt8.htm*.

some creative contracting. A client may need to protect its intellectual property (IP) or determine whether it is infringing on anyone else's IP.

Furthermore, as a consumer of technology, a lawyer may decide to use a new product or may be required to do so by a client. In each of these situations, having someone available with technical expertise can be invaluable, particularly for unique or unusual technologies.

Success Driven from the Top, Carried Out Through Collaboration

A client of mine once called to explain that an edict had come down from management that a federated authentication solution needed to be implemented...and quickly. It turned out that this financial institution had more than one client that understood the many benefits that could result from launching a federated authentication program. Not only would system costs be reduced but security would be increased, in part because the client was going to roll out a hardware, token-based solution and thus supplement its traditional username and password combination to create a two-factor authentication system.

Since the project had management support from the beginning, we were able to easily pull together the necessary personnel to draft the policy. To address the combination of technical, legal, policy, and business issues, the team brought in a multidisciplined cross-departmental group of internal folks to work with my team on the legal issues.

We held weekly teleconferences that discussed the work accomplished during the preceding week, outstanding issues that needed to be addressed, and the activities to be covered by each functional group (or combinations thereof) during the following week. Although at first blush it might seem to be administratively burdensome, having a weekly call turned out to be tremendously productive, and indeed the conversion went smoothly.

A Data Breach Tiger Team

Early cyber attacks often involved unsophisticated individuals using relatively well-known "tools" to launch attacks against websites (i.e., the so-called "script kiddies"). In recent years, because of the increasing complexity in electronic technology, the attacks have been getting more and more sophisticated. (This is covered by other chapters, notably Chapter 4, *The Underground Economy of Security Breaches,* by Chenxi Wang, and Chapter 6, *Securing Online Advertising: Rustlers and Sheriffs in the New Wild West,* by Ben Edelman, both on the economics of security attacks.)

Because attacks can be so complex and multifaceted, having someone with technical expertise glued to the hip of the legal team is almost an imperative when investigating a data breach. In this section, I'll describe a recent client engagement where we needed a cross-functional team to understand sufficiently how a data breach occurred (and subsequently should be handled). This "tiger team" consisted of several technical members of the company, the general counsel, three outside attorneys, the internal marketing and PR folks, and a third-party forensic team that had been hired by the law firm to perform the technical part of the investigation.

Such a tiger team doesn't have to be an administrative burden or even require formal recognition, although in larger organizations, recognition could be helpful. The security tiger team can simply be a handpicked group of people representing key company interests (and even outsiders, as in our case) that has such responsibilities as security awareness and advocacy, developing and promoting a security policy, proactive security activities, investigation of any security breaches, and handling any deviations from the security policy.

In this engagement, we actually held daily meetings (and sometimes multiple meetings each day) in the days immediately after the breach, in order to give each other the background we needed to make fast progress. To drive these meetings, we utilized an open issues list that described each issue, identified the "owner" of the particular issue, and indicated the projected due date for resolution of the issue, the priority of that issue, and its current status.

Two really important lessons can be derived from this. First, getting your attorney involved in a data breach investigation can provide unusual advantages. For example, you may be able to claim that certain materials produced during the investigation for the purposes of rendering a legal opinion (and any related communications) are protected by the attorney-client privilege. Consequently, those materials could be protected from being produced in the event anything ever reaches trial related to the data breach (e.g., if a major vulnerability or noncompliant activities are discovered). Similarly, if your legal counsel hires an outside security or forensic firm for the investigation, as we did, certain materials such as draft reports and other results produced by that outside company during the security audit for the purposes of rendering a legal opinion can claim attorney-client privilege.

The second lesson is that an open issues list that assigns owners to specific items and ties those to a particular due date can speed up the resolution of issues tremendously. Empowering people to take action and holding them to a due date cuts away a lot of excuses and barriers, as in most goal-oriented projects.

Doing the Right Thing

Often while speaking in public, I ask my audiences to consider whether "compliance equals security" or "security equals compliance." Once an attendee challenged me by asking, "Are those trick questions?" I answered that they weren't, but instead that they were somewhat rhetorical questions that both have "no" as the answer.

Certainly, compliance cannot equal security. We know numerous cases where a company or agency complied with relevant standards or requirements but was still compromised in that area of security. For example, several breached organizations—including CardSystems, TJX, and Hannaford—had passed their PCI DSS audits prior to their breach.

In a similar fashion, just because a company is secure does not necessarily mean it is compliant. As a hypothetical example, an entity could be very secure from a technical perspective but might not comply with a particular security standard or guideline.

In wrapping up this chapter, I would repeat that security should be approached pragmatically—meaning that the notions of culture, balance, and communication I covered all aim at "doing the right thing." To some extent, the phrase sounds more idealistic than pragmatic, but I have seen organizations achieve this synthesis, so it can be done. Generally speaking, "doing the right thing" in the area of information security means taking into account not only numerous technical factors but also many policy and process issues. It is in the latter areas that legal issues often arise and where the legal team (consisting of both attorneys within the organization and outside counsel) can be leveraged.

In particular, a seamless relationship between the security folks and the attorneys can head off numerous problems that might otherwise plague you. More generally, perhaps it won't necessarily have to be *plus c'est la même chose*—perhaps we can, as an industry, effect real change that will improve the overall security landscape. Wouldn't that be beautiful?

CHAPTER THIRTEEN

Beautiful Log Handling

Anton Chuvakin

A WELL-THRASHED MAXIM PROCLAIMS THAT **"KNOWLEDGE IS POWER,"** but where do we get our knowledge about the components of information technology (IT) for which we're responsible—computers, networking gear, application frameworks, SOA web infrastructure, and even whatever future, yet-uninvented components come our way? The richest source of such information, almost always available but often unnoticed, are the logs and audit trails produced by the systems and applications. Through logs and audit trails, along with alerts, information systems often give signs that something is amiss or even allow us to look into the future and tell us that something will be amiss soon.

The logs might also reveal larger weaknesses, such as lapses in our controls that affect regulatory compliance. They even impinge on IT governance and, by extension, corporate governance, thus going even beyond the IT realm where they surfaced.

However, more often than not, such logs contain merely data (and sometimes junk data!) rather than information. Extra effort—sometimes gargantuan effort—is needed to distill that data into usable and actionable information about IT and our businesses.

Logs in Security Laws and Standards

To start at a very high level, *logs equal accountability*. This idea is not new; it goes all the way back to the venerable Orange Book ("Department of Defense Trusted Computer System Evaluation Criteria"), first released in 1983. Under the "Fundamental Requirements" section, we find a requirement for logging:

Requirement 4 — ACCOUNTABILITY — Audit information must be selectively kept and protected so that actions affecting security can be traced to the responsible party. A trusted system must be able to record the occurrences of security-relevant events in an audit log.

Wikipedia defines accountability as follows:

Accountability is a concept in ethics with several meanings. It is often used synonymously with such concepts as responsibility, answerability, enforcement, blameworthiness, liability and other terms associated with the expectation of account-giving.*

There are many other mechanisms for accountability in an organization, but logs are the mechanism that pervades IT. And if your IT is not accountable, neither is your business. Thus, if you tend to not be serious about logs, be aware that you are not serious about accountability. Is that the message your organization wants to send?

Along the same lines, logs are immensely valuable for regulatory compliance. Many recent U.S. laws have clauses related to audit logging and the handling of those logs; just a few of the most important laws are the Health Insurance Portability and Accountability Act (HIPAA), the Gramm-Leach-Bliley Financial Services Modernization Act (GLBA), and the Sarbanes-Oxley Act (SOX).

For example, a detailed analysis of the security requirements and specifications outlined in the HIPAA Security Rule sections §164.306, §164.308, and §164.312 reveals items relevant to auditing and logging. Specifically, section §164.312 (b), "Audit Retention," covers audit, logging, and monitoring controls for systems that contain a patient's protected health information (PHI). Similarly, GLBA section 501, as well as SOX section 404 and other clauses, indirectly address the collection and review of audit logs.

Centralized event logging across a variety of systems and applications, along with its analysis and reporting, all provide information to demonstrate the presence and effectiveness of the security controls implemented by organizations. These practices also help identify, reduce the impact of, and remedy a variety of security weaknesses and breaches in the organization. The importance of logs for regulatory compliance will only grow as other standards (such as PCI DSS, ISO2700x, ITIL, and COBIT) become the foundations of new regulations that are sure to emerge.

Focus on Logs

With regulatory lecturing out of the way, what are some examples of logfiles and audit trails? We can classify logfiles by the source that produced them, since it usually broadly determines the type of information they contain. For example, system logfiles produced by Unix, Linux, and Windows systems are different from network device logs produced by routers, switches,

---

* In the interest of accountability, I'll note that this definition began the Wikipedia entry on "Accountability" (*http://en.wikipedia.org/wiki/Accountability*), last accessed on January 10, 2009.

and other network gear from Cisco, Nortel, and Lucent. Similarly, security appliance logs produced by firewalls, intrusion detection or prevention systems, and messaging security appliances are very different from both system and network logs.

In fact, security systems display a wide diversity in what they log and the format in which they do it. Ranging in function from simply recording suspicious IP addresses all the way to capturing full network traffic, security logs store an amazing wealth of data, both relevant and totally irrelevant—or even deceitful!—to the situation at hand.

LOG TERMINOLOGY

Many of the terms used in the realm of logging (including the definition of the log itself!) have vague, misleading, or multiple meanings. In some cases, the terms are "borrowed" from other disciplines or just used differently by different people. This vagueness only muddies the waters of what is already a difficult sea to navigate. Here are our definitions of the terms used in this chapter:

Log message (sometimes just message) or log record
　　A record of some activity or an event observed on a system, network, or application.

Log or logfile
　　A collection of one or more log messages stored in a file, which may be a text file, a file in binary format, or a database or other storage medium.

When Logs Are Invaluable

Logs turn up as an essential part of an investigation, and in fact are often the first data one needs to look at. Once recorded, logs are not altered through the course of normal system use, meaning they can serve as a permanent record (at least as long as the logs are retained). As such, they provide an accurate complement to other data on the system, which may be more susceptible to alteration or corruption. (This assumes that the administrator has followed recommended procedures for logging to a system that's off the Internet and hard to corrupt.)

Since logs have timestamps on each record, they provide a chronological sequence of events, showing not only what happened but also when it happened and in what order.†

In addition, logs forwarded to a dedicated logging collector host provide a source of evidence that is separate from the originating source. If the accuracy of the information on the original source is called into question (such as the issue of an intruder who may have altered or deleted logs), the separate source of information may be considered more reliable. Logs from different

---

† Keep in mind the challenges to correct log timing mentioned earlier.

sources, and even different sites, can corroborate other evidence and reinforce the accuracy of each data source.

In addition, logs serve to reinforce other evidence that was collected during a forensic investigation. Often, the re-creation of an event is based not on just one piece or even one source of information, but on data from a variety of sources: files and timestamps on the system, user command history, network data, and logs. Occasionally logs may refute other evidence, which in itself may indicate that other sources have been corrupted (e.g., by an attacker). When a host is compromised, the logs recorded remotely on other systems may be the only source of reliable information.

As I'll explain in the following section, the evidence in logs is at times indirect or incomplete. For example, a log entry might show a particular activity, but not who did it. As an example, process accounting logs show what commands a user has run, but not the arguments to those commands. So logs can't always be relied on as a sole source of information.

Challenges with Logs

In light of the chaos we've explored in formats, syntax, and meaning, logs present many unique challenges to analysis or even just collecting and retaining them for future use. We will review some of the challenges and then illustrate how they come to life in a representative story about investigative use of log data:

Too much data

This is the first challenge that usually comes to mind with logging. Hundreds of firewalls (not uncommon for a large environment) and thousands of desktop applications have the potential to generate millions of records every day. And log volume is getting higher every day due to increasing bandwidth and connectivity, if not for other reasons.

The sheer volume of log messages can force analysis to take significant time and computing resources. Even simply using the Unix *grep* utility (which looks for strings in a file, line by line) on a multigigabyte file can take 10 minutes or more. Some types of analysis, such as data mining, can take hours or even days with this volume of data.

Not enough data

This is the opposite of the preceding problem. The processing of incident or event responses could be hindered because the application or security device could not record essential data, or because the administrator did not anticipate the need to collect it. This challenge is also often caused by a log retention policy that is too short.

Poor information delivery

This is similar to the previous challenge. Many logs just don't have the right information— or the right information needs to be wrangled out of them with some pain. For example, some email systems will record sent and received emails in different log messages or even different files, thus making it harder to follow the sequence of messages and correlate an email message with its responses.

Some logs just miss key pieces of data in records of interest. One blatant example is a login failure message that does not indicate the user account on which somebody tried to log in.

False positives

These are common in network intrusion detections systems (NIDS), wasting administrators' time and occluding more important information that may indicate real problems. In addition to false positives (benign events that trigger alerts), systems overwhelm administrators with false alarms (events that may be malicious but have no potential of harming the target).

Hard-to-get data

For political or technical reasons, data is frequently unavailable to the person who can benefit from analyzing it, undercutting log management projects. A less common variant is data that is hard to get due to the use of legacy software or hardware. For example, getting mainframe audit records is often a challenge.

Redundant and inconsistent data

Redundant data comes from multiple devices recording the same event, and confusion can arise from the different ways they record it. This adds extra steps to log analysis because data "deduplication" needs to be performed to remove the records that "say the same thing."

There has never been a universal logging standard. Most applications log in whatever format was developed by their creators (who are sometimes creative to the point of bordering on insanity), thus leading to massive analysis challenges. Logs come in a dizzying variety of formats, are logged via different ports, and sometimes look different while meaning the same thing or look the same while meaning something different. For example, the following strings all indicate successful access to a system, albeit on different systems:

```
login
logon
log on
access granted
password accepted
```

Along with the diversity of messages, many are also rather obscure. Many systems do not provide a catalog of messages that they can produce or explanations of how to interpret them. In an extreme case, an individual programmer makes a decision about logging something as well as about the format, syntax, and content of a message, often making it completely inscrutable. Hence the maxim, "log analysis is an art."

In addition, one has to deal with binary as well as text logs, some of the latter being freeform logs that are hard to parse or to convert from text to structured data.

Heterogeneous IT environments

How many folks only use one platform, one piece of network gear and security device type, and a single vendor? Not many. Most companies have multiple types of devices from multiple vendors.

Heterogeneous IT environments boost some of the preceding problems as well as bring forth new ones. For example, more peculiar file formats need to be understood and processed to get to the big picture. Volume gets out of control, NIDSs get confused by what they're monitoring, and custom application logs complicate this already complex problem dramatically.

We will illustrate these and other challenges in the following case study of the investigative use of logs.

Case Study: Behind a Trashed Server

The example in this section is loosely based on several real investigations led by the author, combined to provide an interesting illustration of several concepts in a small space.

Architecture and Context for the Incident

The company in question, a medium-sized online retailer, understands the value of network and host security because its business depends upon reliable and secure online transactions. Its internal network and DMZ setup was designed with security in mind and protected by the latest in security technology. The DMZ was a bastion network with one firewall separating the DMZ from the hostile Internet and another protecting internal networks from DMZ and Internet attacks (with all connections from the DMZ to the internal network blocked).

A network intrusion protection system (IPS) was also deployed inside the firewall that separated the network from the outside. In the DMZ, the company gathered the standard set of network servers: web, email, and a legacy FTP server dedicated to support for some long-running operations, a remainder from the old times. A few of the network services, such as DNS, were outsourced to external providers.

The Observed Event

On Monday morning, the company support team was alerted by one of their field personnel who was trying to download a large ZIP file from the FTP server. He reported that his browser was "timing out" while trying to connect to the company's FTP server. Upon failing to log into the FTP server remotely via secure shell from the internal network, the support team member walked to a server room, only to discover that the machine had crashed and was unable to boot. The reason was simple: it had lost its operating system.

At that point, the company's incident response plan was triggered. Since the security team has long argued that the FTP server needed to be retired in favor of more secure file transfer methods, this situation was used to "drive the final nail in the FTP coffin" and stop using the server. However, the security team was told to complete an investigation to prevent other critical network services from being disrupted. Note that at this point we didn't know whether the system crash was due to a malicious attack and whether there were any other persistent effects.

The Investigation Starts

Thus, the primary purpose of the investigation was to learn what had happened and, in case it was of a malicious nature, to secure other system servers against its recurrence. The main piece of evidence for the investigation was the server's disk drive. No live forensics were possible because the machine had crashed when running unattended, and memory contents or other live data were totally lost.

However, we did have a set of logfiles from the firewall and IPS as well as logs from other DMZ systems, collected by a log management system. We would have been delighted to find logs collected by the log management system from the FTP server; however, due to an omission, remote logging was not enabled on the FTP server. Thus, no firsthand attack information was available from the FTP server itself.

We started the investigation by reviewing the traffic log patterns.

First, by analyzing the firewall log data from its network firewall, we found that somebody had probed the company's externally visible IP addresses at least several hours prior to the incident. That person had also tried to connect to multiple servers in the DMZ. All such attempts were unsuccessful—and logged, of course.

Here are the firewall log records that provided us with the evidence of the rapid attempts to access all external-facing systems. (All IP addresses in all the log records in this section have been sanitized to be in the LAN 10.10.0.0/16 range.)

```
Oct 1 13:36:56: %PIX-2-106001: Inbound TCP connection denied from \
  10.10.7.196/41031 to 10.10.15.21/135 flags SYN  on interface outside
Oct 1 13:36:57: %PIX-2-106001: Inbound TCP connection denied from \
  10.10.7.196/41031 to 10.10.15.21/80 flags SYN  on interface outside
Oct 1 13:36:58: %PIX-2-106001: Inbound TCP connection denied from \
  10.10.7.196/41031 to 10.10.15.21/443 flags SYN  on interface outside
Oct 1 13:37:15: %PIX-2-106002: udp connection denied by outbound list \
  1 src 10.10.7.196 3156 dest 10.10.175.7 53
```

He finally connected to the FTP server, as indicated by this log record:

```
Oct 1 13:36:59: %PIX-6-302001: Built inbound TCP connection 11258524 \
  for faddr 10.10.7.196/3904 gaddr 10.10.15.16/21 laddr 10.10.16.120.122/21
```

Having gained access, the attacker finally uploaded a file to the FTP server, as shown by the following firewall log record:

```
Oct 1 14:03:30 2008 11:10:49: %PIX-6-303002:  10.10.7.196 Stored \
    10.10.15.66:rollup.tar.gz
```

We suspected that the file *rollup.tar.gz* contained a rootkit, which was later confirmed by a more complete investigation.

The last item shown was another unpleasant surprise. How was the attacker able to get onto the system if no connectivity from the DMZ was allowed? The company system administrative team was questioned and the unpleasant truth came out: the FTP server had a world-writable directory for customers to upload the logfiles used for troubleshooting. Unrestricted anonymous uploads were possible, as on many classic FTP servers, to a directory named *incoming*, and it was set up in the most insecure manner possible: anonymous users were able to read any of the files uploaded by other people. Among other things, this presents a risk of an FTP server being used by anonymous outside parties to store and exchanges pirated software.

Bringing Data Back from the Dead

After network log analysis, it was time for some forensics on the hard drive. We decided to look for fragments of logfiles (originally in */var/log*) to confirm the nature of the attack as well as to learn other details. The investigation brought up the following log fragments from the system messages log, the network access log, and the FTP transfer log (fortunately, the FTP server was verbosely logging all transfers):

```
Oct 1 00:08:25 ftp ftpd[27651]: ANONYMOUS FTP
  LOGIN FROM 10.10.7.196 [10.10.7.196], mozilla@
Oct  1 00:17:19 ftp ftpd[27649]: lost connection to 10.10.7.196 [10.10.7.196]
Oct  1 00:17:19 ftp ftpd[27649]: FTP session closed
Oct  1 02:21:57 ftp ftpd[27703]: ANONYMOUS FTP LOGIN FROM
  10.10.7.196 [10.10.7.196], mozilla@
Oct  1 02:29:45 ftp ftpd[27731]: ANONYMOUS FTP LOGIN FROM
  10.10.7.196 [192.168.2.3], x@
Oct  1 02:30:04 ftp ftpd[27731]: Can't connect to a mailserver.
Oct  1 02:30:07 ftp ftpd[27731]: FTP session closed
```

(At this point, an astute reader will notice that one of the challenges I have discussed manifested itself: the timestamps between the FTP server and firewall logs were not in sync.)

This sequence indicates that the attacker looked around first with a browser (which left the standard footprint mozilla@). Then, presumably, the exploit was run (password x@). The line showing an attempt to access the mail server looks ominous as well.

Also from the FTP logs on the hard disk come the following:

```
Oct  1 00:08:25 ftp xinetd[921]: START: ftp pid=27692 from=10.10.7.196
Oct  1 00:17:19 ftp xinetd[921]: EXIT: ftp pid=27692 duration=255(sec)
```

All downloads initiated from the FTP server to the attacker's machine have failed due to rules on the company's external firewall. But by that time the attacker already possessed a root shell from the exploit.

Summary

Two conclusions can be drawn from this incident. First, the server was indeed compromised from outside the perimeter using a machine at 10.10.7.196 (address sanitized). Second, the attacker managed to get some files onto the victim host.

Overall, this teaches us that despite the challenges they present, logs are of great use while investigating an incident; they can often be retrieved even if erased.

Future Logging

How will the humble logfile evolve and continue to play critical roles in system administration and security?

A Proliferation of Sources

First we should consider the increase in the breadth of log sources. There used to be just firewall and IDS logs, then came servers, and now it is expanding to all sorts of log sources: databases, web servers, applications, etc.

A few years ago, any firewall or network administrator worth her salt would at least look at a simple summary of connections logged by her baby PIX or Checkpoint router. Indeed, firewall log analysis represented a lot of early business for log management vendors. Many firewalls log their records in syslog format, which fortunately is easy to collect and review.

At the next historic stage, even though system administrators always knew to look at logs in case of problems, massive operating system log analysis on servers didn't materialize until more recently. It is now *de rigeur* for both Windows and Unix/Linux. Collecting logs from all critical (and many noncritical) Windows servers, for example, was hindered for a long time by the lack of agentless log collection tools such as LASSO. On the other hand, Unix server log analysis was severely undercut by a total lack of unified format for log content in syslog records.

Electronic mail tracking through email server logs languished in a somewhat similar manner. People turn to email logs only when something goes wrong (email failures) or even horribly wrong (an external party subpoenas your logs). Lack of native centralization and, to some extent, the use of complicated log formats slowed down initiatives in email log analysis.

Database logging probably wasn't on the radar of most IT folks until last year. In fact, IT folks were perfectly happy never to turn on the extensive logging and data access auditing capabilities that DMBSs offered. That has certainly changed now! It will be all the rage in a very near future. Oracle, MS SQL, DB2, and MySQL all provide excellent logging, if you know how to enable it (and know what to do with the resulting onslaught of data).

What's next? Web applications and large enterprise application frameworks used to live largely in worlds of their own, but people are finally starting to realize that log data from these sources provides unique insight into insider attacks, insider data theft, and other trusted access abuse. It is expected that much more of such logs will be flowing into log management solutions. Desktop log analysis should not be too far behind.

In a more remote future, various esoteric log sources will be added into the mix. Custom applications, physical sensors, and many other uncommon devices and software want to "be heard" as well!

So, we have observed people typically paying attention first to firewall logs, then to server logs, then to other email and web logs, then to databases (this is coming now), and ultimately to other applications and even non-IT log sources.

Log Analysis and Management Tools of the Future

To conclude this chapter, let's imagine the ideal log management and analysis application of the future—one that will help solve the challenges we presented earlier and address the needs we brought up.

Such an ideal log management tool will have the following capabilities:

Logging configuration

> The application will go out and find all possible log sources (systems, devices, applications, etc.) and then enable the right kind of logging on them, following a high-level policy that you give it. As of today, this requires the tools to have "God-like powers" that are far beyond current products.

Log collection

> The application will collect all the logs it finds securely (and without using any risky super-user access) and with little to no impact on networks and systems. As of today, this also is impossible.

Log standards

> The tool will be able to make use of logging standards that I hope to see adopted in the future. Today's growing log standard efforts (such as MITRE's Common Event Expression, or CEE) will lead first to the creation of log standards and ultimately to their adoption. It might take a few years, but at least partial order will be imposed on the chaotic world of logs.

Log storage

> The application can securely store the logs in the original format for as long as needed and in a manner allowing quick access to them in both raw and summarized/enriched form. This is not impossible today, as long as one is willing to pay for a lot of storage hardware.

Log analysis

> This ideal application will be able to look at all kinds of logs, even those previously unknown to it, from standard and custom log sources, and tell the user what he needs to know about his environment based on his needs. What is broken? What is hacked?

Where? What is in violation of regulations/policies? What will break soon? Who is doing this stuff? The analysis will drive automated actions, real-time notifications, long-term historical analysis, and compliance relevance analysis (discussed later). Future development of AI-like systems might bring this closer to reality.

Information presentation

The tool will distill the data, information, and conclusions generated by the analytic components and present them in a manner consistent with the user's role, whether an operator, an analyst, an engineer, or an executive. Interactive visual, advanced, text-based data presentation with drill-down capabilities will be available across all log sources. Future log visualization tools will not only present "pretty" pictures but will fit the tasks of their users, from operators to managers. The user can also customize the data presentation based on her wishes and job needs, as well as information perception styles. This might not take more than a bunch of daring user interface designers who deeply understand logs.

Automation

The tool will be able to take limited automated actions to resolve discovered and confirmed issues as well as generate guidance to users so that they know what actions to take when fully automatic mode is not appropriate. The responses will range from fully automatic actions, to assisted actions ("click here to fix it"), to issuing detailed remediation guidance. The output will include a to-do list of discovered items complete with actions suggested, ordered by priority. This is also very far from today's reality.

Compliance

This tool can also be used directly by auditors to validate or prove compliance with relevant regulations by using regulation-specific content and all the collected data. The tool will also point out gaps in data collection relevant to specific regulations with which the user is interested in complying. Again, this capability calls for "God-like" powers and might never be developed (but we sure can try!).

Conclusions

Logs are extremely useful for investigative and regulatory purposes, as I've demonstrated in this chapter. Despite the challenges I outline, log handling is indeed "beautiful." At the very least, it serves the beautiful purpose of discovering the hidden truth in an incident.

Finally, if we cast a look ahead to the potential world of logging in the future, we will see more logging: more volume, more log sources, and more diversity. Second, we will see more and more need for log information and more uses for such data. Third, we will hopefully see better tools to deal with logs. Fourth, the log standardization efforts of today should bear fruit and make the world of logs better. When it will happen is anybody's guess, but the author of this chapter is working hard to make it a reality.

But before the logging challenge "gets better," it is likely to "get worse" in the coming years. It will be interesting to watch the race between slowly emerging log standardization efforts and the sharply rising tide of new log types (such as messages logged by various applications) as well as new uses for logs. Developing credible and workable log standards, such as CEE, will take years and the efforts of many people. Standard adoption will also be a challenge because there are so many legacy logging systems.

On the other side, compliance efforts as well as incident investigation requirements are driving increased logging across platforms and applications today. Developers are asked to "add logging" before the community has a chance to give them guidance on how to do it effectively and in a manner useful for security, compliance, and operations. I have confidence that logging will be more uniform in the future, but I am not willing to say when this future will come.

CHAPTER FOURTEEN

Incident Detection: Finding the Other 68%

Grant Geyer
Brian Dunphy

MIDNIGHT ON SATURDAY, JANUARY 25, 2003—AND SOMETHING DEVASTATING was about to happen across the Internet. Hundreds of thousands of computer systems across the globe in data centers, corporations, and even homes were exposed to the massive attack that would soon be launched. The worm would exploit a known vulnerability in Microsoft SQL Server first reported a full six months earlier on July 24, 2002.

From our point of view at Symantec on that quiet night, analysts at our Security Operations Centers went through their normal routines, analyzing security incidents from hundreds of customers worldwide and looking for signs of cyber attacks. But the quiet shift erupted into a sudden storm, with our analysts' queues filling with tens of thousands of alerts within minutes. From the analysts' view, the monitored intrusion detection systems were all concurrently alerting us of an "SQL buffer overflow" as the monitored firewalls were detecting a flood of traffic on port1434/udp.

For organizations allowing port 1434/udp through their firewalls, the worm wreaked havoc within their internal infrastructure within hours, causing denials of service as the worm attempted to propagate. For companies who were blocking port 1434/udp, when Monday morning arrived, many users with MS SQL on their laptops unknowingly carried the worm past the perimeter as they plugged in their computers, allowing the exploit to occur from within.

This was our view of SQL Slammer—a wide-scale exploitation of the Internet through a known vulnerability in Microsoft SQL that almost took down the Internet temporarily.

With 10 years of experience in Managed Security Services at Symantec, we've had the opportunity to witness a significant number of security incidents. Slammer, although lethal to IT infrastructures, was fairly straightforward to detect. The vulnerability was known, the exploit was identified, and the worm's aggressive propagation methodology ensured that every security tripwire would be triggered.

While Slammer was easy to detect, the profiles of many cyber attacks today are much more cunning. Attacks have transformed from compromising systems for notoriety to seeking financial gain through cyber crime, where stealth and anonymity are paramount. As the sophistication and serious intent of attackers increases, they use more subtle attacks that are increasingly difficult to detect—attacks that leave, at most, modest footprints in logfiles and that masquerade as normal traffic.

Without a doubt, the stakes have never been higher for security practitioners to protect their information assets from cyber attacks. It is our contention that many security practitioners are unknowingly operating an incident detection program that can at best identify only 32%[*] of the incidents occurring on their network. This chapter explores some of the limitations of traditional incident detection that inhibit the effectiveness of security monitoring programs, and reviews the use of several technologies and techniques to create a resilient incident detection model—to find the other 68%.

A Common Starting Point

Chapter 13, *Beautiful Log Handling*, by Anton Chuvakin, describes the challenges associated with managing logs and the importance of using them for investigative, regulatory, and governance purposes. In our chapter, we'll concentrate on getting the most out of your logs for incident detection. Most practitioners perform incident detection by analyzing logs from technology designed specifically to detect—and in some cases block—cyber attacks. These technologies are known as Intrusion Detection Systems or Intrusion Prevention Systems, which we'll refer to heretofore as Intrusion Detection and Prevention (IDP) Systems. These technologies compare network activity against patterns that are indicative of exploit attempts or other unauthorized activity. In doing so, IDPs help practitioners by reducing terabytes of potential problems to a small number of real security events that are occurring. This appears to be straightforward, even simple. So what's the challenge? Let's examine a few examples that demonstrate some of the inherent limitations of IDPs.

---

[*] Based on our monitoring of hundreds of enterprises around the world, we examined validated incidents to determine which methods contributed to their detection. Based on our analysis, 32% of the identified incidents resulted from IDP alerts alone.

During the SQL Slammer incident, signatures specific to the worm were available within hours of its debut.† These signatures were very effective at triggering alerts on packets with a specific pattern of bytes unique to the worm's propagation, resulting in the detection of infected hosts with high confidence. While this sounds encouraging, during the height of Slammer, most companies were detecting millions of infection attempts from the Internet that offered little value, as most were noise that didn't actually cause harm to customers.

There are a myriad of incidents occurring on the Internet at any time, but very few require immediate response to mitigate risk to your business. Identifying those few incidents that require specific and timely action is the primary goal of any effective security monitoring program. In the case of the Slammer worm, it was certainly interesting to be aware of the rapid rate of the worm's infection across the Internet, but this data was not useful in accomplishing the goal of protecting information assets. In this case, the *actionable* incidents were the ones that alerted system administrators to compromised hosts within their environment that were attempting to propagate to other systems.

An effective technique used for Slammer and countless worms like it to detect actionable incidents is to refocus your detection based on *directionality*. Here's the premise: although any network will be attacked frequently, most attempts will be unsuccessful. By looking for hosts within your environment that are initiating outbound attacks and thus require immediate action to resolve, you can very quickly find the compromised systems. This may initially seem counterintuitive. Wouldn't a better approach be to identify inbound attacks and prevent the compromise proactively? In theory, yes—but considering that the timing from attack to compromise in many cases is seconds, anything less than an automated, inline blocking response would leave you in the same situation. Therefore, focusing on outbound incidents enables you to be much more efficient by only having to handle real incidents. While this technique certainly works for worms, it also works against a variety of types of malware and other attacks. To enable monitoring based upon directionality, you could either filter the alerts or reconfigure the signatures to report only on incidents propagating from your network. With a little tuning, a practitioner could turn a chatty signature that triggers on every attempt into one that could detect actionable security incidents with confidence.

There are many other techniques employed by practitioners to tune results from IDP technologies that will enable you to maximize their effectiveness. However, based on our experience, even with the most effective techniques IDPs will at best afford you the ability to spot 32% of the security incidents occurring on your network. While many practitioners believe they are effectively monitoring their environment from threats using IDP technologies, there are other technologies and techniques required to find the other 68% of security incidents.

---

† While Slammer-specific signatures were available from most vendors shortly after the worm's debut, many IDPs had generic SQL buffer overflow signatures available prior to Slammer's appearance, enabling early detection.

Improving Detection with Context

An effective technique to improve detection capabilities is to add contextual information that can help validate attacks that otherwise would be disregarded. Let's look at another incident example from an IDP. If you have a public web server, you can be sure it will be scanned for vulnerabilities daily, if not hourly. Most IDPs have literally thousands of signatures that can detect different attacks. The following are a few Snort signatures that are commonly triggered during a web server attack:

```
WEB-IIS ISAPI .ida attempt
WEB-IIS cmd.exe access
WEB-IIS msadcs.dll access
```

Are these signatures actionable incidents? Maybe. These signatures could be indicative of a failed exploit attempt, but they may also represent a successful compromise of the web server. The problem is that based on these example signatures, a failed attempt and successful compromise may look exactly the same. You need more information to corroborate whether or not the attack was successful. By leveraging directionality, if your web server started to initiate attacks to other hosts on the Internet, the compromise is confirmed. However, if the attacker's footprints are more subtle, you may need to look for other indications of a successful exploit.

One readily available source of additional context can be found in your firewall or router logs. These technologies commonly record when and how a host connects to another host. For example, a connection from host A to host B on TCP port 80 probably represents host A accessing a web server on host B. In addition, depending on the source of the traffic logs, you may also see bytes transferred in the session, whether the session was accepted or dropped, NAT translations, and other pieces of information.

Knowing exactly what else occurred between the hosts in question is critical to ascertain the nature of the attack and provide evidence of a successful compromise. For example, imagine an attack that is recorded by an IDP and a firewall with the following logs:

1. The IDP records Host A attacking Host B on TCP port 80 with multiple signatures triggered.

2. The firewall records this traffic as Host A connecting to Host B on TCP port 80.

3. The firewall subsequently records Host B connecting back to Host A on TCP port 21 (FTP) to download a toolkit or botnet malcode.

It is unlikely that the IDP device would alert on the third connection, as this traffic would otherwise appear to be commonplace. Yet when it follows the attack, this connection provides high confidence that the attack was in fact successful due to the post-compromise FTP session connecting back to the attacker. Considering that public web servers are attacked constantly, analysts are frequently left guessing whether the attack was successful if presented with just the IDP alerts. The follow-on traffic is a critical part of the attack footprint and can easily turn a perceived false positive or low-priority incident into a confirmed compromise. Simply by adding additional context to the IDP logs, detection rates can improve to approximately 40%.

Improving Coverage with Traffic Analysis

Another significant limitation of IDPs is that they only find what they are programmed to detect. New threats and vulnerabilities are introduced with staggering frequency, often requiring updated signatures to ensure detection. According to Symantec's Internet Security Threat Report,[‡] in the second half of 2007, there were 499,811 new samples of malicious code reported to Symantec, a 567% increase over the second half of 2006. Each of these threats represents a potential gap for some period between release of the threat on the Internet and the availability of a signature to detect its existence. Even with the best of the IDP technologies, the window of exposure can last from hours to weeks in length. Using the W32.Gaobot worm as an example, dozens of variants of the worm were written and released in 2004. What would happen if the exploit used was a variant that the IDP's signature didn't match? If you relied solely on your IDPs for detection, you might be blind to the attack.

Instead of looking at individual packets for signatures, what if you analyzed how hosts interact with each other over a period of time? If you could organize the logs in a sufficiently real-time manner, some common attack patterns become apparent. For example, every system infected by Slammer stood out clearly because it attempted to connect to thousands of other hosts on port 1434/udp in a very short period of time. This is aberrant behavior for two reasons: (1) hosts typically don't attempt to connect to a myriad of other hosts on port 1434/udp, and (2) the port 1434/udp connection attempts were occurring at a staggering pace. By analyzing unique connections to and from hosts that you are protecting over time, it is very possible to identify suspicious traffic independent of known signatures. For example, consider the following situations:

Not very suspicious
> Host A connects to Host B on TCP port 25 (SMTP)

More suspicious
> Host A connects to 1,000 different hosts on TCP port 25 (SMTP)

The first example is rather benign and probably represents a host attempting to connect to a mail server to send mail. The second example, however, could represent two very different events. If Host A is a mail server, then this is probably also benign activity, as it should be expected that a mail server connects to other hosts across the Internet to send email on a regular basis. If Host A is not a mail server, however, then this activity becomes much more suspicious and likely represents malcode using SMTP as an infection vector to self-propagate to other hosts. Let's look at one more example:

[‡] Symantec's *Internet Security Threat Report*, Volume XIII (April 2008).

Additional information

    Host A connects to 10 million different hosts on TCP port 25 (SMTP)

Let's first revisit the scenario where Host A is a mail server. This could represent Host A sending an inordinate volume of legitimate mail. On the other hand, what if, in addition to sending mail for your enterprise, your mail server has been taken over by spammers and begins to send out spam to millions of people around the world? In order to alert on this incident, you would also need to consider the volume of traffic as part of your detection criteria. As each server and every enterprise would have a different level of activity, applying a fixed threshold for expected connections would not be effective.

However, a technique that could work would be to establish a baseline of normal mail activity for Host A over time and also determine its variability. Let's say that we determine over 30 days that Host A on average establishes 500,000 connections with a standard deviation of 100,000 within a 24-hour window. If during a subsequent 24-hour window we detect that Host A has established one million connections, the statistics would suggest that this volume of connections is far enough from the mean to require further inspection. While this technique is subject to false positives because of the opportunities for atypical volumes of traffic, it should identify incidents that otherwise may be missed. We have found this technique to be effective at detecting misconfigured mail servers that are used by spammers and a variety of DOS attacks.

While IDPs can be very precise with detailed signatures, this very feature may also blind them to other equally valid means of incident detection. In contrast, by examining network traffic for unusual traffic patterns as described above, it is possible to effectively detect attackers based solely on how they interact with other hosts on the network, regardless of any visibility to the actual exploit. How useful is this? Considering that one of the most common actions a malicious payload attempts in the wake of a compromise is to search for other vulnerable hosts, this technique alone can increase the detection rate of attacks within an enterprise to approximately 66%.

Correlating with Watch Lists

Over the past several years, the motives for cyber attacks have shifted from attempts to gain notoriety to an intent to steal confidential information for financial gain. With the goals of preserving their anonymity and infecting a large number of systems to do their bidding, the hackers have created networks of systems infected with malware called bot networks, or botnets. A single botnet consists of hundreds, thousands, or even tens of thousands of computers across the Internet belonging to unsuspecting home users and corporations that have been clandestinely taken over, typically through exploiting client-side vulnerabilities when visiting infected websites. Each computer taken over is called a bot, or "zombie," and they are each programmed to contact one or several IP addresses of "mothership" systems, known as the bot command and control servers, for follow-on commands over a unique communications channel. The instructions could be as simple as searching the infected host for credit card information or as complicated as concurrently launching a distributed denial of service attack against a target web server.

Bot networks are a significant threat on the Internet today: in the last half of 2007, Symantec identified over five million bot-infected hosts connecting to over four thousand bot command and control servers. To emphasize the magnitude of the problem, at Symantec's Managed Security Services operation, over 50% of actionable incidents that we detect have some evidence of bot infection.

One of the challenges of detecting botnets is that other than the frequent callback communication to the bot command and control server, many infected hosts may not exhibit any other suspicious activity until issued a command days or even months later. While some of the more common, widespread networks of bot-infected hosts are well documented with published signatures available for detection, most are unknown with no detection capabilities in the IDP. Without signatures available, what techniques can be used to detect the infection? Knowledge of the bot command and control server could unmask the actionable incident. Regardless of any other footprint or signature, the mere fact that a host on your network is connecting to a bot command and control server on the Internet should classify it as a system that has probably been compromised.

The same principle holds true for systems on the Internet known to be associated with spam, phishing, port scanning, or any other malicious activity. What if you knew the reputation of the known bad offenders on the Internet? As a managed security services provider, our operation benefits from the visibility into a wide range of malicious attacks. With the ability to flag IP addresses as malicious based upon a single incident, what one of our customers experiences benefits all others. This "neighborhood watch program" for Internet security enables quick identification of offenders. The concept is straightforward, but the implementation is powerful. Simply by alerting on router or firewall traffic denoting connections going to or coming from known bad IP addresses, you should be able to find some of the most dangerous and stealthy pathogens on your network.

Creating and maintaining such a list is neither an easy nor exact activity. Bot command and control servers can be assigned to one system one day and a completely different system the next. A high-risk IP address may in fact also be a victim computer of an unknowing corporate or home user, simply relaying attacks on to the next host. While most practitioners will not have an organic capability to build a comprehensive watch list, such lists are available commercially and in the public domain.§ Depending on the reliability and timeliness of your intelligence feeds and the source of your traffic logs,‖ you can easily improve your detection rates to approximately 80%.

---

§ Examples of public watch lists can be found at *http://www.spamhaus.org* and *http://cbl.abuseat.org/*.

‖ Some enterprises opt to disable logging for select outbound traffic, such as HTTP. Obviously, if your enterprise does this, you will be blind to any connections leveraging these ports.

Improving Perspective with Host Logging

Monitoring an enterprise from network devices—namely routers, firewalls, and IDPs—benefits from a broad vantage point. With good network device coverage, an analyst should be able to monitor most if not all of the hosts in the enterprise. However, in addition to the limitations of network-based analysis described previously, there is one further limitation: the network alerts can't provide insight into how the systems are affected by an attack. Were accounts created or successfully accessed? Were files changed or downloaded? Did key services fail?

The host can contribute perspective to security incidents by logging from three key technologies: operating systems, server applications, and security technologies. In theory, the concept of leveraging operating system logs sounds important, but unfortunately, these logs by themselves have somewhat limited value. Logging is typically limited and most logs on a system are designed to record a limited set of activities and expected conditions and errors. Considering that most vulnerabilities are explicitly bypassing some control within the operating system, you can reasonably expect it to be logged only partially, or not at all.

In contrast, some server applications, specifically network-based applications such as databases and web servers, tend to log all requests obtained from the network and host alike. They can capture in detail arguments passed and commands executed, and provide a wealth of contextual information that can contribute to an incident's discovery. The challenge with server applications' logs tends to be associated with efficiently gathering these logs together from all hosts within an enterprise. Centrally collecting application logs from a large enterprise comprised of different operating systems is challenging and in many cases unfortunately is not a priority.

As in the network, there are also purpose-made security technologies that are specifically designed to protect hosts from malcode and intrusions, and to detect any attempts. The more comprehensive technologies combine anti-virus, personal firewall, anti-spyware, anti-spam, and host IPS capabilities together. Generally, these technologies focus first on prevention and second on detection, so while there is certainly more value in the logs, there are still some limitations on what they will and won't record during an attack, and there is a wide variance of capabilities between vendors. As most enterprises have anti-virus deployed and many are actively upgrading to a more unified endpoint security solution, there is certainly value in gathering and including these logs in your analysis. Not only do they offer more precision, but they also fill in detection gaps that may exist within your IDP infrastructure due to network placement.

So with this additional host logging, are you going to get to 100%? Probably not, but you are certainly a lot closer than the 32% you were at when we started.

Building a Resilient Detection Model

Even the best security practitioners are prone to the pitfall of relying too heavily on one technology or log source for detecting security incidents. In our experience managing the security for hundreds of the world's largest companies, we have had countless conversations with security officers. We found many are frustrated that their security monitoring efforts aren't achieving the desired results, yet their monitoring program is limited to deploying IDP sensors throughout their enterprise. We find that many security teams are missing compromises of their systems due to an incomplete security architecture and are inundated with false positive alerts without the means to highlight the real attacks. As described previously, an approach of monitoring only IDP technologies is certain to yield positive results, but will probably catch only 32% of the incidents. For some companies, finding one third of the security incidents is a risk they are willing to accept based on budgetary limitations or the non-mission-critical nature of their information assets. However, for most organizations, having an incident detection capability to find a very limited number of attacks is not acceptable, especially in segments of their network that contain employee or customer sensitive data.

If the goal of an organization is to truly mitigate the risk associated with cyber attacks, it must broaden its visibility of incidents across the network, and leveraging some or all of the techniques described earlier will provide a solid foundation for incident detection. Each of these techniques will be effective at highlighting some key attack characteristics, such as unexplained traffic volumes, connections to known bad offenders, or obvious signatures denoting a compromise. However, the goal cannot be achieved by utilizing each technique in isolation. By examining a combination of logs from a variety of sources to provide different perspectives on an event, your ability to detect the real incidents increases dramatically. As an example, let's review the attack indicators associated with the compromise of a host (Figure 14-1).

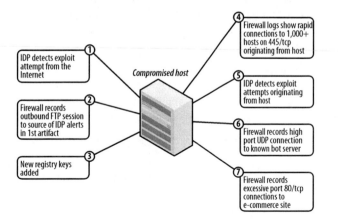

FIGURE 14-1. Evidence of compromise

The indicators shown in the figure are:

1. The IDP detects exploit attempts from the Internet from known signatures. Since IDP alerts didn't contain sufficient details to indicate that the attack was successful, this indicator only notes that the attack was attempted.

2. The firewall recorded reply traffic of an FTP session back to the attacking host. This additional context confirms with high confidence that the first attack was successful.

3. Logs from the host reveal that the string values to the following registry key: *HKEY_LOCAL_MACHINE\Software\Microsoft\Windows\CurrentVersion\Run* were added at approximately the same time. This results in the malcode being executed on system startup. As registry key changes are made with great frequency, the timing of the change is critical. A registry change that occurs concurrently with indicators 1 and 2 could suggest that the attack is successful.

4. The compromised host connects to other systems' file shares, in an effort to propagate malcode or search for credit card information. These connection attempts are logged by the firewall only. A quick check of the host's history reveals that this is atypical for the host in question, so this is another high-confidence indicator that the system has been compromised.

5. Outbound exploit attempts are certainly not expected or typical. This is a third high-confidence indicator that the system has been compromised.

6. The high port UDP connection to a known bot command and control server is a moderate-to high-confidence indicator that the system has been compromised.

7. The excessive traffic to an e-commerce site by itself could be benign, depending on the volume of traffic, but when associated with the previous indicators, this likely reveals that the system is participating in a distributed denial of service attack.

Based on the corroboration of these discrete pieces of evidence, there is little doubt that the host is compromised. In this example, we have the benefit of an incident that exhibits suspicious activity when analyzed from a variety of different perspectives, but we don't always have that advantage. Whereas some attacks will trigger every tripwire placed, some are designed to be stealthy and may only alert us from a single detection technique. What if the exploit leveraged in Figure 14-1 was not detected by the IDP due to unavailable signatures? Indicators 1 and 5 would not have been available. In addition, indicator 2 adds context to the first exploit attempt, so it also would not be present. Even with close to half of the attack footprint missing due to gaps in signatures, there would still be sufficient information to identify and confirm this attack.

By utilizing a broad set of detection techniques, we have created an incident detection model that is highly *resilient*. In this context, we use resiliency to describe an incident detection model capable of finding the majority of attacks that could be launched against your environment. If one technique fails to detect an attack, there is a high probability that one or several others will. While the concept of resiliency is simple, surprisingly it is a trait often overlooked by many security practitioners as they design their detection capabilities. The danger of not having a resilient incident detection model is that you frequently aren't aware that you are missing incidents, and you may only discover the gaps in coverage when real damage has been done to your information assets. Here are some real examples of events that have tested the resiliency of the practitioner's incident detection model:

- An attacker targets a host with a new attack or variant that does not match a signature.

- A signature is frequently triggering false positives.

- Due to a recent network change, the IDP that previously monitored inbound and outbound traffic is now monitoring only outbound traffic.

- A network administrator accidentally turns off port spanning, making your IDP blind to all network traffic.

- The server used for logging firewall traffic becomes unavailable to the network.

- Outbound firewall rules are configured not to log due to performance limitations of the firewall.

- Your watch list of known malicious IP addresses is out of date.

All of these potential gaps work against your ability to see the complete picture of the incident. In fact, you should assume that most of the time, you will see only a partial footprint of an attack. The more comprehensive your capability to see different parts of attacker's footprint, the more likely you are to confirm the incident, even in less optimal circumstances.

In addition to correlating varied detection capabilities together into a single holistic incident, many enterprises also find it useful to enrich the incident with asset information for the affected host. Let's review an example with a less obvious attack footprint than the previous scenario (see Figure 14-2).

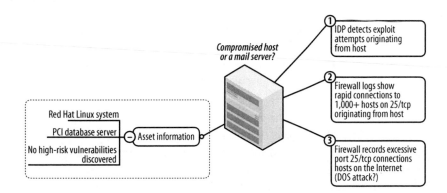

FIGURE 14-2. More subtle evidence of compromise

In Figure 14-2, the attack footprint is less clear, as all three indicators could lead us to two very different conclusions: either a host is attempting to propagate malcode or a mail server is operating as expected. Let's look at each attack indicator in more detail:

1. The IDP alerted on multiple signatures. Depending on which IDP alerts triggered, it is not uncommon at all for a mail server to trigger a variety of lower-confidence signatures as false positives. For the purpose of this example, let's assume these signatures were suspicious, but not sufficient to classify as an incident.

2. This indicator highlights attempted connections by the host to multiple other hosts on port 25/tcp (SMTP). The actual sequencing of destination hosts could be revealing. If the host connects to incrementing IP addresses in order, this is likely malcode searching for other mail servers, as they would not typically connect to other servers in this manner. A mail server attempting to connect to seemingly random IP addresses is nondeterministic, as it could be the result of normal mail operations or malcode that was programmed to connect to hosts randomly rather than sequentially. Hence this indicator could either be very valuable or not at all. Let's assume it's attempting to connect randomly, and hence a low-confidence indicator.

3. The final indicator is the increased traffic on port 25/tcp (SMTP). Also suspicious, but a mail server's load can vary quite dramatically. Unless the observed traffic is significantly above a normal baseline, it is unlikely that an analyst would classify this as an actionable incident based on this indicator.

In this case, the tipping point is not what the system is doing, but what the system is—namely a database server and not a mail server. What were otherwise low-confidence indicators become a high-confidence compromise when corroborating with asset attributes.

There are a variety of asset attributes that are similarly useful to detect security incidents. Some examples of useful asset attributes are:

Operating system of the host
Either obtained from a current Configuration Management Database or a recent vulnerability scan. For example, if the server is Unix-based and it is being targeted with Microsoft exploits, there is no chance of successful compromise.

Vulnerabilities present on the host
For an attack to be successful, the system has to be unpatched for that exploit, and hence vulnerable. Vulnerability information provides good context, but is valuable only if the vulnerability scan has been recently performed, as stale information can lead to spurious conclusions. Additionally, vulnerability scans carry their own false positives and false negatives, which complicate or even mislead your analysis.

The business or network functions of the host
A network management server will send and receive a great deal of SNMP traffic, and a mail server will communicate on SMTP. This information is critical to understand expected

network traffic to reduce false positive rates, but also helps business managers understand systems associated with critical business functions.

Type of data stored on the host

Depending on whether the host contains credit card information, Social Security numbers, patient health information, intellectual property, or just day-to-day operational files and emails is an important consideration in developing a security architecture and protection strategy. While not critical for incident determination, less critical systems may lower your threshold for further investigation. On the other hand, a compromise of a system that is part of your PCI DSS audit may have enormous implications for regulatory compliance and risk to your clients.

DHCP lease logs

Most of your attack footprint is going to revolve around an IP address. Most enterprises assign dynamic IP addresses for all but their servers, so responding to an incident affecting 192.168.5.4 may be useless, as the physical host may have renewed a different IP address. Available access to DHCP logs allows you to look up the MAC address, which is unique for every physical network interface.

Each of these attributes adds a new dimension to the incident assessment that can ultimately increase confidence that the incident is in fact actionable. They also provide contextual information about the business functions of the host to allow for a rapid business impact assessment so that an appropriate response can ensue.

Summary

Although IDPs provide the foundation for performing incident detection, they have some inherent limitations that require the use of other technologies and techniques to enable more complete coverage. In this chapter, we learned how important a variety of data sources and perspectives are to improve detection rates. Most importantly, a resilient model for incident detection allows for a broad set of technologies and techniques, so that incidents invisible to one or several detection methodologies will be caught by others. A resilient incident detection model will also ensure that the inevitable failures in one part of your monitoring infrastructure—whether due to human error, application failures, or networking mistakes—will be buffered by other detection capabilities. With the right data sources and detection techniques, you should be able to build a resilient and robust security monitoring program capable of finding the majority of security incidents occurring in your network.

CHAPTER FIFTEEN

Doing Real Work Without Real Data

Peter Wayner

THE LARGEST PRIVACY BREACHES ARE CAUSED BY DATA THIEVES STEALING the contents of corporate or government databases. Imagine a database that can do useful work without having any useful information in it. For instance, imagine a server that can answer questions about the items you purchased, your schedule for next Thursday, your favorite movies, or countless other details like other databases hooked up to the Internet—but if someone snuck through the firewalls, cracked the password layer, or found some way to get superuser control on the machine, he would find nothing he could use. Even if the evil hacker/ninja snuck into the server room and hooked the hard disk up to a forensic analyzer, there would be no juicy info available.

A database like this sounds impossible. How could the database answer questions about next Thursday without knowing something about what's going to happen next Thursday? It's got to have the data there somewhere, right?

Others have suggested suboptimal solutions to protecting sensitive data. But even if it's locked away inside some electronic safe hidden in a virtual stonewalled chamber buried inside a cyber castle wrapped by an impenetrable software moat filled with digital acid that dissolves any bad bits that come in contact with it, the data is present and remains vulnerable to someone smart enough to simulate a privileged user.

The solution I've developed in this chapter is unique. The data is present, I admit, but not in a form that's *useful to anyone but the end user*. The data is scrambled by the end user or client *before* sending it to the server and unscrambled *after* the client fetches it back. While it lives on the database, the information remains inscrutable and virtually useless to everyone but the rightful owner.

This approach is a bit different from simply encrypting the database using the built-in encryption functions that are part of most databases. That encryption is handled by the database itself, leaving the server with a readable version of the data at both the storage and retrieval ends. The data might live in encrypted form, but the database itself will decrypt it to search it and make decisions. If the server knows what is going on, so can anyone who can hack into the server or the network carrying the traffic.

The trick is to stop thinking of the database as an all-seeing oracle and start imagining it as a mathematical switching network that knows nothing about the information flowing through it. Then you cloak the data selectively and store it translucently so the sensitive bits are hidden while the not-so-sensitive information is kept in the clear. In other words, stop thinking of the database as a fortress to be protected, and start imagining it as a diffuse, unattackable translucent cloud of data dispersed throughout space.

This approach does not require any revolutionary mathematics or sophisticated computer science. The tools for encrypting and decrypting information are well understood, reasonably efficient on modern CPUs, and relatively stable. Thirty-five years of public research has given us a wide range of encryption functions with a surprisingly varied set of options for creating databases that store information without knowing anything about it.

There are limitations and compromises to this system. If the database doesn't know anything, it cannot offer the same trusted foundation, the same all powerful Oz-like stability to the programmers who tend it and the people who rely on it. If someone forgets her password—the key for unlocking all of the data—well, the data is gone forever. Pace Yeats, the center cannot hold, because the center doesn't know anything.

Is this approach worthwhile? It is, more often than many expect. When I first started exploring the idea, a friend said something like, "That's nice. But not for anything real. If the Internet is going to read our minds, it's going to need to track our movements." That didn't seem right to me. So to test it, I sketched out the architecture for a big online store much like Amazon and found that such a store could offer almost all of the features of the best online stores without keeping any personalized information. They just have to store data *translucently* so some parts are visible and some parts are opaque.

How Data Translucency Works

What would such a store look like? The best way to explain some of the basic design patterns is with an example. Table 15-1 shows a traditional database table in a traditional store.

TABLE 15-1. Sample traditional database

Customer	Item purchased	Size	Color
James Morrison	Loafing Khakis	34W–32L	Moondust
James Morrison	Pure White Shirt	16–32	Supernova White
Richard James	Loafing Khakis	32W–32L	Moondust
Harrison James	Tread-On-Me Socks	L	Blackhole

This is the kind of information needed by the folks who stock the shelves and make decisions about marketing. They need to know what is being sold and, so they think, to whom.

People have different instinctual reactions to the existence of these databases. Some welcome them and see the efficiency as a net gain for society (Brin 1998). Others fret about how the information might be used for other purposes. We have laws protecting the movie rental records of people because the data became a focal point during the Senate confirmation hearings of Robert Bork (Etzioni 1999). Times and mores change, and no one knows what will be made of this information in the future. Cigarette smoking was once widespread and an accepted way to push the pause button on life. Now, companies fire people for smoking to save medical costs. What will the society of the future do with your current purchase records?

A store selling clothes might try to placate customer worries by announcing a privacy policy and pledging to keep it locked up, a strategy that often works until some breach happens. This may be intentional (Wald 2004, Anon. 2003, Shenon 2003) or unintentional (Wald 2007, Zeller 2006, Pfanner 2007, and many more), but it's impossible to prevent when you use the fortress model of security.

The translucent model can solve the problem by scrambling some of the columns with a one-way function such as SHA256, a well-known hash function that's designed to be practically impossible to invert. That is, if you start with the string x, you can reliably create SHA256(x), but if you get your hands on SHA256(x), it's infeasible to figure out x.[*] If the customers hash their names, the plain-text name can be replaced by the 256 bits produced by the computation BASE64(SHA256(name)). The result might look like Table 15-2.[†]

---

[*] Users should pay close attention to research into how to break hash functions like SHA256 because this function and many similar ones are proving to be far from perfectly one-way. It makes sense, for instance, to use the HMAC construction to add more security to the average hash function like SHA256.

[†] 256 bits are normally 42 and 2/3 characters long. Space can be saved by keeping only the first n characters of BASE64(SHA256(name)). A shorter string that is still a reasonable length is likely to still be unique, which is the goal.

TABLE 15-2. Sample database with hashes in customer field

Customer	Item purchased	Size	Color
ick93LKJ0dkK	Loafing Khakis	34W-32L	Moondust
ick93LKJ0dkK	Pure White Shirt	16–32	Supernova White
98JOID30dsl0	Loafing Khakis	32W-32L	Moondust
8JidIklel09f	Tread-On-Me Socks	L	Blackhole

The stock department can still track how many pairs of khakis were sold. The marketing department can still try to look for patterns, like the fact that the same customer, ick93LKJ0dkK, bought pants and a shirt at the same time. The names, though, are obscured.

The value of a one-way function is that it combines the two seemingly incompatible goals of hiding information while making it reliably persistent. That is, James Morrison can give the store a hash of his name in the form ick93LKJ0dkK and the store can be sure that his records in the database belong to him, but they can't find his real name. This can be useful with warranties, frequent shopper programs, and automated suggestion tools. Websites that compute suggestions for customers based on their past purchases can still compute them for someone with the digital pseudonym ick93LKJ0dkK.

When James Morrison returns, he can provide his name and look up these values. He doesn't need to remember ick93LKJ0dkK, because the software on his computer can reconstruct it by calculating BASE64(SHA256(name)). After that, ick93LKJ0dkK acts just like a regular name.

The raw data in the scrambled table isn't much use. A drug fiend on a crime spree couldn't use a translucent database from a pharmacy to find houses with narcotic prescriptions[‡] (Meier 2007, Harris 2004, Butterfield 2001).

There are still limitations. If James Morrison's neighbor works at the store, that neighbor can still find out what James Morrison bought by just typing in the right name with the right spelling. This weakness can be reduced by forcing James Morrison to remember a secret password and computing a pseudonym from SHA256(name+password). This is a good solution until James Morrison forgets the password, effectively destroying all of the records.[§] This is why this level of security may be best for more casual applications, such as online stores. It might not make sense for highly valuable records, such as certificates of deposit at banks.

[‡] Pharmacies have recordkeeping requirements that force them to track sales to individuals, a requirement that might limit the use of translucency. But it still might make sense to keep a translucent database at the local store while locking up the real names in a hardened vault at headquarters.

[§] Errors caused by misspelling or forgetting parts of a key can be limited with various techniques, such as removing whitespace, converting everything to uppercase, or using a SOUNDEX code. Other solutions are described in *Translucent Databases* (see "References" on page 246).

A Real-Life Example

There are a number of ways in which translucent databases can save system administrators the time and energy of worrying about the data under their care. Imagine a database that holds the schedule of babysitters so that parents can search for the babysitter who's available on a particular evening, a service that can save parents and babysitters many annoying rounds of phone tag. I built a version of this system to explore the value of the idea; it required distributing a solid hash function to the client. The central server didn't require any code change because the hashed identities were strings that could replace the names.

This information falls into a troubling limbo in terms of security motivation. The potential for malice is large and the downside is catastrophic, but there's no great economic support for the system. The babysitters—unlike the U.S. government, for instance—don't have the money to support the kind of system that protects the nuclear launch codes.

Translucent databases reduce the danger of aggregating so much information in one place protected by one root password. Instead of storing the name of each babysitter, the schedules can be stored under pseudonyms, as shown in Table 15-3.

TABLE 15-3. Babysitter availability table with hashed names

Name	Free/busy	Start time	End time
8a9d9b999d9da9s	Free	Saturday 15:30	Saturday 22:30
8a9d9b999d9da9s	Busy	Sunday 11:00	Sunday 23:00
Aab773783cc838	Free	Saturday 18:30	Saturday 23:00

How do parents get access to the schedules? The babysitters choose who can have access by computing SHA256(*parent's name+parent's password*). Then, they put an entry into an access table that looks like Table 15-4.

TABLE 15-4. Babysitter access table

Babysitter's pseudonym	Parents' pseudonym	Encrypted babysitter name
8a9d9b999d9da9s	4373A73CC83892	91Ab3638dc99390203
Aab773783cc838	4373A73CC83892	2Ab37838DDcc83922
Aab773783cc838	99919a9b9bbb933	AB888329394CC9324

The parents log in by typing in their name and password to generate their pseudonym. They can then search the access table to find the pseudonyms of the babysitters' names. This allows them to search the schedules and find a babysitter with an open schedule. If the babysitter keeps the parents' pseudonym out of the second table, the parents are locked out. The babysitter is in control.

How do the parents locate the babysitter? The third column contains the babysitter's name encrypted with the parents' name and password. Thus, the babysitter's real name in each row can be decrypted only by the parent indicated in that row. In this case, the second column with the pseudonym might be constructed from SHA256(*parent's name+parent's password*), as already described, while the key might be computed a bit differently with SHA256(*parent's password +parent's name*). Thus, parents need just one set of information (name and password) to calculate their pseudonyms and keys, but no one can guess the secret key from the public pseudonym.

Personal Data Stored As a Convenience

The great benefit of my system is in protecting data kept by a store as a convenience. Many stores, both brick-and-mortar and online, keep the customers' shipping addresses, credit cards, and other personalized information on file to avoid the trouble of retyping these for every purchase.

One solution is to combine traditional encryption with the one-way function and use the one-way function to compute the key from a name and a password. That is, encrypt the addresses and credit card number with a key defined by SHA256(*password+name+padding*), where *padding* is some random value added to ensure that the value is different from the digital pseudonym, SHA256(*name+password*), used to replace the name.

A store needs to keep track of a customer's shipping address until the package leaves the building. Then they can delete the data and keep only the encrypted version until the customer comes back again.

Trade-offs

Does it make sense to turn your database into an inscrutable pile of bits? Here are the advantages as I see them:

Lower security costs
> The bits should be useless to anyone who gets root access. This system makes it even easier to distribute the entire database to several sites because there's less placed in the individual sites. Betrayal isn't a problem if the data is inscrutable.

Lower computation costs
> The server doesn't need to encrypt the data or support an SSL session. Clients, which usually have plenty of cycles to burn, do it instead.

More efficient database operations
> This may be a minor effect, but a good one-way function should distribute the database keys evenly across the space. If you use something like a name, you'll end up with clusters around common words or names, slowing the index.

There are, however, prices to be paid:

No superuser to the rescue

If the server administrator has no power to read the data, she has no power to fix the data either.

The center can't initiate action

A store with a translucent database can't help users until they initiate service by presenting the pseudonym. A store wouldn't be able to send out email notices saying effectively, "You bought A, B, and C in the past, so we know you would love $correlation\_function(A,B,C)$." But some see this limitation as a feature, reducing spam.

Clients become the target

If the server is neutered, hackers will attack the client instead with sophisticated key sniffers, social engineering, and other malware. The users may not be as adept at blocking the action as a good system administrator. The advantages of attacking an individual client, however, is dramatically lower than hitting a centralized server.

Encrypted data is more fragile

A single spelling error in a name is often recoverable with clear text, but even a one-bit change can lead to big differences in the value of $SHA256(x)$.[‖]

These considerations suggest that this approach is best for protecting mildly sensitive data that can be lost without real consequences. A customer who loses access to the purchase history at a store is not seriously inconvenienced. A patient who can't access medical records, however, may be pretty upset.

One of the best uses for this approach may be with multitiered databases. A hospital could keep its patient records intact in one centralized vault, but distribute depersonalized, translucent solutions to researchers conducting statistical studies. These researchers could still work with real data without the worry of protecting personal data (Schneier 2007).

Going Deeper

One-way functions are just the beginning of the possibilities for working with protected data. Other traditional mathematical tools developed by cryptologists can be used with applications in the same way to preserve privacy. Steganographic applications, for instance, can mix a hidden layer of data in with the real layer, effectively creating a two-tier database. Only the users with the right keys for unscrambling the steganographic layer can extract the second tier. Public-key solutions can create functions that are one-way except for people who possess the secret key for unlocking the data. All of these solutions are explored in greater detail in *Translucent Databases* (see "References" on page 246).

[‖] There are a number of partial solutions described in *Translucent Databases* that can minimize these dangers and even eliminate them in some cases (see "References" on page 246).

The digital fortress is the traditional approach to storing sensitive information. The best database companies are filled with talented individuals who wrap adamantine layers around the data with access levels, security models, and plenty of different roles that allow the right queries while blocking the suspicious ones. These "unbreakable" systems have their place, but they are complicated, expensive, and fragile. A better solution is often keeping no real data at all and letting the user control the fate of his own information.

References

Anonymous. "Betraying One's Passengers," *New York Times*. September 23, 2003.

Brin, David. *The Transparent Society*. New York: Basic Books, 1998.

Butterfield, Fox. "Theft of Painkiller Reflects Its Popularity on the Street," *New York Times*. July 7, 2001.

Etzioni, Amitai. "Privacy Ain't Dead Yet," *New York Times*. April 6, 1999.

Harris, Gardiner. "Tiny Antennas to Keep Tabs on U.S. Drugs," *New York Times*. November 15, 2004.

Meier, Barry. "3 Executives Spared Prison in OxyContin Case," *New York Times*. July 21, 2007.

Pfanner, Eric. "Data Leak in Britain Affects 25 Million," *New York Times*. November 22, 2007.

Shenon, Philip with John Schwartz. "JetBlue Target Of Inquiries By 2 Agencies," *New York Times*. September 23, 2003.

Schneier, Bruce. "Why 'Anonymous' Data Sometimes Isn't," *Wired*. December 13, 2007. *http://www.wired.com/politics/security/commentary/securitymatters/2007/12/securitymatters_1213*.

Wald, Matthew L. "U.S. Calls Release of JetBlue Data Improper," *New York Times*. February 21, 2004.

Wald, Matthew L. "Randi A.J. v. Long Is. Surgi-Center, No. 2005-04976." N.Y. App. Div, September 25, 2007.

Wayner, Peter. *Translucent Databases*. Flyzone, 2003. *http://www.wayner.org/books/td/*.

Zeller, Tom Jr. "U.S. Settles With Company on Leak of Consumers' Data," *New York Times*. January 27, 2006.

CHAPTER SIXTEEN

Casting Spells: PC Security Theater

Michael Wood
Fernando Francisco

STORM CLOUDS GATHER AND THERE IS UNREST IN THE LAND; THIEVES WANDER the highway with impunity, monsters hide in every tree along the road, and wizards cast spells while handing travelers amulets for their protection. Believing in the power of the talismans, our hero strides forth, wrapped in his magical invincibility, confident he will be the master of any threat he encounters.

Our hero, however, has been deceived. The pratings of amulet peddlers were repeated endlessly by the untutored peasants around him, but he will soon discover that incantations and alchemy are poor substitutes for a real suit of armor, a sturdy sword by his side, and a good plan in his head.

Although this might seem like the start of a fantasy novel, it parallels the state of today's computer security.

The problem is not in the quality of the solutions we use to protect our computers; truly, many of today's security offerings are nothing short of wondrous, developed by dedicated, experienced, and uncommonly talented people. Yet when we look at the overall state of security, the achievements resemble misdirection and magic more than a responsible and effective strategy.

What we need is a new security strategy that makes better use of our current tools and guides the development of new ones. The alchemists and apothecaries of old made many valuable discoveries in chemistry and medicine, but their insights proved effective only when modern views of science were developed. So too with anti-virus and anti-spyware products, firewalls, sandboxes, etc. Unless we adopt a new approach to security, these common tools will prove unsustainable over the near future and irrelevant (for the most part) in the long term.

Our research and development has opened up new possibilities for ensuring security through management of virtual and real (persistent) systems, through the use of artificial intelligence (AI) to detect anomalous behavior, and through accelerated anti-virus development. This chapter looks at the problems that drove us to this solution, and our current work on a product named Returnil.

Growing Attacks, Defenses in Retreat

To understand where we are now, we have to take a trip back to where the mass security market got off track. We don't have to go as far back as the creation of the first true viruses in the 1970s or even the introduction of new malware designed for the increasingly popular IBM-compatible PCs in the early 1980s, but just to the period during and shortly after the Internet bubble of the late 1990s. A huge amount of expertise went into developing defenses, but the battle still goes to the spammers and the spyware distributors.

On the Conveyor Belt of the Internet

The first link in the chain was the end of distinctions between anti-virus vendors. Up until the mid-1990s, malware spread mostly through the exchange of affected files between people who worked together or knew each other. Therefore, it either did not travel very far or traveled very slowly between geographical locations. This led to the creation of many small, region-specific solution providers.

With the increasing adoption of the Internet and the harvesting of email addresses by malware, it became obvious that anti-virus vendors would need to expand their world view and deal with what was heretofore "someone else's problem." While many of the larger providers resisted this change, others who jumped into the breach reaped the rewards of being able to advertise a larger detection capability.

This in turn led to a period of consolidation, where larger companies began merging and acquiring competitors or OEM licensing for the competitors' technology and research. From a practical sense this was the most straightforward way to quickly obtain large sample databases without having to spend an inordinate amount of time trying to obtain samples the traditional way and reproducing the research that had already been done by the competitor.

The industry was thus transformed by "bigger is more secure" marketing messages, bolstered by the media attention malicious programs began to generate. Some readers will remember the anxiety generated by attacks such as Pakistani Flu (1986), Jerusalem (1987), Morris (1988), Michelangelo (1992), Melissa (1999), VBS/Loveletter—"I Love you" (2000), Code Red (2001), Nimda (2001), Klez (2001), Blaster (2003), Slammer (2003), Sobig (2003), Sober (2003),

MyDoom (2004), and so on.* Each newly discovered virus would generate ever-increasing gloom in the media, which the anti-virus industry leveraged to their advantage to generate fear and drive more customers to their products.

Another key contributor to cyber fears, interestingly enough, had nothing whatsoever to do with the Internet but has colored everyone's mindset: September 11, 2001. Whether or not you were personally affected by the tragedy, there can be no doubt that it heightened fears and, as a result, put a greater emphasis on all types of security.

Although consolidation in the consumer security field continues to this day, its imperative has lessened because vendors no longer invest the necessary time and capital to develop unique databases. Now they compete on specialization, claiming to focus on a particular type of attack (banking trojans, gaming trojans, rootkits, spyware, key loggers, spam/phishing, hostile websites, etc.). These distinctions are frequently irrelevant, but provide compelling advertising copy.

Even with the improvements in features, new detection techniques, and added complexity of anti-viral services, you may be shocked to learn that the overall effectiveness of anti-virus solutions has actually dropped over time. Recent studies of random PC populations have reported that 1 in 6 were actively infected with malware, despite running mainstream anti-virus products. This alone demonstrates that existing security technologies, whilst useful, are inadequate.

The same studies show that this problem is becoming worse. The products' success in detecting the types of attacks for which they're designed dropped from an average of 50% in 2006 to closer to 30% in 2007.

To be fair, most if not all of these studies are flawed because they use limited sample sets that do not represent the true population of all possible malware samples. One shouldn't take precise numbers seriously, but the results still indicate an alarming trend. Regardless of the statistical realities, the studies don't instill a great deal of confidence in the current approaches, do they? Later we'll look at reasons for the failure of anti-virus and anti-spyware products.

Rewards for Misbehavior

The next link in our chain came directly out of the Internet bubble, when investors threw bucket loads of money at anyone who could pitch an idea that had even a minimal connection to the Internet, not too far removed from strangers who walk up to you on the street and whisper, "Hey bud, I have this incredible idea for making you money...."

One of the survivors of this devastation was the advertising industry, who hit the mother lode when they enthusiastically embraced the Internet. Their Holy Grail was targeted advertising, and they recognized opportunity in the unprecedented ability of digital networks to record and

---

* See *http://en.wikipedia.org/wiki/Timeline_of_notable_computer_viruses_and_worms*.

sift through data. They therefore rushed to mine user accounts and track surfing habits to build statistics on behavior, preferences, location, etc. They then sold this information to others to design targeted advertising based on real-world data.

Their techniques have been spectacularly successful, generating mountains of profits that fuel the drive for more ways to make revenues from the collection of information. The first modest targeted ads were pop ups in freeware applications promoting payment options and offering web page ads. Then the bundled advertising components became more sophisticated by tracking users' surfing habits and any other relevant information they could scrape from the host computer.

It was only a matter of time before the malware writers discovered that there was money to be made from these advertisers who, blinded by profits, wanted their content on the user's computer no matter how it got there. This incentive provoked malware writers to get serious and apply their knowledge to exploits that fraudulently install advertising components. This enabled them to reap affiliate rewards from legitimate advertisers who were only too willing to throw their money at anything that improved installation numbers. And this new source of revenue, on top of other criminal activities, helped finance the changes that came after, leading to the current and quite effective industrial malware distribution techniques being used today. (See Chapter 4, *The Underground Economy of Security Breaches*, by Chenxi Wang, and Chapter 6, *Securing Online Advertising: Rustlers and Sheriffs in the New Wild West*, by Ben Edelman.)

A Mob Response

The convergence of mainstream advertising and malicious exploits was not readily anticipated and took a while to discover. Separate groups of independent researchers and network administrators, noticing the exploits, formed specialized newsgroups and later online forums to discuss methods for blocking and removing them.

Noting that the privacy and security issues raised by these programs resembled the activities that the anti-virus companies claimed to combat, the researchers and administrators pressured them to take action against fraudulently targeted ads. But the established companies balked at this request, regarding the intrusive ad campaigns as merely a rogue commercial activity rather than malicious attacks.

Both angered and spurred into action by the anti-virus industry's response, activists and enthusiasts in both the privacy and security communities started gathering the scattered information contained in their technical forums with the goal of helping their own members stem the attacks. Information was initially disorganized and of little practical value. Instructions for actually detecting and removing the malware were rare and limited to steps performed manually. Research reports with less complete instructions were slightly more common. The forums also unfortunately contained incorrect and even dangerous advice.

The first step toward a practical implementation of anti-spyware measures was provided by Steve Gibson of GRC.com. Not only did he, along with many others, accomplish much to spread the word about spyware to the public and the media, he also developed the first removal tool, called OptOut, that addressed some of the currently known advertising attacks. Designed primarily as a proof of concept, it had limited effectiveness and served primarily to spur others to take the next step and develop a true commercial privacy solution.

Shortly following the release of OptOut, a developer in Germany who had been following these discussions took the initiative and developed a more robust utility that could be updated regularly like commercial anti-virus programs, rather than being rewritten to address every newly discovered advertising program or threat. He recognized, as did the rest of the community, that the premise underlying the anti-virus approach—an urgent and ongoing search for new attacks and frequent releases of fixes to address them—would ultimately fail. But due to the technical restrictions of the time, researchers accepted this model as the only one they could turn into a practical utility to meet an urgent and growing need.

So a new industry was born to address the threat presented by spyware, ironically benefiting from the same messages of fear (both real and perceived) that the privacy community and the anti-virus services used to force their issues into the public consciousness. The new products garnered more and more media attention, which helped fuel the growth of anti-spyware software from a single company to an integral component of today's anti-virus and even firewall solutions.

The movement gave a new lease on life to the anti-virus companies and even opened the door to a new round of consolidation. Now there was a new pool of unique databases of malware signatures that anti-virus companies wanted to incorporate into their products. Given the obvious similarities between the viruses and spyware, it was only a matter of time before they came together.

What was wrong with that? Its very success dulled any imperative to develop new paradigms and address the glaring flaws in their products. As long as companies could claim a competitive advantage, expand offerings in appealing ways, and increase revenues, the incentive lagged to engage in developmental research and innovation. Along with the tight competitive environment they operated in, this put the brakes on any real change in strategy.

To summarize our history, despite earnest and often brilliant contributions by increasing numbers of security experts, the anti-virus and anti-spyware industry of the past 15 years has been characterized by a brute-force collection and analysis of existing malware. In a "bigger is better" approach, the products slurp up the contributions of competing products—as well as the innovations of researchers who are critical of the original products—and multiply their complexity to deal with creative new threats. We can now examine why we have reached the limits of this approach, and why it is already insufficient.

The Illusion Revealed

In this section, we'll review each type of security solution to see how it protects your computer and where it fails.

Strict Scrutiny: Traditional and Updated Anti-Virus Scanning

The first solution is the traditional, signature-based anti-virus/anti-spyware filter. The program compares files against a regularly updated "blacklist" of bad content. If the file is on the list, the filter will block or remove it based on instructions in the blacklist. Anything not on this list is presumed to be good.

The evolution of the blacklist method

The blacklist approach really became obsolete as soon as people connected to the Internet, allowing malware to cross geographic borders and spread in the blink of an eye.

The anti-virus providers undoubtedly realized quite early that the signature approach would at best be a short-term solution, and would eventually fail to provide reliable frontline protection. To provide protection using this method, the manufacturer first has to have a sample of the malware in hand. Then, it has to generate an update to its signatures that will properly identify and remove the targeted content.

The problem is that the researcher can isolate and view the sample only after the malware has been released, sometimes months or even years previously. Rustock.C, one of the most dangerous Windows-based rootkits found to date, is a good example of this, having been in the wild for over a year before it was discovered, analyzed, and added to detection signatures. Even daily updates would not give manufacturers enough time to find, analyze, and distribute defenses against new malware, so users are vulnerable to yet unknown attacks (zero-day exploits).

From this description, it would be legitimate to assume that a researcher is seeing an old version of the malware and that it has had time to make the rounds with other malware developers and "users." Each malicious attack quickly changes into something completely new or incorporates some of its capabilities into something else.

Furthermore, although anti-virus companies maintain research teams that can number in the hundreds, they are facing an ever-growing backlog of malware identification and signature production. They receive tens of thousands of new suspect items a day from their "honeypot" networks and other sources. In short, the costs of finding malware are rising while the products' detection rate across the total malware population is falling.

It has long been understood that signature-based scanning systems, whilst effective in the past, are doomed as a single defense by the sheer volume and rate of change demonstrated by malware, especially with the recent introduction of industrialized, organized malware development that has increased its volume upwards of 100% over a single year (2007).

The next solution is a variant of the first, but with the addition of heuristics. This approach broadens the effectiveness of the defensive programs, but has an unfortunate tendency to increase false positives: flagging good files as bad. Rather than make the user more secure, it serves to either desensitize him (crying "Wolf!" one too many times) or heighten his fear. The first leaves the system open to exploit because alerts are ignored. The second leads the user to seek more talismans of protection, as no single anti-take-your-pick scanner can detect 100% of all malware, regardless of what the advertising says.

The whitelist alternative

Another approach is to move away from reliance on blacklisting and focus instead on what is actually good, an approach called whitelisting. It should be simple to do an end run around the anti-virus simply by disallowing anything that is new or unknown.

One way to do this is through the use of *anti-executables*. As the name implies, these defenses block programs from running or being activated. This strategy lies behind the recurring dialog boxes that annoy Windows Vista users by forcing them to click a button right after requesting some routine administrative activity.

Conventional wisdom would tell you that if a malicious file cannot activate, it cannot infect your system. But proper functioning depends entirely on maintaining a clean whitelist. If the user makes a mistake and allows a malicious file to be added to the list, the game is up and your protection fails.

Even more disturbing is that anti-executables cannot distinguish between a truly good program and a good program that has been hijacked to run malicious content. Once this happens, the game is again up and the user is left unprotected.

Host-based Intrusion Prevention Systems

A variation of this approach is to use Host-based Intrusion Prevention Systems (HIPS). Conceptually, HIPS is a cross between a type of signature-free anti-virus program, a firewall, behavioral control, and sandboxing (described later). Although large organizations usually run powerful monitoring software on dedicated devices, scrutinizing every host on their networks, a HIPS application actually resides on your computer (the host).

What the program looks for is malicious or suspicious behavior based on a set of rules it has learned or been programmed with. Unfortunately, good and bad programs display similar behavior, so the HIPS has to determine the actual intent behind those behaviors. This is its fatal flaw, because the program relies on the user to determine what is good or bad. As soon as the user makes the wrong decision, as with anti-executables, her protection is breached. Meanwhile, these programs are extremely resource hungry and can adversely affect both system performance and user experience.

Anti-virus and anti-spyware scanning is a desperate and shockingly intrusive approach, even when it works well. Users routinely notice and complain about the degradation in performance they cause, particularly at application startup. The degree of integration with the operating system required by the products leads to its own fragilities, and bugs in the software even introduce new attack vectors.

Security is partly a function of simplicity. The more complex a strategy, the more likely it is to fail. We believe the end user does not need multiple scanners, advanced firewalls, process monitors, filters, and blockers—the common elements of modern anti-virus systems—to be secure.

Applying artificial intelligence

At our company, Returnil (*http://www.returnil.com*), we're trying to streamline the identification of malware through behavioral analytics, artificial intelligence, and machine learning. Returnil runs in conjunction with a virtualization environment, also possessing innovative features, which we'll describe in a later section.

The analysis is performed by our Advanced Monitor System (AMS), which blocks any process demonstrating behavior that we've previously defined as malicious (a form of blacklisting, in other words) and reports processes with unrecognized behavior to the central AI systems. Thus, anything new or with substantially different behavior from before is processed by the AI systems.

Our AI/Knowledge Base puts the processes submitted to it into one of three categories: good, bad, or indeterminate. Indeterminate items are continuously monitored by the AI system learning engines and are either subsequently categorized or, in a minority of cases, passed on to a human researcher to make a definitive determination. False positive and false negative results are continuously directed into feedback loops to improve the AI/Learning engine.

Sandboxing and Virtualization: The New Silver Bullets

As users come to realize the intrusive nature of anti-virus software, they look at current technologies for an escape. They say, "If I can't kill malware with my anti-virus product, can I at least isolate it and keep it from harming my computer?"

Yes and no. Sandboxing, as the name implies, allows the user to put an unknown or potentially harmful application inside of a "bubble" that keeps it from interacting with files and other sensitive parts of your system while letting security programs watch it closely for malicious behavior. Think of this as putting the application on an island to which you control all access.

This is a secure idea in and of itself, but it fails too often in practice. Both user mistakes and specific design elements in the malware can cause "leakage," exploiting the limited connections between the isolated "island" and the "mainland" of your computer. Sandboxing can also have a significant effect, just like the other solutions we've described so far, on the performance of both the program within the "bubble" and the overall operating system. This effect, however, is not as extreme as with traditional virtualization.

Virtual machines, host and guest

Some have suggested using traditional, full-blown virtualization as a security tool. The concept is simple on its face, but involves a great deal of effort and cost to work properly. In the end, it fails to provide any real protection. Most have heard or know of programs such as VMware that run a simulation of a real computer as a "guest" inside their actual "host" computer. Indeed, these types of programs are used frequently by malware researchers to test malicious content on a variety of different operating systems, so they don't have to set up and use a real computer that would need to be serviced frequently in order to reset it for each testing session.

This does not, however, mean that the real computer is protected or secure. It is relatively simple for the user to mistakenly drop a virus-infected application onto his real (host) computer, accidentally allow a virus to migrate from the guest operating system to the host system using shared folders, or become infected from the Internet if the guest operating system is allowed a connection.

Virtualization also takes up a significant amount of resources, as you will need to divide things like your available RAM and hard disk space. This can adversely affect performance of the guest system, and performance of the host system if you try running other programs natively on it. In addition, you will still need to use the same security applications you use on your real computer, which will consume even more resources.

Security-specific virtualization

Instead of cobbling a secure environment on top of virtualization technologies meant for other purposes, we have developed a sleek virtualization solution at Returnil that directly addresses the need to isolate critical system files from everyday user behavior. When the user's system boots, we lock down the "real-world" system from modification and create a virtual system to present to the user.

To the user, the system looks like any other Windows box, and, in theory, the user doesn't even have to know the system's running in a sandbox. Incidentally, a side effect of making the user work in a virtual sandbox is that the system as a whole suffers less from fragmentation or wear and tear on the disk.

By default, the virtual system is a fresh copy that bears no changes from previous sessions. But the user can choose to save system folders in the virtual system (e.g., My Computer, Favorites, System logfiles) so that she can access data she really wants to save upon reboot. Furthermore, there is a mechanism for saving a file to the real environment; the security of that procedure is described in the following section.

If the AMS monitoring software described earlier (in the section "Applying artificial intelligence" on page 254) detects bad behavior, it immediately and automatically reboots the virtual system, usually a fast operation that does not greatly inconvenience the user. Even if malicious content is in one of the folders the user wants to save between reboots, changes to the registry that would make this content dangerous are stored only in the virtual system's registry and therefore wiped out during the reboot. Users are not asked to make decisions they cannot reasonably make about the safety of the programs they run.

Figure 16-1 illustrates the interaction of our monitoring system and virtualization sandbox.

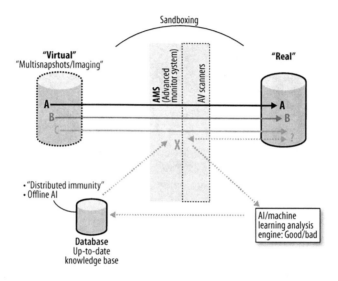

FIGURE 16-1. Returnil procedure for trapping malware

Security of saved files in Returnil

As mentioned, our virtual environment allows users to save files to the real environment. When they do so, we apply a comprehensive scan that uses both traditional signature databases and behavioral analysis to detect malware.

Most anti-virus and anti-spyware programs are continuously scanning huge swaths of the system while the user is trying to get work done: all running processes, the PC registry, and key areas of the disk. At regular intervals, the software spends an hour or more scanning all files. This is a huge and time-consuming task, involving hundreds of thousands of objects. Returnil bypasses all this overhead by using relatively lightweight behavior monitoring on a dynamic basis, and saving exhaustive scans for the occasional file saved to the real environment. Why scan 100,000 objects when you need to scan only one?

Better Practices for Desktop Security

What can computer users do to improve on the current, unsatisfactory security situation?

First, you will need to embrace the fact that there is no silver bullet or all-powerful talisman that will make your computer invulnerable to malware infection. We suggest dual principles to guide you:

- Security is about assessing and reducing risk, not making intrusions impossible.
- Simpler solutions tend to be better ones.

A related and well-known principle—defense in depth—suggests using a mix of solutions.

This does not mean you have to resort to the "more is better" approach of resource-hungry, intrusive, and annoying HIPS products or sandboxing. Although these approaches have merit in expert hands for specific situations, we don't find them appropriate for average users who cannot make the choices they require and don't really need such über-paranoid configurations.

The real magic comes from making the right decisions and selecting your lineup so that each link in the chain combines to provide a solid whole with minimal overlap. In other words, use an intelligent layered approach focused on the threats you are most likely to encounter. We believe the combination of artificial intelligence and virtualization used at Returnil is a good start. You should also make sure you have reliable backups and emergency recovery procedures.

Though there are a dizzying number of programs out there to choose from, each with its own unique pros and cons, it will not be as difficult as you might think to narrow your choices if you take a logical approach.

The first step is to identify your goals. Then, you can select programs that best fulfill the goals in your environment. You generally need to cover three major categories:

Prevention
> This can be accomplished through a firewall, the separation of programs from data storage on different partitions, attention to regular security updates of your software, email filters, Internet content advisors, parental controls, user account control (i.e., granting users limited permissions), executable and driver control, policy restrictions, and safe practices (often called safe surfing or safe HEX). Although "security through obscurity" is disdained among researchers, it can't hurt to disguise sensitive files and data through unconventional naming conventions.

Detection, analysis, and removal
> This is still the place for a solid and consistent anti-malware solution. Stick to a single leading product because they all can now address viruses, trojans, worms, rootkits, spyware, and what are euphemistically called "potentially unwanted or harmful applications" (mostly adware).

Cure

Virtualization, data backup or replication, and emergency recovery provide means for recovering from infections (along with routine user errors, such as deleting key files). The latter is not always well known; it consists of imaging solutions that take a "picture" of your hard drive at certain intervals and can restore that image at a later time, removing any and all malware by simply overwriting the disk.

Conclusion

The computer security industry and the media have combined to create an environment where fear, misleading information, flawed comparisons, and aggressive advertising have cast a hypnotic spell over the public. The industry claims to provide the protection we need, but their promises are not borne out by reality.

Visit any security or privacy discussion forum and you will see that the majority of the "discussions" involve assisting members to identify and remove malicious or advertising content after they thought they were protected. Over time, in fact, such topics have become the overriding mission of these communities. Rather than solving the malware issue, the industry has allowed it to grow to the point where it supplants the previous constructive discourse about general privacy and security issues.

In short, approach PC security the same way you would address personal security. Be aware of your surroundings, make sure your tools are working properly, be cautious about where you travel, and prepare for emergencies. Simplify your lineup and configure your security strategy so that each piece of the puzzle is providing the highest level of protection for its core competence with a minimum of overlap with any other piece.

For example, if you were traveling on vacation, you would not rent a hotel room and then bring a tent with you just in case the roof leaked. Instead, you would get another room or go to a different hotel. Similarly, why would you need to have a firewall with a spyware detector if you already have an anti-malware program running resident in the background? If you judge a solution to be inadequate, you simply change to one that better serves your needs.

Security is not mysterious and does not need to be complicated to be effective. Take a deep breath and use your head. Like our hero at the beginning of this chapter, all you need is a good suit of armor (a simple software firewall, and virtualization and emergency imaging), a sturdy sword at your side (a highly rated anti-virus scanner), and a simple but effective plan for dealing with the threats you are most likely to encounter during your travels.

Contributors

ED BELLIS is currently VP and chief information security officer for Orbitz Worldwide, where he is responsible for the protection and security of all information and electronic assets, as well as compliance and ethics across Orbitz Worldwide's broad, international array of business units. These assets include Orbitz, CheapTickets, eBookers, Away.com, HotelClub, RatesToGo, AsiaHotels, and Orbitz for Business.

With over 16 years of experience in information security and technology, Ed has been involved in protecting information assets at several Fortune 500 companies. Prior to joining Orbitz, Ed served as VP of Corporate Information Security for Bank of America within its Global Corporate and Investment Banking division. His credentials also include security technology and management roles at Ernst & Young, Ford Motor Company, Computer Sciences Corporation, and Young & Rubicam.

Ed is a CISSP, CISM, and CPISM, a contributor to the ISM Community, and a member of the advisory board to the Society of Payment Security Professionals. He has been a frequent speaker at information security events across North America and Europe. Past talks have included venues such as OWASP, the MIS Institute, CXO Media, the Association of Information Technology Professionals, the Technology Executives Club, and the National Business Travel Association. You can find more of Ed's writing on his blog at *http://cleartext.wordpress.com*.

JON CALLAS, security expert and cryptographer, is the chief technical officer and cofounder of PGP Corporation. He has worked at a number of firms, including Counterpane Internet Security, Apple, and Digital Equipment Corporation. He is also the coauthor and codesigner of a number of security protocols, including OpenPGP, DKIM, ZRTP, and Signed Syslog.

Dr. Anton Chuvakin is a director of PCI compliance solutions at Qualys, where he is charged with defining product road maps, creating product requirements, market positioning, and working with key partners.

Anton is also a recognized security expert and book author. He cowrote *Security Warrior (http://oreilly.com/catalog/9780596005450/index.html)* (O'Reilly) and contributed to *Know Your Enemy*, Second Edition (Addison-Wesley), *Information Security Management Handbook* (Auerbach), *Hacker's Challenge 3* (McGraw-Hill), *PCI Compliance* (Syngress), *OSSEC HIDS* (Syngress), and other books. Anton also publishes numerous papers on a broad range of security subjects and, in his spare time, blogs at *http://www.securitywarrior.org*. His recent speaking engagements include appearances in the United States, the United Kingdom, Singapore, Spain, Canada, Poland, the Czech Republic, Russia, and other countries.

Anton comes to Qualys from LogLogic, where he held the title of chief logging evangelist and was tasked with educating the world about the importance of logging for security, compliance, and operations. Before LogLogic, Anton worked at a security information management company in a strategic product management role.

Anton holds a Ph.D. degree from Stony Brook University. His website is *http://www.chuvakin.org*.

Mark Curphey graduated from Royal Holloway, University of London, with a master's degree in information security in the mid-1990s (as a mature student). Royal Holloway recently became famous as the cryptography school where the cryptographer Sophie Neveu was educated in the bestselling novel *The Da Vinci Code*.

After spending several years at investment banks in the city of London, working on a variety of technical projects, including PKI design, Windows NT security, policy development, and single sign-on systems, Mark moved to Atlanta to run a consulting team performing security assessments at Internet Security Systems (now part of IBM).

In late 2000, he took a job at Charles Schwab to create and manage the global software security program, where he was responsible for ensuring the security of all business applications, protecting over a trillion dollars of customer investments. During this period he started OWASP, the Open Web Application Project.

In 2003, he joined a small startup called Foundstone to take the experience learned at Schwab to other Fortune 1000 companies. The company was sold to McAfee in October 2004, and Mark joined the McAfee executive team, reporting directly to the president.

Mark was awarded the Microsoft MVP for Visual Developer Security in 2005 in recognition of his community work in advancing the discipline of software security. In November 2006, he left Foundstone, moved back to Europe, and took a year out to think seriously about the design of an information security management platform. A year later, he joined Microsoft as a director and product unit manager to make that platform a reality. He currently has a house in the U.K. and lives on a plane to Redmond!

BRIAN DUNPHY is senior director of operations for Symantec's Managed Security Services organization, where he is responsible for intrusion monitoring 24/7 at over 800 companies globally, including 92 of the companies listed on the Fortune 500. Prior to Symantec, he was director of analysis operations for Riptech's Managed Security Services (acquired by Symantec in August 2002). He applied his experiences from government to build a best-of-class security monitoring team from the ground up, and contributed to the analysis behind Riptech's Internet Security Threat Report in 2001—the first analysis to empirically document the state of Internet attacks.

Prior to Riptech, Brian was the Incident Response lead for the Department of Defense's Computer Emergency Response Team (DOD-CERT) as an officer in the United States Air Force. In this capacity, he led technical investigations, responses, and countermeasures for multiple high-profile DOD incidents, including Solar Sunrise and Moonlight Maze. He worked closely with the intelligence community, federal law enforcement agencies, and other response teams from around the world. As a result of Solar Sunrise, Brian contributed to the creation of the Computer Network Defense Joint Task Force in 1998 and provided technical guidance for its first two years of operations. He also created a next-generation backbone intrusion detection capability known as Centaur that provides the DOD with visibility of Internet attacks throughout the DOD's unclassified networks.

Brian has presented internationally on a variety of security topics over the past several years, including the state of security threats, techniques in identifying attacks, risks, and challenges facing corporate America. In addition, he is one of Symantec's primary spokespersons for communicating critical information about security outbreaks to the public. He holds a B.S. in electrical and computer engineering from Carnegie Mellon University and is a Certified Information Systems Security Professional (CISSP).

BENJAMIN EDELMAN is an assistant professor at the Harvard Business School. His research focuses on market design, particularly regarding electronic markets and Internet advertising. His recent work compares the revenue of alternative structures of pay-per-click advertising auctions, quantifying the losses caused by early, inefficient auction systems. He has also analyzed the stability and truth-telling properties of certain online advertising mechanisms, and he has designed a simulated bidding environment to evaluate bidding strategies empirically.

During his research, Ben has uncovered all manner of online advertising fraud—from invisible banners to click fraud and spyware. In postings on his website, Ben frequently "outs" major advertising scams and assists networks and advertisers in preventing such practices.

FERNANDO FRANCISCO has over 10 years of experience in information security and technology, having held senior executive positions with several major PC security firms. He began his information security career at F-Secure, a Finnish Internet security company, and subsequently became one of the early members of the Lavasoft Ad-Aware team as its VP of strategy and business development. He and his team established Ad-Aware as one of the world's most downloaded, used, and distributed PC security products. Recently he served as VP of channel marketing at Prevx, a British security software company. Drawing on profound experience and a track record in bringing new, innovative security products to market and driving rapid market penetration, Fernando cofounded the PC security firm Returnil, where he is CEO.

GRANT GEYER presently serves as vice president of Symantec's Managed Security Services (MSS) organization, where he is responsible for the business's strategy, operations, service delivery, and profit and loss. Symantec's MSS delivers a range of highly engineered, remotely delivered, scalable offerings to over 800 large enterprise customers from Security Operations Centers around the world, managing thousands of devices on behalf of its customers.

Grant previously served as senior director for Symantec MSS for the North American and Asia Pacific regions. In this role, he was responsible for providing around-the-clock protection to Symantec MSS customers from network security threats. He launched the Security Operations Center in Sydney, Australia, helping it achieve its ISO 27001 and SAS 70 Type II certifications. While at Symantec, Grant also launched initiatives to deliver log management services and bot-aware protection services, managed threat analysis services, integrated Symantec's DeepSight Early Warning Services with MSS, and integrated vulnerability data to provide comprehensive protection.

Prior to joining Symantec, Grant served as vice president of business development at Riptech, a managed security service provider, where he developed and managed relationships with the company's major Service Provider and Technology Alliance partners. He joined Riptech from Lucent Technologies, where he was a senior consultant leading the execution of various large network infrastructure and operations engagements for global clients in a number of industries. Prior to Lucent, he served as a Military Intelligence officer for the U.S. Army for several years, where he led operational teams in critical intelligence missions. He earned a bachelor's degree in computer science with honors from the United States Military Academy at West Point, and a master's degree in engineering management from the University of Maryland, Baltimore County.

DR. JOHN MCMANUS is the chief information officer for Watermark, a professional services firm. John leads the definition and development of Watermark's Information Technology architecture and ensures that it meets the needs of the enterprise and its clients.

John joined Watermark after serving as the deputy CIO and chief technology officer for NASA and the Department of Commerce. Prior to working at NASA, he served as vice president of the Software Technology Center at Lucent Technologies' Bell Laboratories in Murray Hill, New Jersey. John has also served as vice president for research at Cigital, Inc., following a career in flight simulation research, development, and management at NASA's Langley Research Center.

John received his Ph.D. and M.S. in computer science from the College of William and Mary and his B.A. from Randolph-Macon College.

ELIZABETH (BETSY) A. NICHOLS is a serial entrepreneur who has applied mathematics to develop solutions in satellite mission optimization, industrial process control, war gaming, economic modeling, enterprise systems and network management, and most recently, security metrics. In 2007, with her husband, Joseph, she cofounded PlexLogic LLC, a firm that offers metrics on-demand using the Software as a Service delivery model. She is the CTO and VP of engineering.

Prior to starting PlexLogic, Betsy cofounded two other software companies in the role of CTO and VP of engineering. The first company, Digital Analysis Corporation (DAC), implemented network and systems management software. DAC was acquired by Legent Corporation, which was in turn acquired by Computer Associates (CA) during the Internet bubble in the mid-1990s when Unix, the Web, and networks were booming. Betsy became one of two principal architects for Unicenter TNG, CA's flagship product. The DAC technology became the real-time agent infrastructure for Unicenter. In the time Betsy was at CA, Unicenter's annual revenues grew from $50 million to over $3 billion. Her second company, ClearPoint Metrics, founded in 2000, was the first company dedicated to implementing software products for security metrics.

Betsy has coauthored five textbooks on microprocessor programming and interfacing, as well as numerous articles in both the trade press and academic journals. Most recently, she has chaired several MetriCon Workshops and contributed to Andrew Jaquith's book *Security Metrics: Replacing Fear, Uncertainty, and Doubt* (Addison-Wesley).

Betsy graduated with an A.B. from Vassar College and a Ph.D. in mathematics from Duke University. With her husband, Joseph Nichols, who is also a mathematician, cofounder, and coauthor, she has two sons who are currently in school at Caltech and MIT.

ANDY ORAM is an editor at O'Reilly Media. An employee of the company since 1992, Andy currently specializes in open source, programming, and software engineering. His work for O'Reilly includes the first books ever released by a U.S. publisher on Linux, the 2001 title *Peer-to-Peer (http://oreilly.com/catalog/9780596001100/)*, and the 2007 title *Beautiful Code (http://oreilly.com/catalog/9780596510046/)*. His modest programming and system administration skills are mostly self-taught. Andy writes often for the O'Reilly Network (*http://community.oreilly.com*) and other publications on policy issues related to the Internet and on trends affecting technical innovation and its effects on society. His website is *http://www.praxagora.com/andyo*.

JIM ROUTH, CISM, has over 20 years of experience in information technology and information security as a practitioner, a management consultant, and a leader of technology functions and information security functions for global financial service firms.

He is currently a managing director and chief information security officer for the Depository Trust & Clearing Corporation (DTCC). In this position, Jim designed and implemented an enterprise-wide information security program based on risk-management best practices and the COBIT and ISO 27001 standards. He implemented an innovative information security risk-assessment process and a security program for software development that has been recognized as an industry leader. Jim was selected as the 2007 Information Security Executive of the Year for the Northeast.

Prior to joining DTCC, he led a customer information management function within the Risk Management group for the American Express Advisors' U.S. card businesses; ran the Information Technology function for American Express Financial's Institutional Services and Investment Management businesses; became the first CISO for American Express; and led enterprise-wide implementations of GLBA-specific controls and practices within two different banking entities in North America. He was also a management consultant in information technology for dozens of leading financial service firms for over 12 years.

Jim is a member of the board of directors for the Financial Services Information Sharing and Analysis Center (FS-ISAC) and the Wall Street Technology Association. For FS-ISAC, he is the 2009 Program Committee Chairman and the Chairman of the Product & Services Committee. He is a steering committee member for the Security and Risk Management Committee for BITS and a member of the Executive Advisory Committee for the BITS Shared Assessments Program. He is a member of the Security and Risk Management Committee for the Securities Industry and Financial Markets Association (SIFMA). He is also the current chairman of the Archer User Group.

RANDY V. SABETT, J.D., CISSP, is a partner in the Washington, DC, office of Sonnenschein Nath & Rosenthal LLP, where he is a member of the Internet, Communications & Data Protection practice group and the Venture Technology Group. He counsels clients on information security, privacy, IT licensing, and patents, dealing with such issues as Public Key Infrastructure (PKI), digital and electronic signatures, federated identity, HIPAA, Gramm-Leach-Bliley, Sarbanes-Oxley, state and federal information security laws, identity theft, and security breaches.

Randy was a commissioner on the Commission on Cyber Security for the 44th Presidency and has been recognized as a leader in Privacy & Data Security in the 2007 and 2008 editions of *Chambers USA: America's Leading Lawyers for Business*. He has also been recognized as one of the Top 50 Under 45 by the American Lawyer's *IP Law and Business* and is listed in the International Who's Who of Business Lawyers.

Within the American Bar Association, he is a member of the Council of the Section of Science and Technology Law. He is also the Immediate Past Co-Chair of that section's Information Security Committee, having previously served as a Co-Vice Chair (2002–2004). Within that committee, he has also served as editor for the book *Information Security: A Legal, Business, and Technical Handbook* (2004) and the Digital Signature Guidelines (1996), and was a Co-Rapporteur for the PKI Assessment Guidelines (PAG) (2003).

Randy is an active member of the Information Systems Security Association (ISSA), for whom he authors a monthly column. He is a member of the bars of Maryland, Virginia, the District of Columbia, and the United States Patent and Trademark Office (USPTO). He teaches

Information Policy as an adjunct professor at George Washington University and is on the faculty of the Institute for Applied Network Security. He also participates on the advisory boards of various information security startup companies.

Randy also has several years of engineering experience in the information security marketplace and has worked in the field of active noise cancellation, and also has served with the National Security Agency as a crypto engineer. He holds two U.S. patents, one in the area of information security (U.S. Patent No. 6,981,149) and the other in the area of active noise cancellation (U.S. Patent No. 5,440,642).

JIM STICKLEY is CTO and vice president of strategic operations at TraceSecurity, Inc., of which he was one of the founders. A renowned security expert, he has been involved in thousands of security services for financial institutions, Fortune 100 corporations, health care facilities, legal firms, insurance companies, and government agencies. He is the author of *The Truth About Identity Theft* (FT Press) and has been featured in *Time Magazine*, *BusinessWeek*, *Fortune Magazine*, and *The New York Times*, along with many industry-specific publications, such as *PC Magazine* and *Security Focus*. He also has been showcased on NBC's *Nightly News*, CNN's *NewsNight*, and several CNBC programs, including *The Big Idea* and *Business Nation*, and has appeared numerous times on NBC's *Today Show*. He has breached the physical security of more than 1,000 facilities nationwide and has gained access to billions of dollars through stolen identities.

When not on assignment, Jim continues to serve as a speaker and has delivered hundreds of speeches at security-related trade shows, conventions, seminars, and forums throughout the U.S. and other countries, covering topics ranging from identity theft to national cyber terrorism. His website, *http://www.stickleyonsecurity.com*, features security tips and the latest alerts.

JOHN VIEGA is CTO of the SaaS Business Unit at McAfee, his second stint at McAfee. Previously, he was the chief security architect, after which he founded and served as CEO of Stonewall Software, which focused on making anti-virus technology faster, better, and cheaper. John was also the founder of Secure Software (now part of Fortify).

John is author of many security books, including *Building Secure Software* (Addison-Wesley), *Network Security with OpenSSL (http://oreilly.com/catalog/9780596002701/index.html)* (O'Reilly), and the forthcoming *The Myths of Security (http://oreilly.com/catalog/9780596523022/index.html)* (O'Reilly). He is responsible for numerous software security tools and is the original author of Mailman, the GNU mailing list manager. He has done extensive standards work in the IEEE and IETF, and he coinvented GCM, a cryptographic algorithm that the National Institute of Standards and Technology (NIST) has standardized. John is also an active advisor to several security companies, including Fortify and Bit9. He holds an M.S. and a B.A. from the University of Virginia.

Dr. Chenxi Wang is a member of Forrester's Security and Risk Management research team and a frequent keynote speaker in research and industry conferences. Most recently, Chenxi was an invited speaker for the OWASP North America and Asia conferences.

Prior to joining Forrester, Chenxi was the chief scientist for KSR, Inc., a risk management service provider firm. Before that, she was an associate professor at Carnegie Mellon University for computer security. At CMU, Chenxi led a number of large research projects, including research efforts funded by the Department of Defense and National Science Foundation. Chenxi conducted consultative projects for the Federal Trade Commission, HP Labs, Lucent, and a number of Venture Capital companies. Earlier in her career, she held one of the first research associate positions at Citibank's Corporate Information Security Office (CISO), the very first CISO designation in the country.

Chenxi holds a Ph.D. in computer science from the University of Virginia. Her Ph.D. thesis research received an ACM Samuel Alexander award.

Kathy Wang is a cofounder and chief technology officer of AlphaDetect, Inc. Prior to founding AlphaDetect, she was an information security engineer at The MITRE Corporation.

In 2004, Kathy began to research and develop an open source honeyclient prototype, which was released and presented at a conference in June of 2005. Following that, the Honeyclient Project was funded through a research grant at The MITRE Corporation, and Kathy became the lead researcher of the project, providing direction to a team of engineers to develop a much more effective honeyclient prototype. Past projects of Kathy's include Morph, an OS fingerprint cloaking tool.

Prior to working at MITRE, Kathy worked at Counterpane, the University of Michigan's Computer-Aided Engineering Network (CAEN), and Digital Equipment Corporation. Kathy graduated with a B.S. and M.S. in electrical engineering from the University of Michigan, Ann Arbor. She has presented her works at numerous conferences internationally, including RSA, DEFCON, AusCERT, ToorCon, and RECON, and she has been invited as a presenter for several malware-detection expert panels.

Peter Wayner is the author of 15 books, including *Translucent Databases* (CreateSpace), which expands on the ideas described in his *Beautiful Security* chapter; *Disappearing Cryptography* (Morgan Kaufmann), an exploration of steganography; and *Free for All* (HarperBusiness), a small subset of the history of open source. He often consults on these topics and teaches classes about how the ideas can be implemented. He lives in Baltimore and writes frequently for *The New York Times*, *InfoWorld*, and other major publications.

Michael Wood has had the unique and humbling experience of serving on both the front lines and the boardroom in the fight against malware. His perspective comes from a 10-year history of online privacy and security advocacy, involving endless hours as a volunteer helping others in technical support forums. He was part of the original team that launched Lavasoft (makers of Ad-Aware) and, consequently, an entire industry. Michael is currently VP of product management at Returnil, where he is responsible for guiding the development of

Returnil products while working closely with customers and the security community to provide cutting-edge PC security solutions.

PEITER "MUDGE" ZATKO is perhaps best known as the hacker who told the U.S. Senate that he could take down the Internet in 30 minutes. He has testified to the United States Senate Committee on Government Affairs as a subject-matter expert in regard to government systems, and to the House and Senate Joint Judiciary Oversight Committee as a subject-matter expert on legislation regarding cyber crime. He is currently technical director, National Intelligence Research and Applications, for BBN Technologies.

Mudge has published in ACM and CORE/CQRE refereed journals, as well as the USENIX Security refereed journal. He has taught offensive cyber warfare techniques and tactics courses at various Department of Defense entities and was recently a visiting scientist at Carnegie Melon University.

As the leader of the hacker think tank known as "The L0pht," Mudge is the inventor of L0phtCrack, an industry-standard Microsoft password auditing tool, and several other well-received software security solutions.

Mudge was recognized by the National Security Council, Executive Office of the President, as a vital contributor to the success of the President's Scholarship for Service Program. He was also recognized as contributing to the CIA's critical national security mission. He is an honorary plank owner of the USS McCampbell (DDG-85). His mission remains constant: "Make a dent in the universe."

PHILIP ZIMMERMANN is the creator of Pretty Good Privacy (PGP), an email encryption software package. Despite the lack of funding, the lack of any paid staff, the lack of a company to stand behind it, and the opprobrium of government persecution, PGP nonetheless became the most widely used email encryption software in the world.

After the government dropped its case in early 1996, Zimmermann founded PGP, Inc. That company was acquired by Network Associates, Inc. (NAI) in December 1997, where he stayed on for three years as Senior Fellow. In August 2002, PGP was acquired from NAI by a new company called PGP Corporation, where Zimmermann now serves as special advisor and consultant.

Zimmermann currently is consulting for a number of companies and industry organizations on matters cryptographic, and is a Fellow at the Stanford Law School's Center for Internet and Society. He was a principal designer of the cryptographic key agreement protocol for the wireless USB standard. His latest project is Zfone, which provides secure telephony for the Net.

Zimmermann has received numerous technical and humanitarian awards for his pioneering work in cryptography. In 2008 *PC World* named him one of the Top 50 Tech Visionaries of the last 50 years. In 2003 he was included on the Heinz Nixdorf MuseumsForum Wall of Fame, and in 2001 he was inducted into the CRN Industry Hall of Fame. In 1999 he received the Louis Brandeis Award from Privacy International, in 1998 a Lifetime Achievement Award from

Secure Computing Magazine, and in 1996 the Norbert Wiener Award from Computer Professionals for Social Responsibility for promoting the responsible use of technology. In 1995, *Newsweek* named Zimmermann one of the "Net 50," the 50 most influential people on the Internet.

Zimmermann received his bachelor's degree in computer science from Florida Atlantic University in 1978. He is a member of the International Association of Cryptologic Research, the Association for Computing Machinery, and the League for Programming Freedom. He served on the Roundtable on Scientific Communication and National Security, a collaborative project of the National Research Council and the Center for Strategic and International Studies.

Numbers

3-D Secure protocol
  account holder domain, 76
  acquirer domain, 76
  e-commerce security and, 76–78
  evaluation of, 77
  issuer domain, 76
  transaction process, 76
802.11b standard, 51, 52
802.11i standard, 51

A

ABA (American Bar Association), 203
Access Control Server (ACS), 77
accountability, 213, 214
ACS (Access Control Server), 77
ActionScript, 93
ad banners (see banner ads)
Adams, Douglas, 158
Advanced Monitor System (AMS), 254, 256
advertising (see online advertising)
adware (see spyware)
Aegenis Group, 66
Agriculture, Department of, 196
AHS (Authentication History Server), 77
AI (artificial intelligence), 254, 257
AllowScriptAccess tag, 94
Amazon Web Services platform, 152
Amazon.com, 102
American Bar Association (ABA), 203
AMS (Advanced Monitor System), 254, 256
analyst confirmation traps, 12
Anderson, Chris, 165
Andreessen, Marc, 165, 166
Anna Carroll (barge), 206
anti-executables, 253
anti-spyware software
  evolution of, 251
  initial implementation, 251

intrusive performance, 254
  strict scrutiny, 252
anti-virus software
  diminished effectiveness, 249
  functional fixation, 15
  functionality, 232
  historical review, 248–249
  honeyclients and, 141
  intrusive performance, 254
  malware signature recognition, 251
  need for new strategies, 248
  strict scrutiny, 252
  zero-day exploits and, 252
Apgar score, 37
Apgar, Virginia, 37
Apple Computer, 8
artificial intelligence (AI), 254, 257
Ascom-Tech AG, 117
Ashenfelter, Orley, 164
Aspect Security, 188
Atkins, Derek, 119
ATMs, early security flaws, 36
attacks (see malicious attacks)
attribute certificates, 111
Attrition.org, 55
authentication
  3-D Secure protocol, 77
  auto-update and, 15
  CV2 security code, 76
  e-commerce security, 83, 84
  federated programs, 210
  NTLM, 6
  password security, 7
  PGP Global Directory and, 127
  portability of, 85
  security pitfall in, 71
  SET protocol, 78
  WEP support, 52
Authentication History Server (AHS), 77
authoritative keys, 123
authorization

We'd like to hear your suggestions for improving our indexes. Send email to *index@oreilly.com*.

3-D Secure protocol, 77
  e-commerce security, 84
  security pitfall in, 71
Ayres, Ian, 164
Azure cloud operating system, 152

B

B.J.'s Wholesale Club, 50
backend control systems, 18–20
backward compatibility
  LANMAN password encoding, 6
  learned helplessness and, 2
  legacy systems, 7
  PGP issues, 117
balance in information security, 202–207
banking industry (see financial institutions)
banking trojans, 141, 249
banner ads
  exploit-laden, 89–92, 143
  honeyclients and, 143
banner farms, 98, 99
Barings Bank security breach, 38–49
Barnes & Noble, 50
Bass-O-Matic cipher, 117
behavioral analytics, 254
Bell Labs
  background, 171, 173
  software development lifecycle, 174–178
Bellis, Ed, 73–86
Bernstein, Peter, 33
Bidzos, Jim, 117, 118
Biham, Eli, 117
biometrics, 37–38
BITS Common Criteria for Software, 193
Black Hat Conference, 161
blacklisting, 252, 254
Blaster virus, 248
blogging, 166
BoA Factory site, 65
Bork, Robert, 241
Boston Market, 50
botnets
  army building software, 67
  attack infrastructure, 66
  challenges in detecting, 231
  client-side vulnerability, 131
  CPC advertising, 100, 101
  cyber underground and, 64
  functionality, 64, 69, 230
  peer-to-peer structure, 66
BPM (Business Process Management)
  levels of effective programs, 157
  multisite security, 156–158
  potential for, 154–158
  supply chain composition and, 155

BPMI (Business Process Management Initiative),
    157
breaches (see security breaches)
bridge CAs, 111
Briggs, Matt, 140
brute-force attacks, 28, 251
buffer overflows
  security vulnerability, 15, 131
  SQL Slammer worm, 225
Business Process Management (see BPM)
Business Process Management Initiative (BPMI),
    157
business rules engines, 157

C

California AB 1950, 207
California SB 1386
  balance in information security, 203–205
  on data sharing, 36, 38
  on reporting breaches, 55
  passage of, 207
call options, 40
Callas, Jon, 107–130
Capture-HPC honeyclient, 138, 145
CardSystems security breach, 211
Carnegie Mellon CMMI process, 185
Carr, Nicholas, 157
Carter Doctrine, 201
CAs (see certificate authorities)
cashiers (cyber underground)
  defined, 65
  drop accounts, 70
CDC (Centers for Disease Control and Prevention),
    36
Center for Internet Security (CIS), 45
Center for Strategic and International Studies
    (CSIS), 201
Centers for Disease Control and Prevention (CDC),
    36
certificate authorities, 112
  (see also introducers in PGP)
  certification support, 111
  DSG support, 203
  establishing trust relationships, 27
  hierarchical trust, 109
  SET requirements, 78
certificates, 109
  (see also specific types of certificates)
  defined, 111
  revoking, 120–122
  self-signed, 109
  verifying, 109
  Web of Trust support, 113
certification
  defined, 111

OpenPGP colloquialism for, 112
OpenPGP support, 111
CFAA (Computer Fraud and Abuse Act), 207
Charney, Scott, 201
Chuvakin, Anton, 213–224, 226
Cigital, 171, 188
Citi, 79
CLASP methodology, 187, 188
click fraud
    botnet support, 66, 101
    CPA advertising, 102
    federal litigation, 102
client-side vulnerabilities, 133
    (see also honeyclients)
    background, 131–132
    malware exploitation, 15, 132, 141–143
    naïveté about, 8–9
Clinton, Bill, 17
cloud computing
    applying security to, 152
    builders versus breakers, 151
    defined, 150
    identity management services, 154
CNCI (Comprehensive National Cybersecurity
        Initiative), 202
CNN network, 16
COBIT regulation, 214
Code Red virus, 248
Commerce, Department of, 180
commercial software (see software acquisition)
Commission Junction affiliate network, 102
Commission on Cyber Security for the 44th
        Presidency, 201
Common Vulnerabilities and Exposures (CVE)
        database, 131
communication
    cyber underground infrastructure, 65, 66
    information security and, 207–211
Comprehensive National Cybersecurity Initiative
        (CNCI), 202
Computer Fraud and Abuse Act (CFAA), 207
confidentiality of data, 85
confirmation traps
    defined, 10
    intelligence analysts, 12
    overview, 10–11
    rationalizing capabilities, 13
    stale threat modeling, 12
contagion worm exploit, 131
cookies, stuffed, 102
cost per action (see CPA advertising)
cost per click (see CPC advertising)
Cost Per Thousand Impressions (see CPM
        advertising)
COTS (see software acquisition)

coverage metrics, 46
CPA advertising
    functionality, 100
    inflating costs, 102–103
    stuffed cookies, 102
CPC advertising
    click-fraud detection services, 101
    functionality, 100–101
    syndication partnerships, 100
CPM advertising
    basis of, 98
    fraud-prone, 100–103
credit card information
    as shared secret, 75–76, 85
    card associations and, 82
    checking site authenticity, 26
    consumers and, 81, 83
    current market value, 66
    CV2 security code, 76
    cyber underground and, 65
    devaluing data, 71
    e-commerce security, 73–75
    financial institutions, 82
    identity theft, 23–25
    merchants and service providers, 81, 83
    PCI protection, 44
    proposed payment model, 86
    spyware stealing, 69
    SQL injection attacks, 69
    TJX security breach, 50
    virtual cards, 79
cross-certification, 111
cross-site scripting, 188
crowdsourcing, 161
Crypto Wars, 118
CSIS (Center for Strategic and International
        Studies), 201
culture, organizational, 200–202
cumulative trust, 110
Curphey, Margaret, 169
Curphey, Mark, 147–169
CV2 security code, 76
CVE (Common Vulnerabilities and Exposures)
        database, 131
cyber underground
    attack infrastructure, 66
    attack methods, 68–70
    cashiers, 65
    combating, 71–72
    communication infrastructure, 65
    CSI-FBI Study, 63
    data exchange example, 67
    fraudsters and attack launchers, 65
    goals of attacks, 63, 226, 230
    information dealers, 64

information sources, 68
makeup and infrastructure, 64–66
malware producers, 64
money laundering and, 70
payoffs, 66–71
resource dealers, 64
Cydoor ad network, 90

D

Danford, Robert, 144
Data Encryption Standard (DES), 4
data integrity, 85
Data Loss Database (DataLossDB), 36, 55–58
data responsibility
  incentive/reward structure, 72
  social metric for, 72
data theft
  as cottage industry, 67
  botnet support, 66
  combating, 71
  from merchant stores, 68
  incident detection considerations, 237
  spyware and, 69
data translucency
  additional suggestions, 245
  advantages, 244
  disadvantages, 245
  overview, 239–242
  personal data and, 244
  real-life example, 243
data-sharing mechanisms
  DHS support, 36
  security flaws in, 35
databases
  data translucency in, 239–246
  logging support, 221
  security breaches and, 239
Dave & Buster's, 50
Davies, Donald, 148
DCS systems, 18
DDoS (distributed denial of service)
  attacks on major ISPs, 16
  botnet support, 66, 231
  client-side vulnerability, 131
  honeyclients and, 138
  LANs and, 28
deceptive advertisements, 94–98
Defense, Department of, 213
Dell computers, 131
Deloitte & Touche, LLP, 201
denial of service (see DDoS)
Department of Agriculture, 196
Department of Commerce, 180
Department of Defense, 213
Department of Homeland Security, 36

deperimeterization, 156
DES (Data Encryption Standard), 4
designated revokers, 121
DHCP lease logs, 237
DHS (Department of Homeland Security), 36
Diffie, Whitfield, 112
digital certificates (see certificates)
Digital Point Systems, 102
Digital Signature Guidelines (DSG), 202–203
direct trust
  defined, 109
  root certificates, 110
directionality, 227
distributed denial of service (see DDoS)
distribution channels, 166
DKIM email-authentication, 124
Dobbertin, Hans, 119
doing the right thing in information security, 211–
    212
drop accounts, 70
Drucker, Peter, 163
DSG (Digital Signature Guidelines), 202–203
DSW Shoe Warehouse, 50
Dublin City University, 144
Dunphy, Brian, 225–237
Durick, J.D., 138
dynamic testing, 190

E

e-commerce security
  3-D Secure protocol, 76–78
  analyzing current practices, 74–75
  authorizing transactions, 84
  broken incentives, 80–83
  confidentiality of data, 85
  consumer authentication, 83
  data integrity, 85
  exploiting website vulnerabilities, 68
  friendly fraud and, 84
  merchant authentication, 83
  new security model, 83–86
  not sharing authentication data, 84
  portability of authentication, 85
  primary challenges, 73
  proposed payment model, 86
  SET protocol, 78
  shared secrets and, 75–76, 85
  virtual cards, 79
EAP (Extensible Authentication Protocol), 51
Earned Value Management (EVM), 173
eBay
  CPA advertising, 102
  DDoS attacks on, 16
  principle of reliability, 160

ECPA (Electronic Communications Privacy Act), 207
Edelman, Benjamin, 89–105, 210, 250
Edwards, Betsy, 178
Einstein, Albert, 147
Electronic Communications Privacy Act (ECPA), 207
email
    log handling, 221
    malware exploits, 248
EMBED tag, 94
encryption
    LAN Manager sequence, 4
    PGP support, 107, 116–120
    security certificates and, 22, 24
    SET support, 78
Encyclopædia Britannica, 94–98
event logs (see logs)
EVM (Earned Value Management), 173
executables, malware exploits and, 143
exportable signatures, 125
extended introducers, 123
Extensible Authentication Protocol (EAP), 51

F

Facebook social network, 159, 165, 166
failing closed, 8
failing open, 8
false negatives, 236
false positives, 217, 236
Federal Sentencing Guidelines, 209
Federal Trade Commission (see FTC)
financial institutions
    banking trojans, 141, 249
    credit card information, 82
    cyber attacks on, 68
    drop accounts, 70
    exploiting website vulnerabilities, 68, 187
    federated authentication programs, 210
    infosecurity and, 208
Finjan security firm, 65
Finney, Hal, 117
firewalls
    energy company vulnerabilities, 18
    host logging, 232
    log handling, 216, 221
    need for new strategies, 248
    SQL Slammer worm, 225
    watch lists, 231
Flash ActionScript, 93
Forester, C. S., 158
Forever 21, 50
forums, online, 250
Foundstone vulnerability management, 151
Francisco, Fernando, 247–258

fraudsters (cyber underground)
    combating, 71
    defined, 65
    information sources, 68
Friedman, Thomas, 154
friendly fraud, 84
FTC (Federal Trade Commission)
    challenging deceptive ads, 96, 97
    deceptive door opener prohibition, 95
    Encyclopædia Britannica and, 95
    exploit-laden banner ads and, 91
    OWASP recommendation, 159
FTP server security breach, 218–221
functional fixation
    costs versus profits examples, 16–20
    defined, 14
    overview, 15
fuzzing technique, 10

G

gaming trojans, 141, 249
Gartner Group, 187
Gates, Bill, 154
Geer, Daniel E., Jr., 34, 35, 60
Geyer, Grant, 225–237
Gibson, Steve, 251
GLBA (Gramm-Leach-Bliley Financial Services Modernization Act), 80, 214
GoDaddy, 109
Gonzalez, Albert, 50
Google
    AdSense service, 104
    CPC advertising, 100, 101
    democratization of production tools, 166
    false ads lawsuit, 97
    honeyclient support, 145
    on malware distribution, 69
    Safe Browsing API, 145
    testing ads, 94
Gore, Al, 149
Gramm-Leach-Bliley Financial Services Modernization Act (GLBA), 80, 214
GRC.com, 251
grep utility, 216
Guin v. Brazos, 206
Gutmann, Peter, 117

H

handshakes, 28
Hannaford Brothers security breach, 67, 68, 211
hash algorithms
    data translucency and, 241
    LAN Manager, 4
    SET procedure, 78

Windows NT, 5
Hasselbacher, Kyle, 127
health care field
    infosecurity and, 208
    security metrics, 34–38
Health Insurance Portability and Accountability Act
        (HIPAA), 80, 214
hierarchical trust
    cumulative trust comparison, 110
    defined, 109
HijackThis change tracker, 92
HIPAA (Health Insurance Portability and
        Accountability Act), 80, 214
HIPS (Host-based Intrusion Prevention Systems),
        253
Holz, Thorsten, 145
Homeland Security, Department of, 36
honeyclients
    defined, 133
    future of, 146
    implementation limitations, 143
    open source, 133–135
    operational results, 139–140
    operational steps, 134, 137
    related work, 144–145
    second-generation, 135–138
    storing and correlating data, 140
honeymonkeys, 144
Honeynet Project, 138, 145
honeypot systems
    defined, 133
    proliferation of malware, 252
Honeywall, 138
host logging, 232–237
Host-based Intrusion Prevention Systems (HIPS),
        253
hostile environments
    confirmation traps and, 10
    specialization in, 249
hotspot services, 22
House Committee on Homeland Security, 201
Howard, Michael, 195
HTTPS protocol, 66
Hubbard, Dan, 144
Hula Direct ad broker, 98, 99

I

IBM, social networking and, 159
IDEA (International Data Encryption Algorithm),
        117, 118
iDefense Labs, 59, 156
identity certificates, 111
identity management services, 154
identity theft
    devaluing credit card information, 71

wireless networking, 23–25
IDS (intrusion detection system)
    building a resilient model, 233–237
    challenges detecting botnets, 231
    false positives, 217
    functionality, 226
    honeyclient support, 133, 144
    host logging, 232–237
    host-based, 253
    improving detection with context, 228–231
    limitations, 227, 229
    log handling considerations, 218
Iframedollars.biz, 132
incident detection, 233
    (see also malicious attacks)
    building a resilient model, 233–237
    host logging and, 232–237
    improving with context, 228–231
    percentage identified, 226, 227
    SQL Slammer worm, 225
InCtrl change tracker, 92
information dealers
    defined, 64
    IRC data exchange, 67
    malware producers and, 64
    sources of information, 68
information security
    as long tail market, 165–167
    balance in, 202–207
    basic concepts, 200
    cloud computing, 150–154
    communication considerations, 207–211
    connecting people and processes, 154–158
    doing the right thing, 211–212
    historical review, 248–251
    host logging, 232
    need for new strategies, 247
    organizational culture, 200–202
    overview, 147–150
    September 11, 2001 and, 249
    social networking and, 158–162
    strict scrutiny, 252–254
    suggested practices, 257
    supercrunching, 153, 162–164
    taking a security history, 44–46
    web services, 150–154
Information Security Economics, 162–164
Information Security Group, 168
injected iFrames, 69
International Data Encryption Algorithm (IDEA),
        117, 118
International Tariff on Arms Regulations (ITAR),
        3
Internet Explorer
    exploit-based installs and, 92

open source honeyclients, 134
recent vulnerabilities, 131
Internet Relay Chat (see IRC)
intranets, security flaws, 25
introducers in PGP, 113
    (see also certificate authorities)
    defined, 109, 112
    extended, 123
    Web of Trust process, 113
intrusion detection system (see IDS)
investment metrics, 47
IRC (Internet Relay Chat)
    botnet communication, 66
    cyber underground communication, 65, 67
ISO 2700x standard, 214
ISPs, costs versus profits, 16–17
ITAR (International Tariff on Arms Regulations), 3
ITIL regulation, 214
iTunes, 165

J

J/Secure, 76
JCB International, 76
Jericho Forum, 156
Jerusalem virus, 248

K

Kaminsky, Dan, 161
KBA (knowledge-based authentication), 68
key loggers
    as information source, 68
    specialization in, 249
key signatures
    bloat and harassment, 124
    certificate support, 111
    exportable, 125
    freshness considerations, 122
    in-certificate preferences, 126
    Web of Trust, 113, 115, 120
keyrings, 112
keys (see certificates; public key cryptography)
keyservers
    defined, 112
    key-editing policies, 126
    PGP Global Directory, 127
Klez virus, 248
knowledge-based authentication (KBA), 68
Kovah, Xeno, 138

L

L0phtCrack
    government interest in, 13
    learned helplessness example, 3–6

Lai, Xuejia, 117
LAN Manager, 4
Lancaster, Branko, 117
Langevin, Jim, 201
LANs, physical security inherent in, 28
Lansky, Jared, 90–92
learned helplessness
    backward compatibility and, 2
    defined, 2, 7
    L0phtCrack example, 3–6
    overview, 2–7
Leeson, Nick, 38–49
legacy systems
    backward compatibility, 7
    e-commerce security and, 74
    end-of-life upgrades, 2, 7
    password security and, 4–6
legal considerations
    balance in information security, 202–207
    communication and information security, 207–211
    doing the right thing, 211–212
    information security concepts, 200
    log handling, 223
    organizational culture, 200–202
    value of logs, 214
Levy, Steven, 119
LinkShare affiliate network, 102
Linux systems, 221
log management tools, 222–223
log messages, 215
logs
    case study, 218–221
    challenges with, 216–218
    classifying, 214
    database, 221
    defined, 215
    email tracking, 221
    future possibilities, 221–223
    host logging, 232–237
    incident detection and, 226, 228
    regulatory compliance and, 214
    universal standard considerations, 217
    usefulness of, 153, 214, 215
long straddle trading strategy, 40
Lucent (see Bell Labs)
Lynch, Aidan, 144

M

machine learning, 254
malicious attacks, 228
    (see also cyber underground; incident detection)
    attack indicators, 233–237
    Blaster, 248

Code Red, 248
confirmation traps, 10
directionality of, 227
energy companies vulnerabilities, 18
identity theft, 22–28
Jerusalem, 248
Klez, 248
Melissa, 248
Michelangelo, 248
Morris, 248
MyDoom, 248
Nimda, 248
Pakistani Flu, 248
Slammer, 248
Snort signatures, 228
Sober, 248
Sobig, 248
SQL Slammer worm, 225–227, 229
Symantec reports on, 229
VBS/Loveletter—"I Love you", 248
W32.Gaobot worm, 229
malvertisements, 92–94
malware
    anti-virus software and, 251
    as cyber attack method, 69
    banking trojans, 141, 249
    client-side exploitation, 15, 132, 141–143
    common distribution methods, 69
    current market values, 67
    directionality of attacks, 227
    gaming trojans, 141, 249
    historical review, 248–249
    polymorphic, 70
    production cycle, 64
    streamlining identification of, 254
    targeted advertising, 250
    testing, 65
    zero-day exploits, 252
malware producers
    defined, 64
    information dealers and, 64
    polymorphic malware, 70
    testing code, 65
man-in-the-middle attacks, 25
manual penetration testing, 190
Massey, James, 117
MasterCard
    3-D Secure protocol, 76
    SET protocol, 78
Maurer, Ueli, 128
MBNA, 79
McAfee
    online safety survey, 187
    SiteAdvisor, 97
    vulnerability management, 152

McBurnett, Neal, 128
McCabe, Jim, 178, 179
McCaul, Mike, 201
McDougle, John, 178
McGraw, Gary, 186
McManus, John, 171–182
Mean Time Between Security Incidents (MTBSI),
        48
Mean Time to Repair (MTTR), 58
Mean Time to Repair Security Incidents (MTTRSI),
        48
Media Guard product, 94
medical field
    infosecurity and, 208
    security metrics, 34–38
Melissa virus, 248
Merchant Server Plug-in (MPI), 77
meta-introducers, 123
metrician, 34
metrics
    Barings Bank security breach, 38–49
    coverage, 46
    for data responsibility, 72
    health care field, 34–38
    investment, 47
    measuring ROI, 163
    scan coverage, 58
    software development lifecycle and, 172–174,
        189
    TJX security breach, 49–59
    treatment effect, 48
MetricsCenter technology, 45
MetricsCenter.org, 54
Michelangelo virus, 248
microchunking, 166
Microsoft, 134
    (see also Internet Explorer)
    Authenticode, 110
    Azure cloud operating system, 152
    Commission on Cyber Security, 201
    CPC advertising, 100
    hierarchical trust, 110
    honeymonkeys, 144
    L0phtCrack example, 3–6
    security controls in SDLC, 194
    SQL Server, 225
    supporting legacy systems, 7
    testing approach, 10
    Unix systems and, 8
MITRE Corporation, 135, 222
money, 44, 70, 141
    (see also financial institutions; PCI)
Monroe Doctrine, 201
Morris virus, 248
mothership systems, 230

Motorola Corporation, 31
Mozilla Firefox
    honeyclient support, 140, 145
    malware exploits and, 141
MPI (Merchant Server Plug-in), 77
MTBSI (Mean Time Between Security Incidents),
    48
MTTR (Mean Time to Repair), 58
MTTRSI (Mean Time to Repair Security Incidents),
    48
Murray, Daragh, 144
MyDoom virus, 248
MySpace social network, 159

N

naïveté
    client counterpart of, 8–9
    learned helplessness and, 2–7
NASA
    background, 171
    perception of closed systems, 172
    software development lifecycle, 172–174, 178–
        181
National Institute for Standards, 159
National Office for Cyberspace (NOC), 201, 202
Nazario, Jose, 145
newsgroups, 250
Nichols, Elizabeth, 33–61
Nichols, Elizabeth A., 30
Nimda virus, 248
NOC (National Office for Cyberspace), 201, 202
NTLM authentication, 6

O

OCC, 191
off-the-shelf software (see software acquisition)
Office Max, 50
online advertising
    advertisers as victims, 98–105
    attacks on users, 89–98
    CPA advertising, 102–103
    CPC advertising, 100–101
    CPM advertising, 100–103
    creating accountability, 105
    deceptive ads, 94–98
    exploit-laden banner ads, 89–92
    false impressions, 98–99
    fighting fraud, 103–104
    malvertisements, 92–94
    special procurement challenges, 104
    targeted, 250
online advertising, targeted, 249
online forums, 250
Open Security Foundation, 55

open source honeyclients, 133–135
Open Web Application Security Project (see
    OWASP)
OpenID identity management, 154
OpenPGP standard/protocol
    background, 108
    certification support, 111, 112
    designated revokers, 122
    direct trust, 109
    exportable signatures, 125
    extended introducers, 123
    in-certificate preferences, 126
    key support, 112
    key-editing policies, 126
    revoking certificates, 122
OpenSocial API, 159
operating systems, host logging, 232, 236
OptOut spyware removal tool, 251
Orange Book, 213
organizational culture, 200–202
outsourcing
    extending security initiative to, 190
    trends in, 154
    vulnerability research, 156
OWASP (Open Web Application Security Project)
    background, 159
    CLASP methodology, 187
    Top 10 list, 187

P

P2P (peer-to-peer) networks
    botnet communication, 66
    honeyclient considerations, 146
packet sniffers, 92
packets
    handshake, 28
    SQL Slammer worm, 227
Pakistani Flu virus, 248
PAN (Primary Account Number), 77
Panda Labs, 69
PAR (Payer Authentication Request), 77
PARAM tag, 94
passive sniffing, 9
passphrases, 29
password grinding, 28
password-cracking tools
    L0phtCrack example, 3–6
    passphrases and, 29
passwords
    authentication security, 7
    identity theft and, 24
    NTLM authentication and, 6
PATHSERVER, 129
Payer Authentication Request (PAR), 77
Payment Card Industry (see PCI)

PayPal, 79
PCI (Payment Card Industry)
    Data Security Standard, 75, 82, 159, 211, 214,
        237
    protecting credit card data, 44
peer-to-peer networks (see P2P networks)
PEM (Privacy Enhanced Mail), 117
perma-vendors, 156
Personally Identifiable Information (PII), 180
Pezzonavante honeyclient, 144
PGP (Pretty Good Privacy), 111
    (see also Web of Trust)
    background, 107, 108, 116
    backward compatibility issues, 117
    Crypto Wars, 118
    designated revokers, 122
    encryption support, 107, 116–120
    key validity, 108
    patent and export problems, 117
    source download, 116
    trust models, 109–116
    trust relationships, 108
PGP Corporation, 108
PGP Global Directory, 127
pharmware, 68
phishing
    3-D Secure protocol, 77
    as information source, 68
    botnet support, 66
    challenges detecting, 231
    spam and, 70
    specialization in, 249
PhoneyC website, 145
PII (Personally Identifiable Information), 180
Piper, Fred, 168
PKI (Public Key Infrastructure)
    authoritative keys, 123
    defined, 111
    DSG support, 203
    revoking certificates, 120
    SET considerations, 79
PlexLogic, 45
Plumb, Colin, 119
port scanning, 231
pragmatic security, 200, 209
Pre-Shared Key (PSK), 28
Pretty Good Privacy (see PGP)
Price, Will, 127
Primary Account Number (PAN), 77
Privacy Enhanced Mail (PEM), 117
proof-of-concept project, 191–193
Provos, Niels, 145
PSK (Pre-Shared Key), 28
psychological traps
    confirmation traps, 10–14

functional fixation, 14–20
learned helplessness, 2
public key cryptography
    cumulative trust systems, 111
    key revocation, 121
    PGP support, 107
    RSA algorithm, 117
    SET support, 78
    steganographic applications, 245
    validity, 108
Public Key Infrastructure (see PKI)
Public Key Partners, 118
put options, 39

Q

Qualys vulnerability management, 151

R

Raduege, Harry, 201
Regular, Bob, 90
regulatory compliance (see legal considerations)
Reiter, Mark, 129
Reliable Software Technologies, 171, 173
reputation economy, 167
resource dealers, 64
Return on Investment (ROI), 163, 205–207
Return on Security Investment (ROSI), 206
Returnil, 254, 255, 256, 257
revoking certificates, 120–122
RFC 1991, 108, 119
RFC 3156, 108
RFC 4880, 108
Right Media, 94
ROI (Return on Investment), 163, 205–207
root certificates
    defined, 109
    direct trust, 110
rootkits
    example investigating, 220
    Rustock.C, 252
    specialization in, 249
ROSI (Return on Security Investment), 206
routers
    DDoS attacks on, 16
    host logging, 232
    watch lists, 231
Routh, Jim, 183–197
RSA Data Security Incorporated, 117
RSA public-key algorithm, 117
RSAREF library, 117
Rustock.C rootkit, 252

S

Sabett, Randy V., 199–212

sandboxing
    functionality, 254
    HIPS support, 253
    need for new strategies, 248
Santa Fe Group, 44
Sarbanes-Oxley Act (SOX), 80, 214
SCADA systems, 18
Schoen, Seth, 127
SDLC (see software development lifecycle)
Second Life virtual world, 159
Secret Service
    Shadowcrew network and, 65
    TJX security breach and, 50
Secunia, 156
Secure Electronic Transaction (see SET)
security breaches
    attorney involvement in investigating, 211
    Barings Bank, 38–49
    California data privacy law, 203–205
    cyber underground and, 63–72
    databases and, 239
    impact of, 208
    logs in investigating, 218–221
    public data sources, 59
    tiger team responses, 210–211
    TJX, 49–59
security certificates
    defined, 22
    encryption and, 22, 24
    fundamental flaw, 25
    paying attention to, 26
    wireless access points, 26, 27
Security Event Managers (SEMs), 153
security metrics (see metrics)
Security Metrics Catalog project, 54
security traps (see psychological traps)
SecurityFocus database, 132
SecurityMetrics.org, 54
SEI (Software Engineering Institute), 176
Seifert, Christian, 138, 145
self-signed certificates, 109
SEMs (Security Event Managers), 153
separation of duties, 39
September 11, 2001, 249
server applications, host logging, 232
Service Set Identifier (SSID), 52
service-oriented architecture (SOA), 150
SET (Secure Electronic Transaction)
    background, 78
    evaluation of, 79
    protections supported, 78
    transaction process, 79
SHA256 hash algorithm, 241
Shadowcrew network, 65
short straddle trading strategy, 39, 40

signature harassment, 125
Sinclair, Upton, 149
Skinner, B. F., 163
Slammer virus, 248
SMTP protocol
    botnet communication, 66
    incident detection considerations, 236
SOA (service-oriented architecture), 150
Sober virus, 248
Sobig virus, 248
social networking
    crowdsourcing, 161
    impact on security, 154, 158, 160–162
    interoperability, 160
    malware distribution and, 69
    PGP and, 107
    potential in, 159
    state of the art in, 159
    Web of Trust and, 128
Social Security numbers
    incident detection considerations, 237
    spyware stealing, 69
software acquisition
    enforcing security, 190–193, 195–197
    implicit requirements in, 184–185
software development lifecycle
    Bell Labs example, 174–178
    business model evolution, 183
    CLASP methodology, 187, 188
    designing security, 171–172, 181–182, 193
    developer training, 188
    fixing security problems, 189
    formal quality processes for security, 187
    improving software security, 185–190
    instituting security plan, 186–188
    NASA examples, 172–174, 178–181
    outsourcing considerations, 190
    proof-of-concept project, 190–193
    static code analysis tool, 188, 189, 194
Software Engineering Institute (SEI), 176
Sophos, 69
SOX (Sarbanes-Oxley Act), 80, 214
spam
    botnet support, 66
    challenges detecting, 231
    client-side vulnerability, 131
    phishing and, 70
    specialization in, 249
    targeted, 70
    traffic analysis, 230
Sports Authority, 50
SpyBye honeyclient, 145
spyware
    as information source, 68
    CPA advertising, 102

Dell estimates, 131
functionality, 69
malvertisements and, 92
OptOut removal tool, 251
specialization in, 249
SQL injection attacks, 69, 131
SQL Server (Microsoft), 225
SQL Slammer worm
    background, 226
    IDS challenges, 227
    port 1434/udp, 225, 229
    signatures, 227
SSID (Service Set Identifier), 52
stale threat modeling, 12
static code analysis tool
    context-sensitive help, 194
    developer training, 188
    threshold of quality, 188
    vulnerability information, 188, 189
steganographic applications, 245
Stickley, Jim, 21–31
storing data
    honeyclients, 140
    logs, 222
strict scrutiny
    blacklisting, 252, 254
    whitelisting, 253
Stubblebine, Stuart, 129
stuffed cookies, 102
supercrunching, 153, 162–164
supervalidity, 114, 128
switches, failing open, 8
Symantec
    DeepSight Threat Management Service, 59
    Internet Security Threat Reports, 60, 229
    Managed Security Services, 231
    on botnets, 231
    on malware distribution, 69
    SQL Slammer worm, 225
SYSLOG format, 221
system development lifecycle (see software
        development lifecycle)

T

targeted advertising, 249, 250
technology economics, 165
testing
    ads, 94
    confirmation traps in, 11
    dynamic, 190
    fuzzing technique, 10
    malware code, 65
    manual penetration, 190
    Microsoft approach, 10
Thomson, William (Lord Kelvin), 33

time-to-market, 174–178
time-to-quality, 174–178
TJX security breach, 30, 49–59, 211
traffic analysis, improving coverage with, 229–230
treatment effect metrics, 48
Truman Doctrine, 201
trust models
    cumulative trust, 110
    defined, 109
    direct trust, 109
    hierarchical trust, 109
    users as certification authorities, 112
trust relationship
    defined, 108, 114
    establishing for wireless networks, 26–28
    PGP support, 107
    validity comparison, 108

U

Unified Compliance Framework, 44
University of London, 168
Unix systems
    grep utility, 216
    log handling, 221
    security vulnerabilities, 8
usernames, identity theft and, 24

V

validity
    defined, 114
    supervalidity, 114, 128
    trust comparison, 108
ValueClick, 97, 103, 105
VBS/Loveletter—"I Love you" virus, 248
VeriSign
    hierarchical trust, 109, 110
    iDefense Labs, 59, 156
Viacrypt, 119
Viega, John, 187
virtual cards
    defined, 79
    functionality, 79
    multiple-use, 80
    single-use, 80
virtual machines, 255
    honeyclient support, 136
    malware detection of, 141
virtualization, 255–256, 257
viruses (see malicious attacks)
VirusTotal.com, 142
Visa, Inc.
    3-D Secure protocol, 76
    SET protocol, 78
    transaction statistics, 75

VMware, 136, 141, 255
VMware Workstation, 92
vulnerability scanners
    breaker mentality and, 151
    false positives/negatives, 236
    functional fixation, 15
    proliferation of malware and, 252

W

W32.Gaobot worm, 229
Wallace, Sanford, 89–92
Wang, Chenxi, 63–72, 210, 250
Wang, Kathy, 131–146
warchalking, 29
wardriving technique, 51
Wason, Peter, 11
watch lists, 230–231
Wayner, Peter, 239–246
Web 2.0, 159
web applications
    exploiting vulnerabilities, 68, 187
    log handling support, 221
    risk of exploits, 193
    trends in exploits, 186, 187
    uncovering vulnerabilities, 188
Web of Trust
    areas for further research, 128
    background, 107
    cumulative trust support, 111
    enhancements to original model, 120–128
    functionality, 112–114
    implications of signing keys, 114–116
    in-certificate preferences, 126
    PGP Global Directory, 127
    revoking certificates, 120–122
    rough edges in original, 114–116
    scaling issues, 123–124
    signature bloat/harassment, 124
    social networking and, 128
    supervalidity, 114, 128
    variable trust ratings, 128
web services
    applying security to, 152
    builders versus breakers, 151
    defined, 150
Websense, 144
WEP (Wired Equivalent Privacy), 21
    authentication support, 52
    security flaws, 28
Western Union, 65
wget tool, 134
Whitehead, Alfred North, 150
whitelisting, 253
Whois website, 97
Wi-Fi Protected Access (WPA), 21, 28

Windows Home Server, 152
Windows Live ID, 154
Windows NT
    hash function, 5
    Internet security and, 8
Windows Vista
    Internet security and, 8
    security warnings, 26
    strict scrutiny and, 253
Windows XP
    exploit-based installs and, 92
    honeyclient support, 137, 139
Wired Equivalent Privacy (WEP), 21
wireless access points
    identity theft and, 25
    scan coverage, 58
    security certificates, 26, 27
    SSID support, 52
    WEP support, 28
wireless networking
    future of, 31
    identity theft, 22–28
    role at TJX, 49–59
    security flaws, 28–31
    wardriving technique, 51
Wireshark packet sniffer, 92
Wood, Michael, 247–258
WordPress, 165
worms
    SQL Slammer, 225–227, 229
    W32.Gaobot worm, 229
WPA (Wi-Fi Protected Access), 21, 28
WS-Security specification, 152

X

X.509 certificates
    authoritative keys, 124
    certification support, 111
    hierarchical trust, 110
    revoking, 120
    SET support, 78
    web services and, 152

Y

Yahoo!
    CPC advertising, 101
    DDoS attacks on, 16
YouTube, 165

Z

Zatko, Peiter "Mudge", 1–20, 205
zero-day exploits, 252
Zimmermann, Phil, 107–130

COLOPHON

The cover image is a cactus from Photos.com. The cover fonts are Akzidenz Grotesk and Orator. The text font is Adobe's Meridien; the heading font is ITC Bailey.